SPECIAL SERIES NO. 14 **MAY 25, 1943**

GERMAN INFANTRY WEAPONS

PREPARED BY

MILITARY INTELLIGENCE DIVISION

WAR DEPARTAMENT • WASHINGTON, DC

Published by Books Express Publishing
Copyright © Books Express, 2011
ISBN 978-1-780390-75-8

Books Express publications are available from all good retail and online booksellers. For publishing proposals and direct ordering please contact us at: info@books-express.com

MILITARY INTELLIGENCE SERVICE
WAR DEPARTMENT
WASHINGTON, May 25, 1943

SPECIAL SERIES
No. 14
MIS 461

NOTICE

1. Publication of *Special Series* is for the purpose of providing officers with reasonably confirmed information from official and other reliable sources. This issue has been prepared with the assistance and collaboration of the Ordnance Intelligence Unit, Technical Division, Office of the Chief of Ordnance.

2. Nondivisional units are being supplied with copies on a basis similar to the approved distribution for divisional commands, as follows:

INFANTRY DIVISION		CAVALRY DIVISION		ARMORED DIVISION	
Div Hq	8	Div Hq	8	Div Hq	11
Rcn Tr	2	Ord Co	2	Rcn Bn	7
Sig Co	2	Sig Tr	2	Engr Bn	7
Engr Bn	7	Rcn Sq	7	Med Bn	7
Med Bn	7	Engr Sq	7	Maint Bn	7
QM Co	7	Med Sq	7	Sup Bn	7
Hq Inf Regt, 6 each	18	QM Sq	7	Div Tn Hq	8
Inf Bn, 7 each	63	Hq Cav Brig, 3 each	6	Armd Regt, 25 each	50
Hq Div Arty	8	Cav Regt, 20 each	80	FA Bn, 7 each	21
FA Bn, 7 each	28	Hq Div Arty	3	Inf Regt	25
	150	FA Bn, 7 each	21		150
			150		

In order to meet the specific request of appropriate headquarters, or in order to conserve shipping space, the distribution of any particular issue of *Special Series* may be modified from the standard. Distribution to air units is being made by the Assistant Chief of Air Staff, Intelligence, Army Air Forces.

3. Each command should circulate available copies among its officers. Reproduction within the military service is permitted provided (1) the source is stated, (2) the classification is not changed, and (3) the information is safeguarded.

4. Readers are invited to comment on the use that they are making of this publication and to forward suggestions for future issues. Such correspondence may be addressed directly to the Dissemination Unit, Military Intelligence Service, War Department, Washington, D. C.

Other publications of the Military Intelligence Service include: *Tactical and Technical Trends* (biweekly); *Intelligence Bulletin* (monthly); *Military Reports on United Nations* (monthly).

Requests for additional copies of publications of the Military Intelligence Service should be forwarded through channels for approval.

CONTENTS

	Page
Section I. INTRODUCTION	1
II. PISTOLS, RIFLES, AND GRENADES	3
1. LUGER PISTOL	3
a. General	3
b. How to Identify	3
c. Characteristics	4
d. How to Operate	5
e. Ammunition	8
f. Maintenance	9
g. Accessories	10
2. WALTHER PISTOL	10
a. General	10
b. How to Identify	10
c. Characteristics	10
d. How to Operate	12
e. Ammunition	14
f. Maintenance	14
g. Accessories	15
3. SUBMACHINE GUN (*M.P. 38* AND *M.P. 40*)	15
a. General	15
b. How to Identify	16
c. Characteristics	16
d. How to Operate	17
e. Ammunition	19
f. Maintenance	20
g. Accessories	21
4. MAUSER *KAR. 98K* RIFLE	21
a. General	21
b. How to Identify	22
c. Characteristics	22
d. How to Operate	23
e. Ammunition	25
f. Maintenance	25
g. Accessories	26
(1) *General*	26
(2) *Grenade launchers and sights*	27

CONTENTS

Section II. PISTOLS, RIFLES, AND GRENADES—Continued.

		Page
4. MAUSER *KAR. 98K* RIFLE—Continued.		
(3) *Grenades*		28
(a) *High-explosive grenade (Gewehr Sprenggranate, G. Sprgr.)*		28
(b) *Armor-piercing grenade (Gewehr Panzergranate, G. Pzgr.)*		29
(c) *Practice projectile (Gewehr Sprenggranate, Übungsmunition, G. Sprgr., Üb.)*		33
(d) *Cartridge and packing*		33
(e) *Range*		33
5. *PZ.B. 39* (ANTITANK RIFLE)		34
a. General		34
b. How to Identify		34
c. Characteristics		35
d. How to Operate		36
e. Ammunition		38
f. Maintenance		38
g. Accessories		39
6. HAND GRENADES		40
7. STICK HAND GRENADE, MODEL 24 (*STIELHANDGRANATE 24*)		40
a. How to Identify		40
b. Characteristics		41
c. How to Operate		41
d. Method of Carrying		43
e. Use as a Booby Trap		43
8. STICK HAND GRENADE, MODEL PH 39 (*STIELHANDGRANATE PH 39*)		45
a. How to Identify		45
b. Characteristics		45
c. How to Operate		45
d. Method of Carrying		46
e. Use as a Booby Trap		47
9. SMOKE HAND GRENADE, MODEL 34 (*NEBELHANDGRANATE 34*)		47

CONTENTS

	Page
Section II. PISTOLS, RIFLES, AND GRENADES—Continued.	
10. EGG-TYPE HAND GRENADE, MODEL 39 (*EIER-HANDGRANATE 39*)	47
a. How to Identify	47
b. Characteristics	47
c. How to Operate	48
d. Method of Carrying	49
e. Use as a Booby Trap	49
11. SPECIAL USES OF STICK GRENADES	50
III. MACHINE GUNS AND MORTARS	53
12. *M.G. 34*	53
a. General	53
b. How to Identify	54
c. Characteristics	56
d. How to Operate	60
(1) *Safety*	60
(2) *To load and fire*	61
(3) *Sights*	64
(4) *Immediate action*	67
(5) *To unload*	72
(6) *To change barrels*	73
(7) *Tripod mount*	74
e. Ammunition	78
f. Maintenance	80
g. Accessories	82
13. *M.G. 42*	83
a. General	83
b. How to Identify	84
c. Characteristics	85
d. How to Operate	88
e. Ammunition	93
f. Maintenance	93
g. Accessories	94
14. 5-CM LIGHT MORTAR, MODEL 36	95
a. General	95
b. How to Identify	95
c. Characteristics	95
d. How to Operate	97
e. Ammunition	101
f. Maintenance	101

Section III. MACHINE GUNS AND MORTARS—Continued.

	Page
15. 8–CM Heavy Mortar, Model 34	102
a. General	102
b. How to Identify	104
c. Characteristics	104
d. How to Operate	105
e. Ammunition	108
f. Maintenance	109

IV. ANTITANK GUNS AND INFANTRY HOWITZERS — 113

16. 3.7-CM PAK	113
a. General	113
b. Table of Characteristics	114
c. How to Operate	114
d. Ammunition	118
e. Maintenance	119
f. Carriage	121
17. 5-CM PAK 38	123
a. General	123
b. Characteristics	124
c. How to Operate	125
d. Ammunition	130
e. Maintenance	130
f. Carriage	135
18. 7.5-CM Light Infantry Howitzer	136
a. General	136
b. Characteristics	137
c. How to Operate	137
d. Ammunition	143
e. Maintenance	145
f. Carriage	143
19. 15–CM Heavy Infantry Howitzer	149
a. General	149
b. Table of Characteristics	151
c. How to Operate	151
d. Ammunition	157
e. Maintenance	159
f. Carriage	159

	Page
Section V. AMMUNITION	161
20. INTRODUCTION	161
21. CALIBERS	161
22. LABELS	162
a. General	162
b. Color of Labels	162
c. Special Marks on Labels	162
d. Special Labels	163
e. Method of Reading Labels	164
23. BASE MARKINGS	172
24. BELTED AMMUNITION	172
25. POSSIBLE DANGERS	172
26. STANDARD PISTOL AND SUBMACHINE-GUN AMMUNITION	173
a. *Pist. Patr. 08, Pistr. Patr. 08 für M.P.,* or *Pist. Patr. 9 mm*	173
b. *Pist. Patr. 08 S.m.E.*	173
27. RIFLE AND MACHINE-GUN AMMUNITION (7.92–MM)	174
a. General	174
b. *Patr.s.S*	174
c. *Patr.S.m.K*	174
d. *Patr.S.m.K.L'Spur*	174
e. *Patr. S.m.K. (H)*	175
f. *Patr.l.S*	176
g. *Patr.s.S.L'Spur*	176
h. *Patr.S.m.E*	176
i. *Patr.P.m.K*	176
j. *B.Patr*	177
28. STANDARD ANTITANK RIFLE AMMUNITION	178
a. Introduction	178
b. *Patr. 318* or *Patr. 318 S.m.K*	179
29. MORTAR AMMUNITION	179
a. *5-cm Wgr. 36, Wgr.Z. 38*	179
b. *8-cm Wgr. 34, Wgr.Z. 38*	180
c. *8-cm Wgr. 34, Nb.Wgr.Z. 38*	181
30. CHART OF PISTOL, RIFLE, MACHINE-GUN, AND MORTAR AMMUNITION	182
VI. GLOSSARY OF GERMAN TERMS	185
VII. GERMAN ABBREVIATIONS	187

ILLUSTRATIONS

Figure		Page
1.	Armament and organization of German infantry regiment	XII
2.	Luger pistol and magazine	4
3.	Cross section of Luger pistol, showing action of toggle joint	6
4.	Close-up of Luger pistol to show operation of extractor	7
5.	Method of using German sights	8
6.	Walther pistol	11
7.	Diagrammatic sketch showing trigger action of Walther pistol	13
8.	Two views of *M.P. 40*, showing skeleton shoulder stock folded, and open	16
9.	*M.P. 40* in action	18
10.	Method of removing receiver of *M.P. 40* from barrel and from magazine housing	20
11.	Mauser *Kar. 98K* rifle	22
12.	Cross section of magazine, trigger, and bolt mechanism of Mauser *Kar. 98K* rifle	24
13.	Mauser *Kar. 98K* rifle with grenade launchers and sights	28
14.	Grenade launcher, showing method of unscrewing it to aid in cleaning	29
15.	Method of inserting rifle grenade	29
16.	Rifle grenade launcher and grenade firing pistol (very light type)	30
17.	Pistol grenade being breech-loaded	30
18.	Three types of grenade projectiles: ① pistol grenade; ② rifle grenade, with percussion detonator fuze; ③ rifle grenade, with hollow charge	31
19.	Method of unscrewing base of rifle grenade and thereby using friction fuze	31
20.	Special projectile 361 for signal pistol (*Wurfkörper 361 für Leuchtpistole*)	32
21.	*Pz.B. 39* (antitank rifle)	34
22.	Overhead view of *Pz.B. 39*, illustrating cutout folding shoulder stock	35
23.	*Pz.B. 39* in position on edge of road	37
24.	Close-up of breech of *Pz.B. 39*	39
25.	Sketch of *Stielhandgranate 24* (stick hand grenade, model 24), showing outside and cross section of grenade and fuze	42
26.	Method of carrying and packing stick-type grenades	44
27.	Sketch of *Eierhandgranate 39* (egg-type hand grenade, model 39)	49
28.	Cross section of shaving-stick grenade	50
29.	Concentrated charge (*geballte Ladung*) made from several stick grenades	51

CONTENTS

Figure		Page
30.	① Stick grenade antipersonnel mine	52
	② Stick grenade cluster mine	52
	③ Cross section of pressure igniter 35 (*Drückzünder 35, D.Z. 35*)	52
31.	Stick grenades used as Bangalore torpedo	52
32.	*M.G. 34* in action without bipod or tripod	54
33.	Two views of *M.G. 34* on bipod mount	55
34.	*M.G. 34* on tripod mount	55
35.	*M.G. 34* on tripod mount, and with antiaircraft adapter	56
36.	*M.G. 34* on antiaircraft mount, using drum feed	57
37.	*M.G. 34* in action on tripod mount, with antiaircraft and telescopic sights	59
38.	*M.G. 34* in action on boat, showing protective shield and drum feed	59
39.	Sketch showing method of inserting loaded belt in feedway of *M.G. 34*	61
40.	Close-up of 75-round saddle-type drum	62
41.	German method of firing *M.G. 34* from bipod mount	64
42.	Rear sight of *M.G. 34*, showing relation between yards and meters	65
43.	Telescopic sight on *M.G. 34*	66
44.	Telescopic sight for *M.G. 34* (rear view)	67
45.	Removal of barrel of *M.G. 34*	73
46.	Rear view of tripod mount for *M.G. 34*	75
47.	Method of joining metallic-link ammunition belt	78
48.	Cross section of trigger, recoil, and feed mechanism of *M.G. 34*	81
49.	*M.G. 42*	84
50.	*M.G. 42* with feed cover raised to show feed mechanism	86
51.	*M.G. 42*, showing method of operating barrel extension	92
52.	Left side of 5-cm mortar	97
53.	Right side of 5-cm mortar	98
54.	8-cm mortar, model 34, in action	102
55.	Right view of 8-cm mortar, model 34	103
56.	Left view of 8-cm mortar, model 34	105
57.	Laying 8-cm heavy mortar for direction during training	107
58.	*3.7-cm Pak*	114
59.	*3.7-cm Pak* in action	115
60.	Close-up of rear of *3.7-cm Pak*	116
61.	Breech mechanism of *3.7-cm Pak* (viewed from top rear)	117
62.	Stick bomb for use with *3.7-cm Pak*	119
63.	Carriage of *3.7-cm Pak*, showing traversing and elevating mechanisms	122
64.	*5-cm Pak 38*	123
65.	*5-cm Pak 38* from rear	125
66.	Breech of *5-cm Pak*	126

CONTENTS

Figure		Page
67.	Gunner's position on *5-cm Pak*, showing traversing and elevating handwheels	127
68.	Extractors of *5-cm Pak*	131
69.	Breechblock of *5-cm Pak*	132
70.	Barrel and breech of *5-cm Pak*	134
71.	7.5-cm infantry howitzer in action	138
72.	Breech of 7.5-cm infantry howitzer	139
73.	Breechblock and firing mechanism of 7.5-cm infantry howitzer	140
74.	Firing mechanism parts of 7.5-cm infantry howitzer	141
75.	7.5-cm infantry howitzer in traveling position	142
76.	Sighting mechanism (side view) of 7.5-cm infantry howitzer	143
77.	Sighting mechanism of 7.5-cm infantry howitzer, showing range-scale drum	144
78.	Manhandling 7.5-cm infantry howitzer	145
79.	Panoramic sight (*Rundblickfernrohr 16, Rbl.F. 16*) used on 7.5-cm infantry howitzer	147
80.	15-cm infantry howitzer in action	149
81.	15-cm infantry howitzer (rear view)	150
82.	15-cm infantry howitzer on self-propelled mount	152
83.	Firing mechanism of 10.5-cm light field howitzer 18 (*l.F.H. 18*)	154
84.	Breechblock of 10.5-cm light field howitzer 18 (*l.F.H. 18*)	153
85.	Breechblock (rear view) of 10.5-cm light field howitzer 18 (*l.F.H. 18*)	155
86–90.	Special labels	163, 164
91.	Label for case of 1,500 rounds of heavy, pointed ball ammunition (*Patronen s. S., Patronen schweres Spitzgeschoss*)	166
92.	Label for super armor-piercing bullet with tungsten carbide core (*Patr. S.m.K.H., Patronen Spitzgeschoss mit Stahlkern gehartet*)	167
93.	Label for 5 rounds of armor-piercing bullet (*Patronen 318*)	167
94.	Label for armor-piercing incendiary bullet (*Patr.P.m.K., Patronen Phosphor mit Stahlkern*)	167
95.	Label for heavy, pointed ball ammunition (*Patr.s.S., Patronen schweres Spitzgeschoss*)	168
96.	Label for 1,500 rounds of heavy, pointed ball ammunition (*Patr. s.S., Patronen schweres Spitzgeschoss*)	168
97.	Labels for steel-core, armor-piercing ammunition (*Patronen S.m.K., Patronen Spitzgeschoss mit Stahlkern*)	169
98.	Label for 1,500 rounds of observation (explosive) bullets (*B.-Patronen, Beobachtungsgeschoss Patronen*)	170
99.	Label for light, pointed ball ammunition (*Patronen l.S, Patronen leichtes Spitzgeschoss*)	170
100.	Label for model 08 pistol cartridges (*Pistolenpatronen 08*)	171

Figure		Page
101.	Label for dummy, drill cartridges, model S (*Exerzierpatronen S.*)	171
102.	Markings on base of German small-arms cartridge	172
103.	Heavy, pointed ball (*Patronen schweres Spitzgeschoss*)	175
104.	Armor-piercing (*Patronen Spitzgeschoss mit Stahlkern*)	175
105.	Armor-piercing tracer (*Patronen Spitzgeschoss mit Stahlkern und Leuchtspur*)	175
106.	Super-armor-piercing with tungsten carbide core (*Patronen Spitzgeschoss mit Stahlkern gehartet*)	177
107.	Light ball, special practice (*Patronen leichtes Spitzgechoss*)	177
108.	Practice tracer (*Patronen leichtes Spitzgeschoss mit Leuchtspur*)	177
109.	Semi-armor-piercing (*Patronen Spitzgeschoss mit Eisenkern*)	178
110.	Armor-piercing incendiary (*Patronen Phosphor mit Stahlkern*)	178
111.	Observation (explosive) bullet (*Beabachtangsgeschoss Patronen*)	178
112.	Dummy cartridges (*Exerzierpatronen*)	179
113.	Blank cartridge (*Platz-Patrone 88*)	180
114.	Cross section of ball cartridge (*scharfe Patrone S.*)	180
115.	8-cm mortar shell	181
—	Graphic comparison of millimeters and inches	*inside back cover*

TABLES

1.	Overhead firing table (in yards)	76
2.	Table of minimum clearance	77
3.	Firing table, 8-cm heavy mortar, model 34 (German)	110

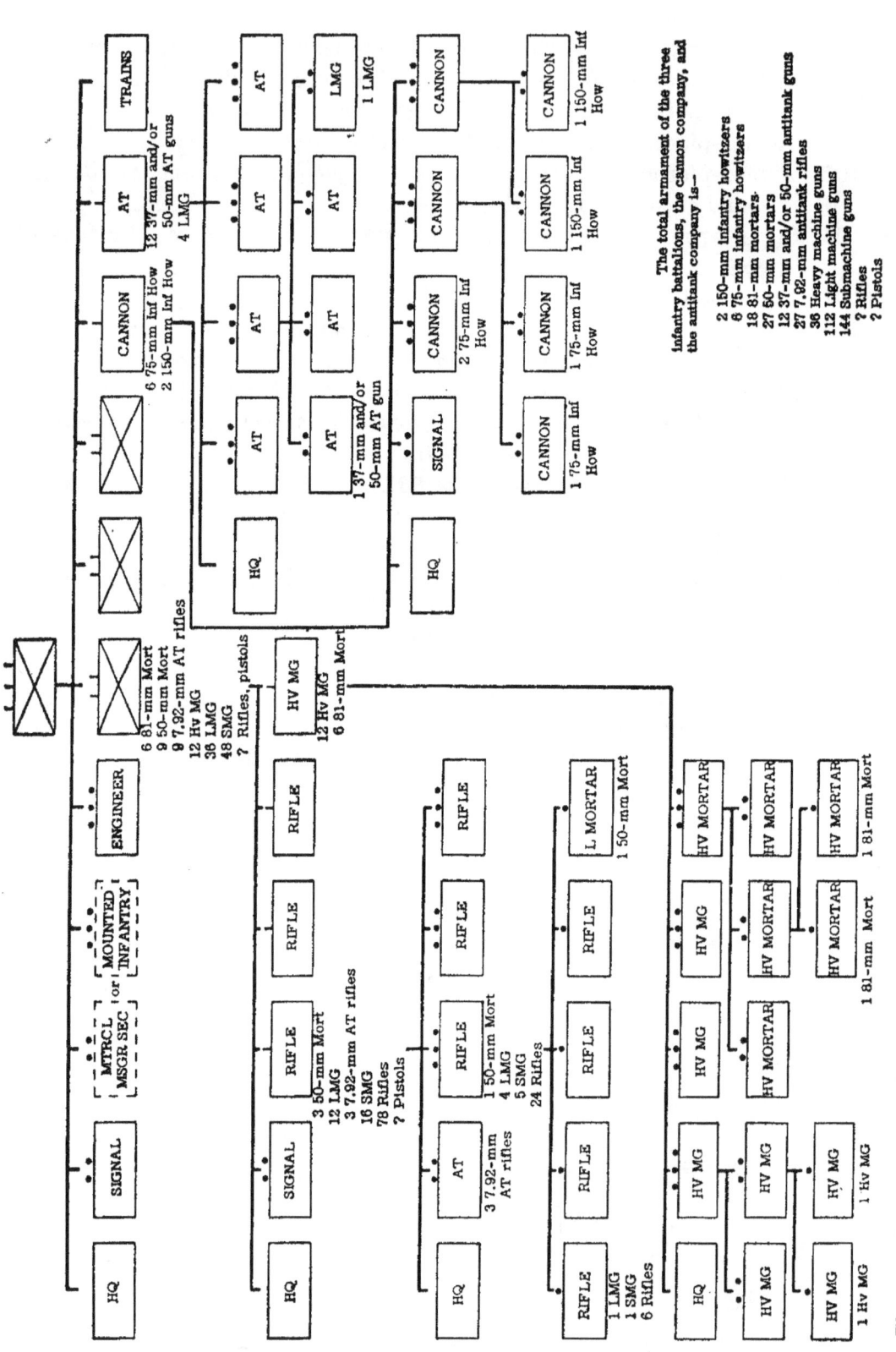

Figure 1.—Armament and organization of German infantry regiment. (This chart shows the principal unit which employs the weapons described herein.)

Section I. INTRODUCTION

The principal German infantry weapons are here described in order to enable U. S. troops to identify and, when the opportunity exists, to operate them.[1] No attempt has been made to provide all the details necessary for the maintenance and repair of the weapons described.

Reports from observers, enemy documents, British publications, and other sources of information have been examined and compared in order to present in a compact and simple form all the pertinent information on the main German infantry weapons. Wherever possible, the exposition is based on an actual examination and operation of the weapon concerned.

The equipment of the German Army in 1939, and its present equipment, reflect the settled policy of the German High Command to have the smallest variety of weapons consistent with meeting operational requirements. While emphasis has been maintained on developing weapons with a high degree of fighting efficiency, only selected types have been designed for mass production.

---

[1] "Abandoned enemy matériel is promptly put into use to augment that of the pursuing force or to replace losses." FM 100–5, "Field Service Regulations, Operations," par. 579, Changes No. 1 (Sept. 16, 1942). The processing of captured matériel for intelligence purposes is described in Training Circular No. 81 (Nov. 6, 1942), Section III. Training Circular No. 88 (Nov. 17, 1942) contains general instructions for the recovery and evacuation of arms and other equipment by combat units in the combat zone.

As the battle fronts have widened and the theaters of operations become more varied, the Germans have been forced to increase the variety of their weapons and to improve existing matériel. In addition, they have augmented their supply of weapons by using captured matériel.

No attempt has been made in the sections which follow to describe experimental or new German weapons which have not yet come into wide use. Nor is captured matériel used by the Germans considered. Therefore, on occasion U. S. troops may encounter German infantry equipped with some weapon not included in this study. However, a good knowledge of the standard German weapons will usually form a sound basis for understanding the operation of the newer German weapons.

For the armament and organization of the German infantry regiment, the principal unit which employs the weapons described herein, see figure 1.

Section II. PISTOLS, RIFLES, AND GRENADES[1]

1. LUGER PISTOL

a. General

Since 1908 the Luger pistol has been an official German military side arm. Georg Luger of the DWM Arms Company[2] in Germany developed this weapon, known officially as *Pistole 08,* from the American Borchart pistol invented in 1893.

The Luger is a well-balanced, accurate pistol. It imparts a high muzzle velocity to a small-caliber bullet, but develops only a relatively small amount of stopping power. Unlike the comparatively slow U. S. 45-caliber bullet, the Luger small-caliber bullet does not often lodge itself in the target and thereby impart its shocking power to that which it hits. With its high speed and small caliber it tends to pierce, inflicting a small, clean wound.

When the Luger is kept clean, it functions well. However, the mechanism is rather exposed to dust and dirt.

b. How to Identify

The Luger may be identified readily by its exposed barrel, curved butt, and generally smooth lines. (See fig. 2.)

---

[1] The weapons discussed in this section may be operated by one man.
[2] *Deutsche Waffen- und Munitionsfabriken, Aktiengesellschaft.*

c. Characteristics

(1) *General.*—The Luger is the most common side arm in use in the German Army. It is a semiautomatic, recoil-operated, 8-shot pistol with a caliber of 9 mm (.354 inch).[3] It has a toggle-joint action very

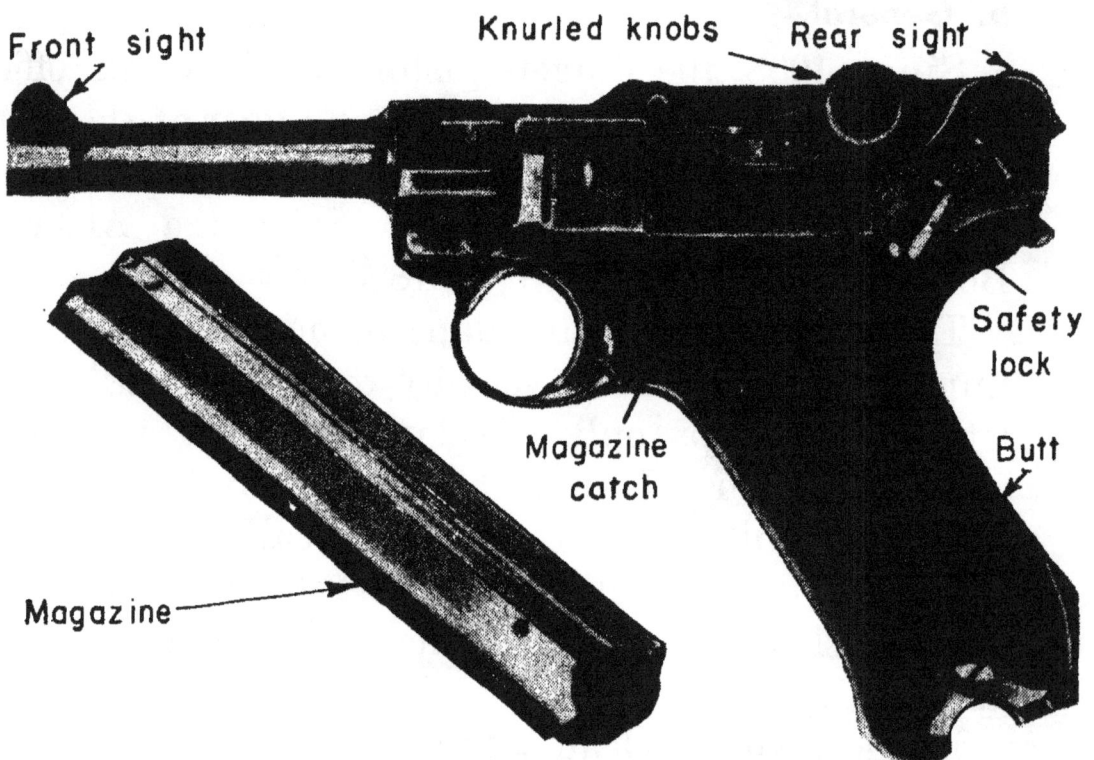

Figure 2.—Luger pistol and magazine.

similar to that of the Maxim machine gun. It is fed by an 8-round magazine that fits into the butt and is held by a magazine catch similar to that on the U. S. service automatic pistol (M1911 or M1911 A1 Colt .45), and located in approximately the same relative position.

---

[3] A scale of inches and millimeters is printed on the inside of the back cover to aid readers to know the exact length of these units.

PISTOLS, RIFLES, AND GRENADES

(2) *Table of characteristics.*—

Principle of operation	Recoil-operated.
Caliber	9 mm (.354 inch).
Ammunition	9-mm Parabellum (German, British, Italian, or U. S. manufacture).
Capacity of magazine	8 rounds.
Sights:	
Front	Inverted V blade.
Rear	Open V notch, nonadjustable.
Length of barrel	4.25 inches.
Weight (empty)	1 pound 14 ounces.
Range:	
Effective	25 yards.
Maximum	1,150 yards.
Muzzle velocity	1,040 feet per second.

d. How to Operate

(1) *Safety.*—The safety is on the left side of the receiver as you hold the pistol in firing. It is a lever pivoted at the lower end. When the safety lock is turned down and to the rear, the safety catch is on and the pistol will not fire. With the lock in this position, the German word *gesichert* ("made safe") is exposed. To release the safety, it is necessary to push the lever forward and up; the word *gesichert* will then be covered by the safety lever arm, and the pistol is ready to fire.

(2) *To load and fire.*—A loaded magazine is inserted into the butt and shoved home until the magazine catch

clicks. This is similar to the operation used in loading the U. S. Colt .45.

In order to move one of the cartridges forward into the chamber for firing, it is necessary to pull the toggle joint to the rear and then let it snap forward, in much

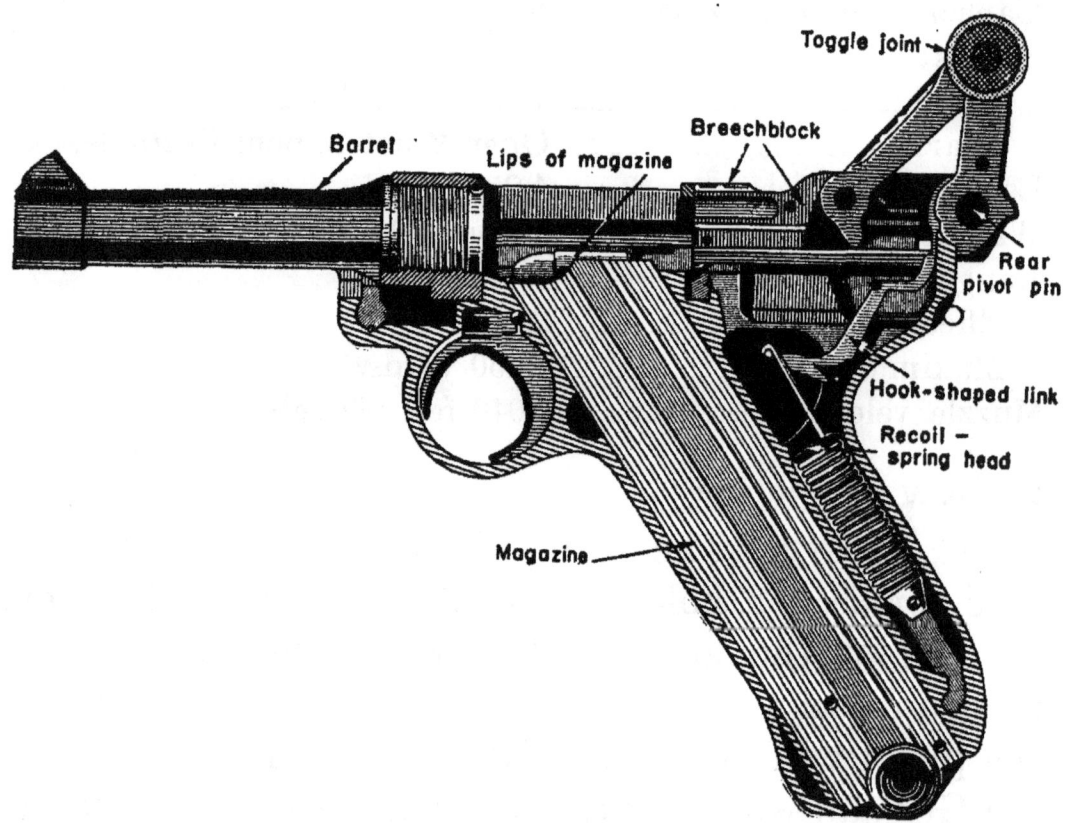

Figure 3.—Cross section of Luger pistol, showing action of toggle joint.

the same fashion as is done with the U. S. Colt .45. With the thumb and forefinger of the left hand, grasp the knurled knobs on both sides of the toggle joint and draw the joint to the rear as far as it will go (see fig. 3). Then release the knobs, and let the breechblock snap forward. This operation will carry forward a cartridge from the lips of the magazine into the chamber.

The pistol should then be locked by moving the safety so as to expose the word *gesichert*.

It is always possible to determine whether there is a cartridge in the chamber by feeling or noting the position of the extractor (see fig. 4). When there is a cartridge in the chamber, the front end of the extractor projects above the level of the top surface of the breech-

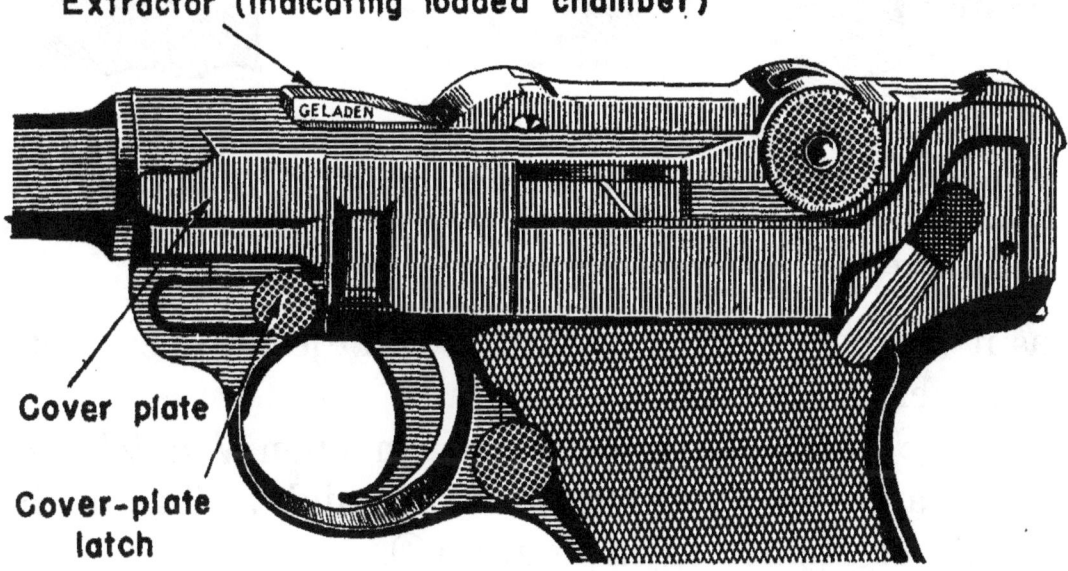

Figure 4.—Close-up of Luger pistol to show operation of extractor.

block, exposing the word *geladen* ("loaded") on the left side of the extractor. If there is no cartridge in the chamber, the extractor is level with the top surface of the breechblock.

(3) *To unload.*—First, press the magazine catch, allowing the magazine to drop out of the butt. Then, to extract any cartridge that may be in the chamber, grasp the knurled knobs of the toggle joint in the same manner as in loading. Pull the joint to the rear as far

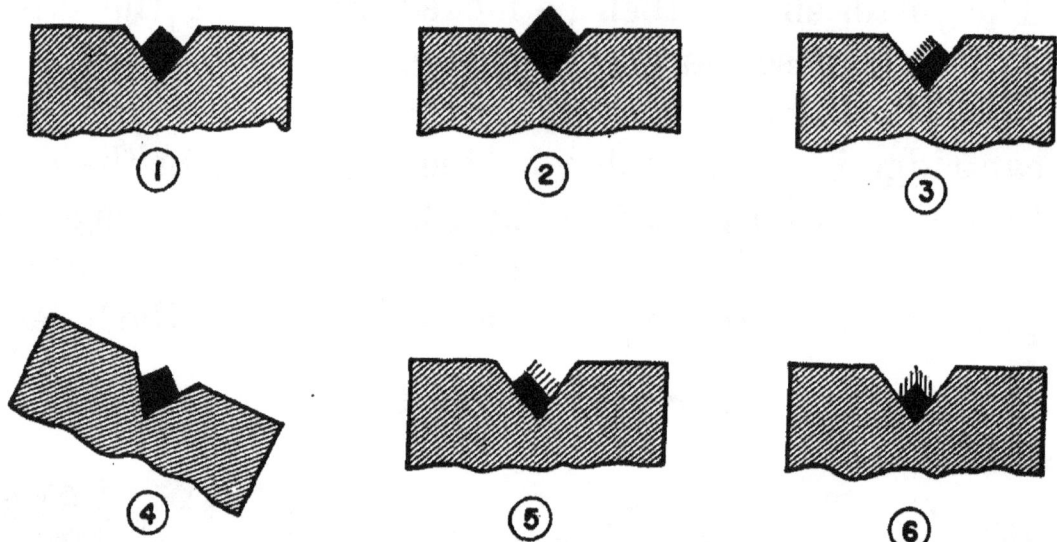

Figure 5.—Method of using German sights. (①) illustrates correct sight picture; ②, firing high; ③, low and right; ④, low and right; ⑤, lower left; ⑥, low shot.)

as it will come. This operation will eject any cartridge in the chamber.

(4) *Sights*.—This pistol has an open V notch rear sight and an inverted V front sight. The sights should be aligned as in figure 5 ①.

e. Ammunition

Rimless, straight-case ammunition is used. German ammunition boxes will read *Pistolenpatronen 08* ("pistol cartridges 08"). These should be distinguished from *Exerzierpatronen 08* ("drill cartridges 08"). The bullets in these cartridges have coated steel jackets and lead cores. The edge of the primer of the ball cartridge is painted black. British- and U. S.-made 9-mm Parabellum ammunition will function well in this pistol; the German ammunition will of course give the best results. (See sec. V, p. 161, below.)

f. Maintenance

(1) *Oiling and cleaning.*—This pistol requires the same type of care as the U. S. M1911 Colt .45 automatic. The cleaning and oiling is done in a similar manner. However, in desert countries, or in other places where dust is prevalent, oil should be used sparingly or not at all.

(2) *Stripping.*—In order to disassemble the weapon, it is necessary to remove the magazine and empty the chamber as indicated in **d** (3), page 7, above. Press the muzzle against a clean, hard surface until the barrel has moved to the rear about a half inch. Then push the knurled section of the cover-plate latch downward and remove the cover plate. Turn the pistol upside down and slide the barrel and receiver forward and separate them. Punch out the rear pivot pin and remove the breechblock from the receiver. This amount of disassembly is sufficient for purposes of cleaning and oiling the pistol.

(3) *Assembly.*—To reassemble the parts of the weapon, first put the breechblock and receiver together and replace the pivot pin. Slide the barrel and receiver back onto the frame, making sure that the hook-shaped link engages in the claws of the recoil-spring head. Push the barrel backward, using a piece of wood against the muzzle, and replace the cover plate. Turn the cover-plate latch until it catches in its locked position.

g. Accessories

There is a leather holster which carries extra ammunition in a separate magazine. This holster also contains a tool which can be used for disassembling the pistol and for loading the magazine.

2. WALTHER PISTOL

a. General

The Walther, officially called *Pistole 38,* is coming into more and more general use as a standard issue in the German Army. Eventually it may replace the Luger. Although the Walther lacks the stopping power of the U. S. M1911 Colt .45, it is nevertheless a handy weapon because of its double-action [4] feature and its good balance.

b. How to Identify

The Walther may be identified by—

(1) Horizontally grooved grips.
(2) Outside hammer.
(3) Marking ("P. 38") on the left side of the slide.
(4) Safety on the left rear of the slide.
(5) Lanyard hook on the left grip.
(6) Double action.

c. Characteristics

(1) *General.*—The Walther is a recoil-operated pistol with a slide that moves directly to the rear (in this respect, like the U. S. M1911 Colt .45 and unlike

---

[4] The double-action feature enables the weapon to be fired simply by pressure on the trigger without cocking the hammer. The Walther is the only military pistol with this feature.

the Luger). The feed is by an 8-round magazine that fits into the pistol handle, but, unlike the U. S. M1911 Colt .45 and the Luger, the magazine catch is located

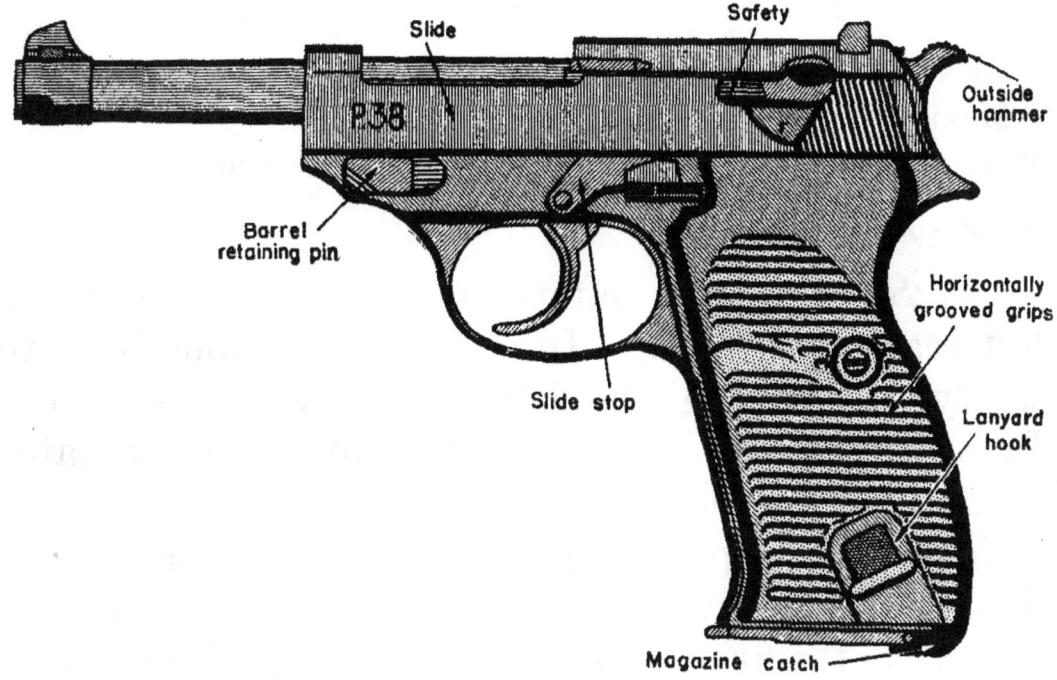

Figure 6.—Walther pistol.

on the bottom rear of the butt and is moved to the rear to release the magazine. (See fig. 6.)

(2) *Table of characteristics.*—

Principle of operation	Short recoil-operated, double-action trigger mechanism.
Caliber	9-mm (.354 inch).
Ammunition	9-mm Parabellum (German, British, Italian, or U. S. manufacture).
Capacity of magazine	8 rounds.
Sights:	
Front	Inverted V blade.
Rear	Open V notch, nonadjustable.

Length of barrel_____ 4.75 inches.
Weight:
  With loaded magazine____ 2 pounds 5.25 ounces.
  With empty magazine____ 2 pounds 1.75 ounces.
Range:
  Effective _____ 25 yards.
  Maximum _____ 1,150 yards.
Muzzle velocity_____ 1,040 feet per second.

d. How to Operate

(1) *Safety.*—The safety is a lever located at the left rear of the slide. In order to fire, thumb up the safety, uncovering the letter "F" (*Feuer*—"fire"). In order to lock the pistol, thumb down the safety uncovering the letter "S" (*sicher*—"safe").

To uncock the pistol, set the safety to the "safe" position. This permits the hammer to fall and at the same time locks the firing pin in its rearmost position. (See fig. 7.)

The Walther has a device which enables a quick check to be made in order to determine whether or not there is a cartridge in the chamber. If there is a cartridge in the chamber, a small pin protrudes about a quarter of an inch from the back end of the slide. If the chamber is empty, this small pin will remain flush with the surface of the back end of the slide. This arrangement is particularly handy in the dark.

(2) *To load and fire.*—(a) *To load, "single action."*—Put the safety on "fire." Insert a loaded magazine into the butt and shove it forward until the magazine catch holds it. Pull the slide back once and

let it snap forward. The pistol is now loaded and cocked. A pull on the trigger will fire the weapon.

(b) *To load, "alternate method."*—Put the safety on "safe." Insert the loaded magazine and work the slide as described in **d** (1), on the opposite page. This pistol is now loaded but not cocked. When ready to

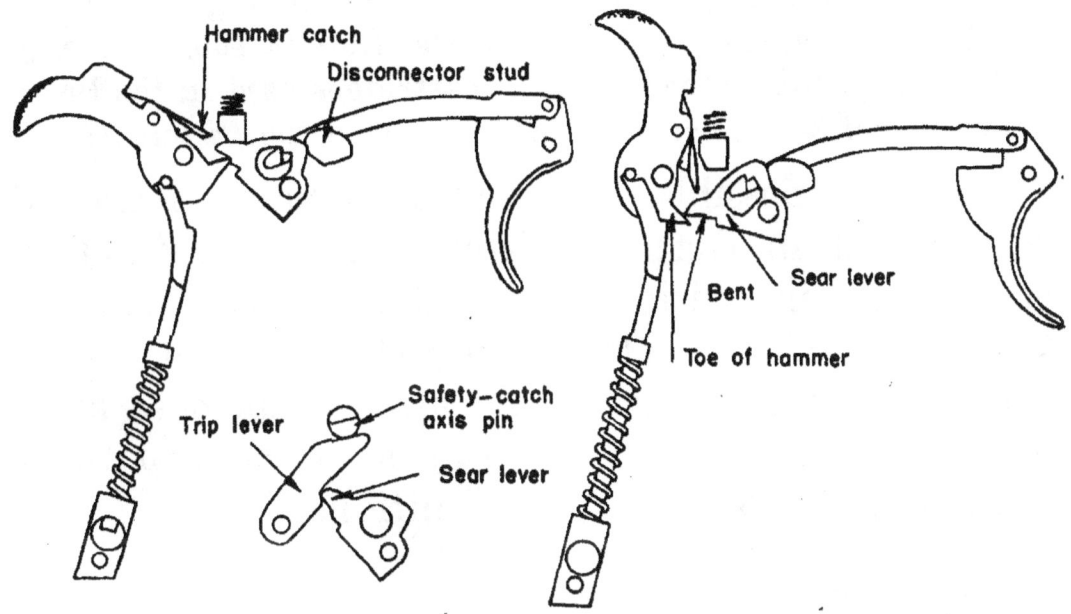

Figure 7.—Diagrammatic sketch showing trigger action of Walther pistol.

fire, put the safety on "fire" and pull the trigger. As this pistol has a double action, the pull on the trigger will cock the hammer and then fire the round. After the first shot, the recoil of the slide will cock the hammer.

(3) *To unload.*—Pull to the rear the magazine catch, located on the bottom rear of the butt, and the magazine will drop out. Work the slide back and forth several times to be sure that the chamber is emptied.

e. Ammunition

The following types of ammunition may be used in the *Pistole 38*:

(1) German standard 9-mm Parabellum cartridge (which is used also in the *Pistole 08*).

(2) British- and U. S.-manufactured 9-mm Parabellum ammunition for the Sten and Lanchester submachine guns.

(3) Italian ammunition used in the Beretta submachine gun and 9-mm pistols (other than the cartridges used in the Beretta pistol, model 34, which will not function in the *Pistole 38*).

Wherever possible, German-issue ammunition should be inserted in German pistols, which are "touchy" about the ammunition used. Italian pistol ammunition, model 38, is likely to cause stoppages in German 9-mm weapons. Care should also be taken so as not to mistake the dummy cartridges (*Exerzierpatronen 08*) used in drills for live ammunition.

f. Maintenance

(1) *Stripping.*—Insert an *empty* magazine in the pistol. Pull the slide back until the slide stop engages and holds the slide in the rear position. Turn the barrel retaining pin clockwise about three quarters of a turn. Remove the magazine, press down on the slide stop, and let the slide snap forward. Pull the trigger, and remove the slide and barrel from the receiver by pulling the slide forward. Unlock the slide from the barrel by pushing in on the locking-cam plunger and pulling down the locking cam.

(2) *Assembly.*—Assemble in the reverse order, but be sure that the slide and barrel are locked together

before being assembled to the receiver. To insure this, pull out the locking-cam plunger and press the locking cam upward into its groove. The barrel and slide will remain locked together if the pistol is assembled upside down, but the ejector and the two levers of the safety mechanism must be pushed in so as to prevent them from catching on the rear end of the slide.

(3) *General care.*—The type of care given the U. S. service pistol will keep the *Pistole 38* in good working order. It should be cleaned and oiled frequently. In extremely sandy or dusty regions, oil should be used sparingly or not at all.

g. Accessories

A leather holster, spare magazines, and a magazine holder are issued with this weapon.

3. SUBMACHINE GUN [5] (M.P. 38 AND M.P. 40)

a. General

Although this weapon was originally designed for use by parachute troops, it can now be found in general use in all combat units of the German Army. The construction is simple, and both the *M.P.*[6] *38* and the more recent *M.P. 40,* which has been issued in large quantities, are reliable weapons. They fire from an open bolt, and the pressure in the barrel forces the bolt back in order to extract and eject the empty

---

[5] A submachine gun shoots pistol ammunition; the ordinary machine gun shoots rifle ammunition.

[6] *M.P.* is an abbreviation for *Maschinenpistole,* literally "machine pistol."

cartridge case. The spring then forces the bolt forward again, chambering and firing a new round.

b. How to Identify

The *M.P. 38* and *M.P. 40* may be identified by—

(1) Folding skeleton shoulder stock.
(2) Absence of wood (these guns are all metal and plastic).
(3) Fixed and folding, open rear sights.
(4) Hooded front sight.
(5) Marking ("M.P. 38" or "M.P. 40") on top of the receiver.
(6) Corrugations on the receiver casing of the *M.P. 38;* smooth surface on the receiver casing of the *M.P. 40.*

c. Characteristics

(1) *General.*—The *M.P. 38* and *M.P. 40* are simple blowback-operated submachine guns; they are maga-

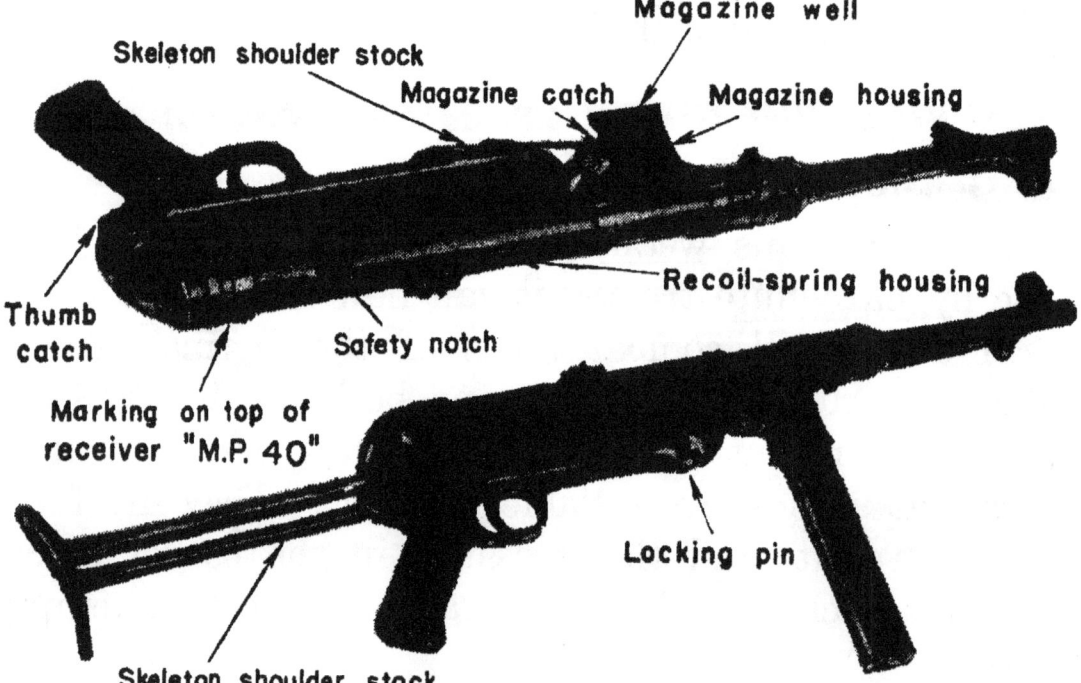

Figure 8.—Two views of *M.P. 40*, showing skeleton shoulder stock folded, and open.

zine-fed, air-cooled shoulder weapons which may also be fired from the hip. They are used for close work and are not effective at the longer ranges. They fire from an open bolt and deliver full-automatic fire only. Although the *M.P. 40* is slightly lighter and has a slower rate of fire, both types are the same for all practical purposes. (See fig. 8.)

(2) *Table of characteristics.*—

Principle of operation	Straight blowback, full-automatic fire only.
Caliber	9 mm (.354 inch).
Capacity of magazine	32 rounds in removable box magazine.
Sights:	
Front	Inverted V blade, with cover.
Rear:	
Fixed	Open V notch, sighted to 100 meters (109 yards).
Folding	Open V notch, sighted to 200 meters (219 yards).
Length	Over-all, with shoulder stock extended, $33\frac{1}{2}$ inches.
Weight	With loaded magazine, 10 pounds 7 ounces.
Range:	
Effective	200 yards.
Maximum	1,850 yards.
Rate of fire (practical)	80 to 90 rounds per minute (in short bursts).

d. How to Operate

(1) *Safety.*—The only safety on these guns is the notch marked "S" (*sicher*—"safe") at the butt end of the cut made for the operating handle in the receiver.

To make the gun "safe," pull the operating handle back as far as it will go and then push it upward into the

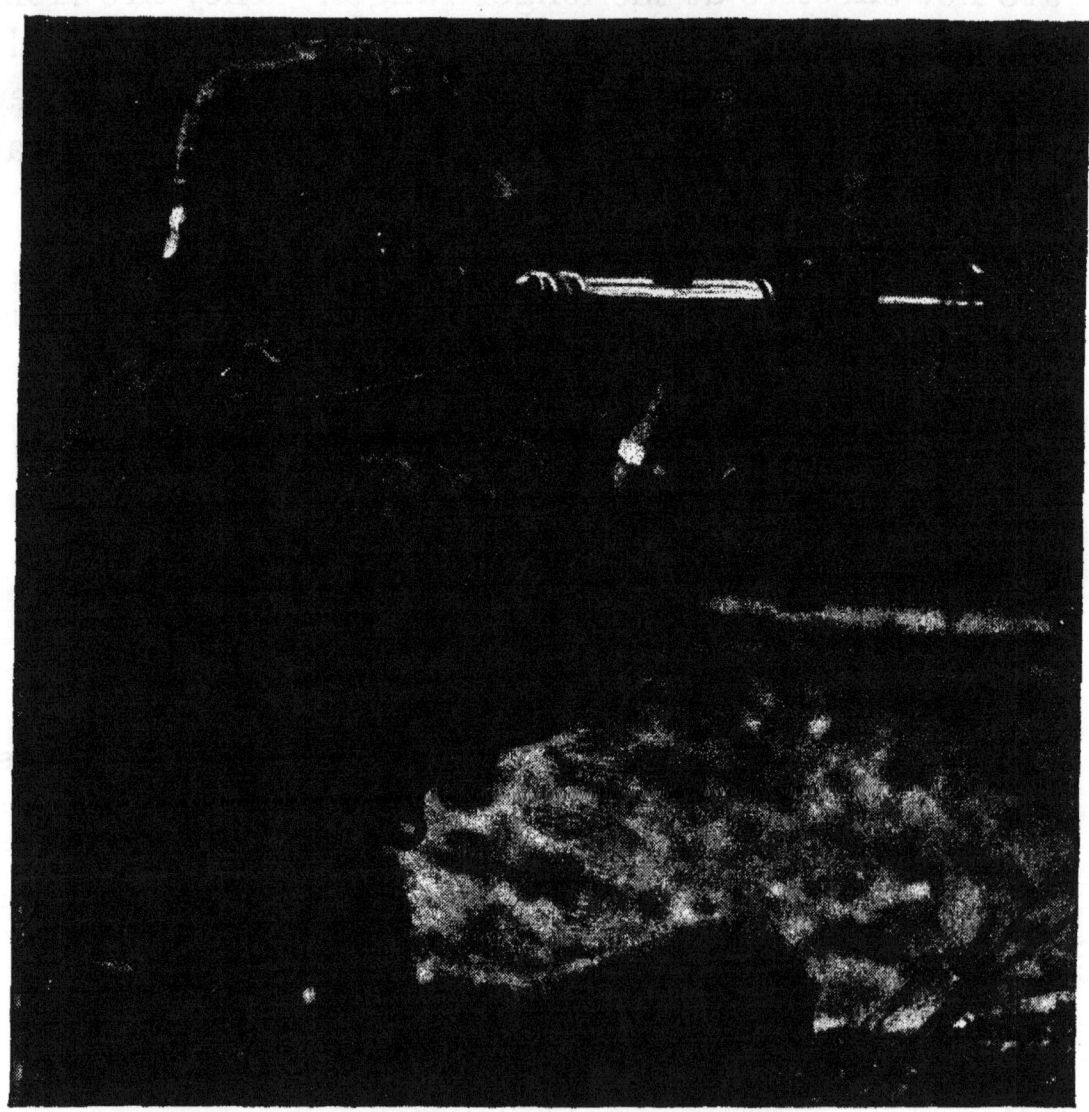

Figure 9.—M.P. 40 in action. (This photograph shows the manner of holding the pistol with the left hand when using the skeleton shoulder stock.)

safety notch. This is not a positive safety, as a jump or a fall may disengage the operating handle from the safety notch and leave the gun ready to fire.

(2) *To load and fire.*—Press the thumb catch above the pistol grip in order to release the skeleton shoulder stock from its folded position. Snap the shoulder stock into extended position and unfold the butt plate. Pull the operating handle back and switch it into the safety notch. Insert a loaded magazine into the feedway on the under side of the receiver until the magazine catch engages. Disengage the operating handle from the safety notch; then aim,[7] and squeeze the trigger. The magazine can serve as a grip while firing (but see fig. 9 for the German method of firing).

(3) *To unload.*—Press the magazine catch and remove the magazine. Check the chamber to be sure that it is empty. After pressing the trigger, let the operating handle go forward slowly.

e. Ammunition

The ammunition used in these guns is the standard 9-mm Parabellum cartridge, used in all German pistols and submachine guns. This is a rimless, straight-case cartridge with a round-nose, jacketed bullet. The German nomenclature for this ammunition is *Pistolenpatronen 08* ("pistol cartridges 08"). It comes in cases containing 4,160 rounds, packed in multiples of 16 rounds in cartons and packages. Ammunition (9-mm) manufactured for the British Sten submachine gun (called a machine carbine by the British) can be used in the *M.P. 38* and *M.P. 40.* Italian 9-mm pistol ammunition other than model 34 will also

---

[7] See fig. 5, p. 8, above, for the method of aligning German sights.

function. But the German-issue ammunition should be used whenever possible.

f. Maintenance

(1) *Oiling and cleaning.*—These submachine guns are cleaned and oiled in the same manner as the U. S.

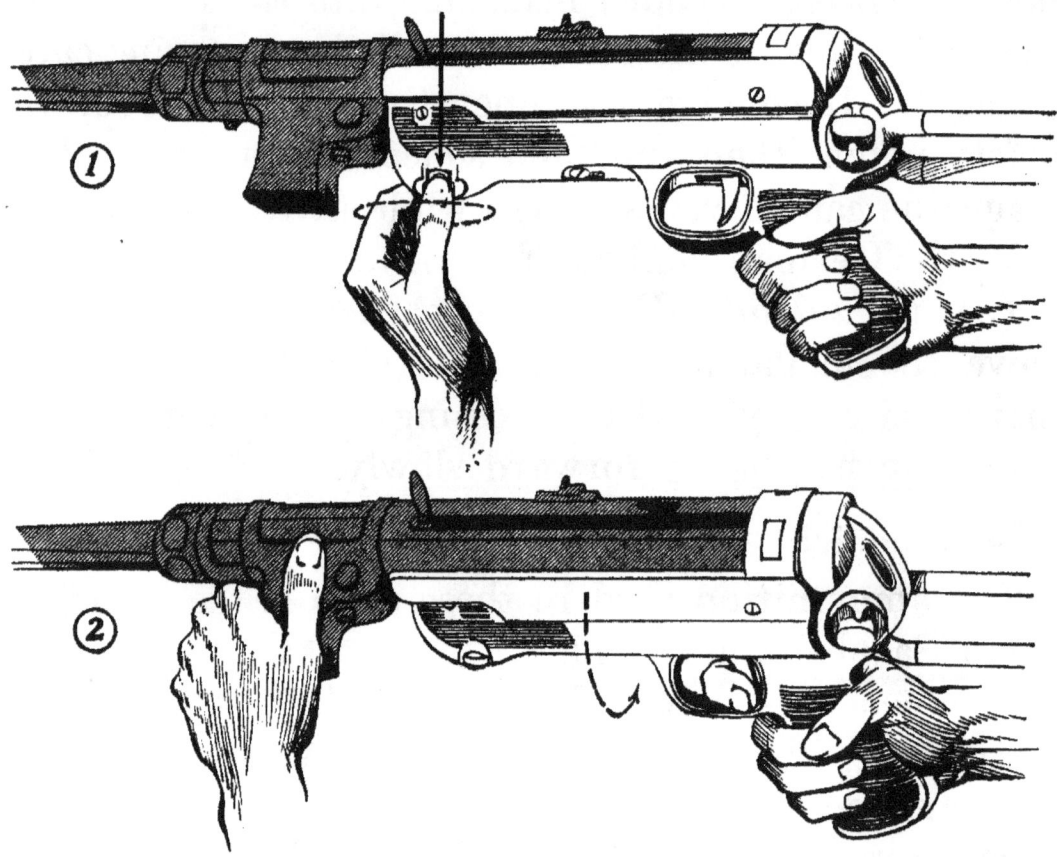

Figure 10.—Method of removing receiver of M.P. 40 from barrel and from magazine housing.

Thompson submachine gun. In sandy or dusty country, oil should be used sparingly or not at all.

(2) *Stripping.*—First, be sure that the gun is unloaded and uncocked. Pull out the locking pin (see fig. 10 ①) located on the bottom front portion of the receiver behind the magazine well, and turn the pin a

little to keep it unlocked. Grasp the barrel with the left hand and the pistol grip with the right; press the trigger, and at the same time turn the receiver in a counterclockwise direction, holding the magazine housing in its normal position (see fig. 10 ②). It will then be possible to separate the receiver from the barrel and from the magazine housing. Remove the bolt and recoil spring from the receiver by means of the operating handle. The recoil spring may be removed from the telescoping recoil-spring housing.

(3) *Assembly.*—Assemble the recoil spring to the recoil-spring housing. Replace the recoil-spring assembly and bolt into the receiver. Hold the trigger back, and assemble the receiver to the barrel and the magazine housing by holding the magazine housing and then inserting the receiver and turning it in a clockwise direction. Turn the locking pin so that it snaps in.

g. Accessories

Six magazines and a magazine filler are carried in a web haversack. Four magazines are sometimes carried on a magazine holder attached to the belt. A small cleaning outfit is carried on the person, and a sling is attached to these guns for carrying purposes.

4. MAUSER KAR. 98K RIFLE

a. General

The Mauser *Kar. 98K,* or Mauser carbine, model 98K, rifle is the standard shoulder weapon of the German Army. Anyone who can use the U. S. M1903 (Springfield) service rifle will have little difficulty in using this German weapon, which is a handy, accurate short rifle. Although the German rifle has no windage adjustment or peep-sight, it will give good results at medium ranges after a little practice.

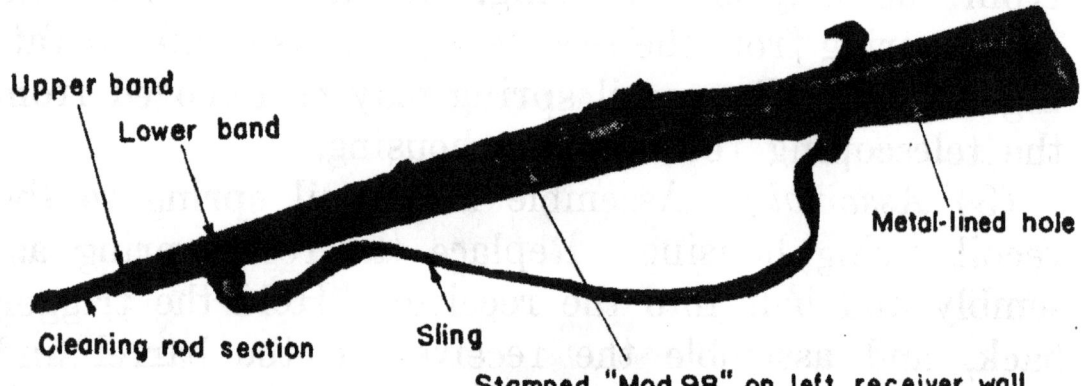

Figure 11.—*Mauser Kar. 98K rifle.*

b. How to Identify

The Mauser *Kar. 98K* rifle may be identified by—

(1) Short barrel (23.4 inches).
(2) Upper and lower bands very close together.
(3) Cleaning rod section fitted into the stock under the muzzle.
(4) Open V notch, leaf rear sight, sliding on a ramp and graduated from 100 to 2,000 (meters).
(5) Bolt action similar to the U. S. M1903 (Springfield) rifle.
(6) Semi-pistol-grip stock, with sling on the left side and a metal-lined hole through the stock, behind the hole for the butt end of the sling.
(7) Marking ("Mod 98") on the left receiver wall.

c. Characteristics

(1) *General.*—The Mauser *Kar. 98K*, a short rifle or carbine, is a bolt-operated, magazine-fed shoulder

weapon very similar to the U. S. M1903 (Springfield) service rifle (see fig. 11). It has a leaf rear sight, with an open V notch that slides on a ramp and is graduated from 100 to 2,000 meters (109 to 2,187 yards). Older models, which operate exactly as does the *Kar. 98K* and differ only in that they have longer barrels and minor variations in fittings, are the *Gew. 98, Kar. 98,* and *Kar. 98B.*

(2) *Table of characteristics.*—

Principle of operation	Manually bolt-operated.
Caliber	7.92 mm (.312 inches).
Capacity of magazine	5 rounds.
Ammunition	7.92 German small-arms ammunition (rifle or machine-gun).
Weight	9 pounds (approximately).
Length of barrel	23.4 inches.
Over-all length	43.5 inches.
Muzzle velocity	2,800 feet per second (approximately).
Sights:	
Front	Inverted V blade (which is sometimes equipped with a hood to provide shade).
Rear	Leaf with open V notch sliding on ramp, graduated from 100 to 2,000 meters; no windage adjustment.
Range:	
Maximum	3,000 yards (approximately).
Effective	800 yards (approximately).

d. How to Operate

(1) *Safety.*—The safety is a thumb-operated lever mounted on the bolt plug, and operates in the same

manner as the safety on the U. S. Springfield service rifle. The rifle can be fired and the bolt worked when the safety lock is moved to the left. When the safety lock is moved to the right, the piece is locked. The safety lock can be moved only when the rifle is cocked.

(2) *To load and fire.*—The rifle is loaded in the same manner as the U. S. Springfield rifle. Open the

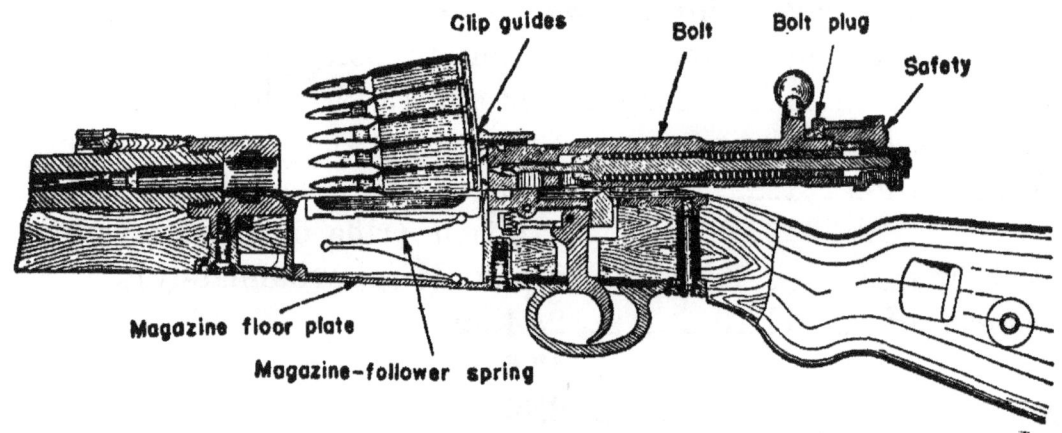

Figure 12.—**Cross section of magazine, trigger, and bolt mechanism of Mauser *Kar. 98K* rifle.**

bolt, place a clip of cartridges in the clip guides, and press them down into the magazine (see fig. 12). Close the bolt; this action will eject any empty clip. The trigger has a double pull; so take up the slack (as in the U. S. service rifles) before squeezing the trigger.[3] Observe all the safety precautions used in firing U. S. rifles.

(3) *To unload.*—Open the bolt and work it back and forth until you empty both the magazine and the chamber. Check the chamber and magazine with your

---

[3] See fig. 5, p. 8, above, for the method of aligning German sights.

finger tip to make sure that they are both clear of cartridges.

e. Ammunition

The ammunition used in this rifle includes various types of 7.92-mm (.312-inch) small-arms ammunition. (See pars. 20 to 30, incl., pp. 161–184, below, for an explanation of the labels on ammunition cases.) Ball ammunition is packed in cases holding 1,500 rounds, and the label is overprinted **i.L.** to indicate that the ammunition in a case is packed in 5-round clips. Do not use ammunition from cases whose labels are overprinted **Ex.**, as this is "dummy," or drill, ammunition.

f. Maintenance

(1) *Stripping.*—(a) *To remove bolt.*—Cock the rifle by working the bolt, and set the safety lever halfway between the safe and the locked positions. Pull the bolt back. Then pull out the near end of the bolt stop, which is located on the left side of the receiver near the cutoff. Hold the bolt stop out while you remove the bolt from the receiver.

(b) *To disassemble bolt.*—The bolt is stripped in the same manner as that of the U. S. Springfield rifle. Press in the bolt-sleeve lock and unscrew the bolt sleeve, firing pin, and spring assembly. Now place the tip of the firing pin in the hole in the stock of the rifle. Compress the spring, pushing down on the bolt sleeve until the bolt sleeve clears the headless cocking piece. Turn the cocking piece a quarter turn in either direction and remove it from the firing pin shaft. Ease up on the bolt sleeve so as not to allow the spring to escape suddenly. Remove the bolt sleeve and firing-pin spring from the firing pin.

(c) *To remove magazine floor plate.*—Insert the point of a bullet or a pointed tool into the small hole in the magazine floor plate, and exert pressure while at the same time pushing the floor plate toward the trigger guard. This will release the catch, and the magazine floor-plate spring and follower can then be removed and broken down into their separate units. Further stripping is not usually necessary.

(2) *Assembly.*—The assembling is done in the reverse order to that described in f(1), above.

(3) *Care and cleaning.*—The care of this rifle is the same as that required for the U. S. M1903 and M1 service rifles.

g. Accessories

(1) *General.*—Each rifle is furnished with a short length of cleaning rod, fitted through the bayonet stud. The rods from 3 rifles will make one full-length cleaning rod. A small metal case carried on the person holds an oiler, a pull-through, brushes, and short lengths of tow used as patches. Ammunition is carried in 2 leather ammunition pouches attached to the belt, which hold 60 rounds in 5-round clips. Additional rifle ammunition is issued in cloth bandoleers similar to the U. S. type. Muzzle and breech covers are sometimes used. Rifle grenade launchers may be attached to the rifle. In addition, a short knife bayonet

is made to be fixed to the rifle in a manner similar to that of U. S. service bayonets.

(2) *Grenade launchers and sights.*—Both types are illustrated in figure 13. (See also figs. 14, 16, and 18.) The grenade launcher at the top of figure 13 is used with the spigot-type, hollow-charge rifle grenade (*Schuss-G.P. 40*); this grenade launcher is fitted to the bayonet lug, and the grenade slips over the cylindrical part of the launcher.

The grenade launcher shown in the lower right-hand corner of figure 13 is used to fire the high-explosive rifle grenade (*G. Sprgr.*) and the armor-piercing rifle grenade (*G. Pzgr.*). These two grenades are inserted with a twisting motion into the cup section of the launcher. (See fig. 15.)

There are two types of sights which are used with the grenade launchers. These are illustrated in figure 13. The sight is a simple attachment clamping to the left-hand side of the rifle behind the rear sight. The sight is composed of a sighting device placed on a base which revolves about an axis and is leveled by a small spirit bubble. There are two range scales reading from 0 to 250 meters for low-angle fire and from 250 to 50 meters for high-angle fire. These graduations apply to the high-explosive grenade only. When the armor-piercing grenade is fired, 75 meters on the low-angle scale corresponds to a range of 100 meters, and 50 meters on the high-angle scale corresponds to a range of 65 meters. (On the pistol grenade, see figs. 16, 17, 18 ①, and 20.)

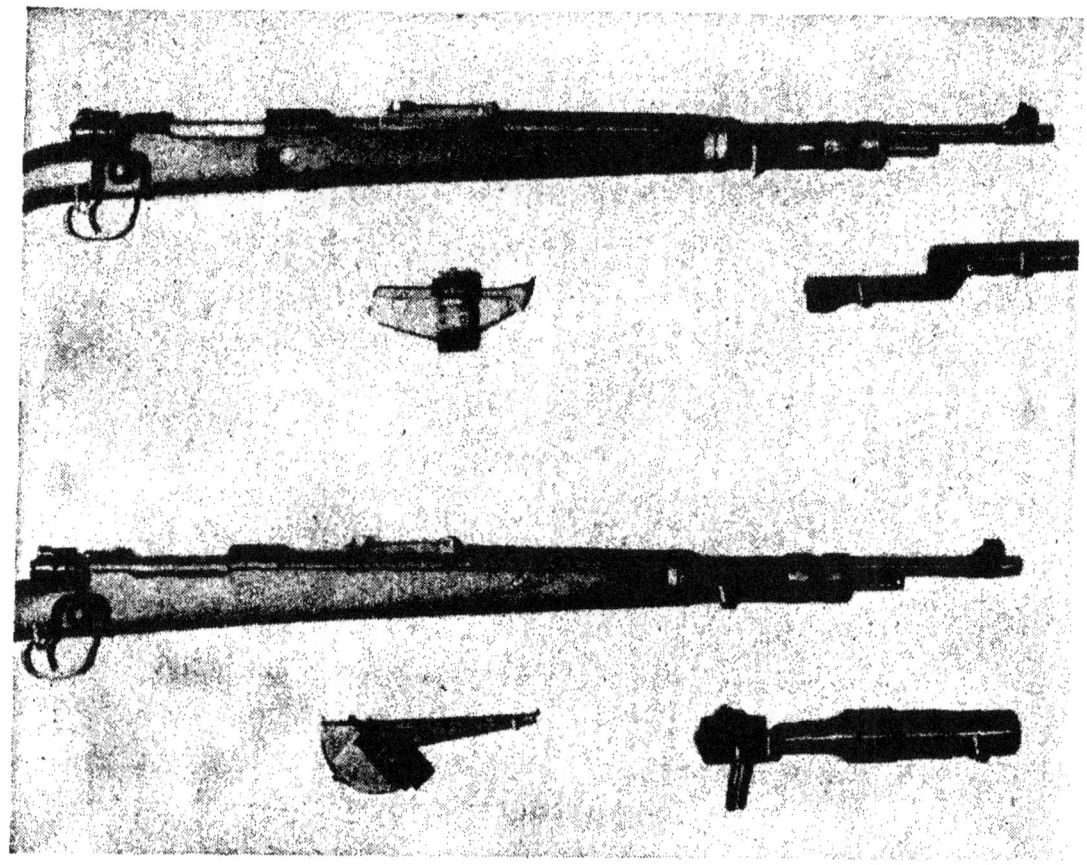

Figure 13.—Mauser *Kar. 98K* rifle with grenade launchers and sights.

(3) *Grenades.*—(a) *High-explosive grenade (Gewehr Sprenggranate, G. Sprgr.).*—The high-explosive grenade consists of a blackened steel body with an aluminum nose fuze and a grooved collar fitting into the rifling of the bore of the launcher (see fig. 18 ②). The fuze operates on impact, but the shock of discharge also initiates a delay system in the base which, in the event of the nose fuze's failing to function, detonates the filling after a delay of 4 to 5 seconds. The collar carrying the rifling may be unscrewed from the body and the igniter string pulled, in which case

the projectile can then be thrown as a hand grenade, operating after 4 to 5 seconds (see fig. 19). The effect is equivalent to that of a "defensive" type of grenade, the radius of fragmentation being described by an enemy document as about 30 yards.

(b) *Armor-piercing grenade (Gewehr Panzergranate, G. Pzgr.).*—The rifle grenade for use against armor incorporates the hollow-charge principle (see

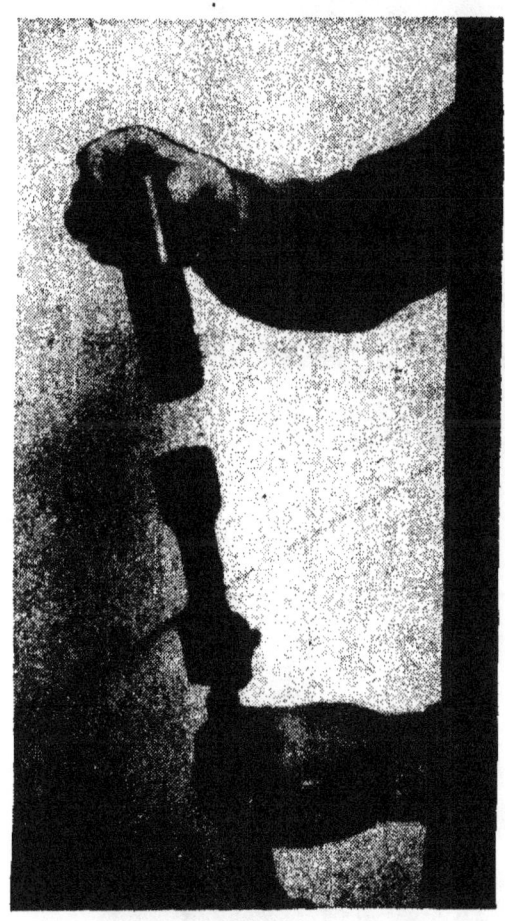

Figure 14.—Grenade launcher, showing method of unscrewing it to aid in cleaning.

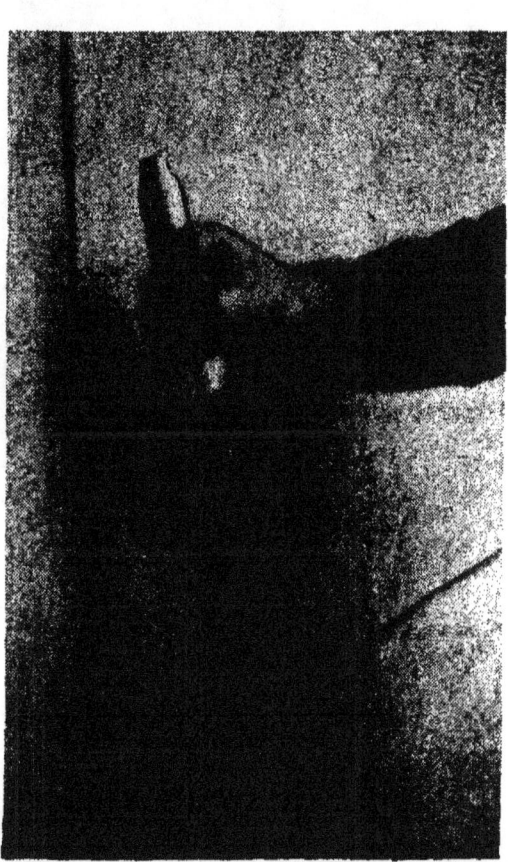

Figure 15.—Method of inserting rifle grenade. (The cup of the launcher being rifled, the grenade is inserted with a twisting motion.)

Figure 16.—Rifle grenade launcher and grenade firing pistol (very light type). (Both the launcher and the pistol are rifled).

Figure 17.—Pistol grenade being breech-loaded.

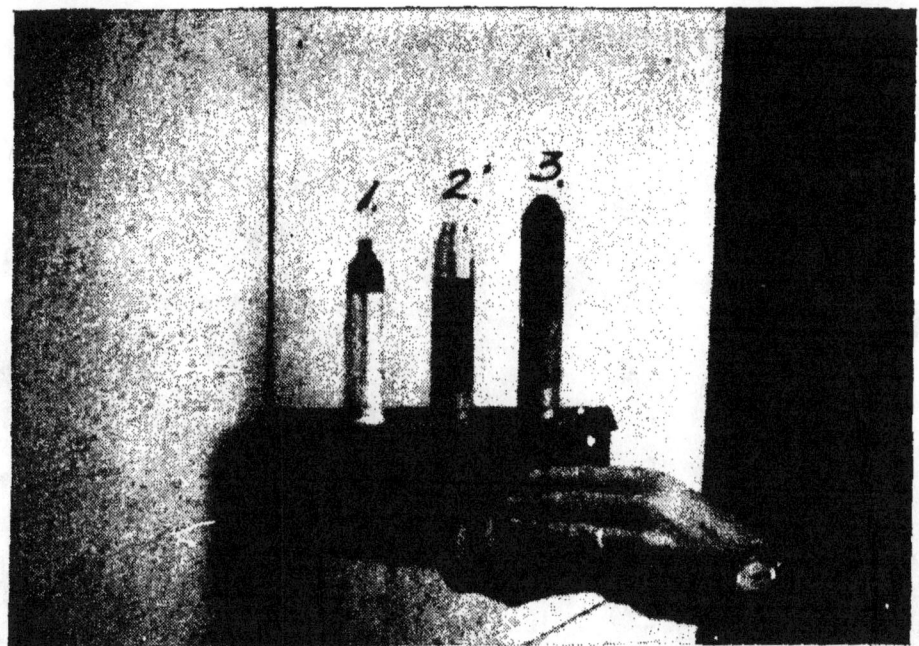

Figure 18.—Three types ow grenade projectiles: ① pistol grenade; ② rifle grenade, with percussion detonator fuze; ③ rifle grenade, with hollow charge.

Figure 19.—Method of unscrewing base of rifle grenade and thereby using friction fuze.

Figure 20.—Special projectile 361 for signal pistol (*Wurfkörper 361 für Leuchtpistole*).

(The projectile consists of the normal egg-type hand grenade (see par. 10, p. 47, below), with a stem in place of the combustion fuze 39. The stem contains a combustion fuze (combustion time, approximately, 4 to 5 seconds) on the upper end of which a No. 8 detonator is fitted. The fuze is inserted into the detonator and then the detonator end is inserted into the grenade. On the lower end of the stem there is the cartridge (propellant charge with percussion cap) which expels the projectile on firing and sets off the combustion fuze. The projectile is secured in the stem by a cotter pin and ring which must be withdrawn before the projectile is loaded into the signal pistol. When withdrawn, the projectile is "live."

For firing the projectile, a barrel-reinforcing tube is inserted into the barrel of the signal pistol. It is pushed in from the rear when the pistol is broken. When the barrel is returned to position, the pistol is ready for loading. (The barrel-reinforcing tube should be cleaned about every 100 rounds.) The stem of the projectile is introduced into the tube until appreciable resistance shows that the base of the tube has been reached. The pistol may now be cocked.

The signal pistol grenades are packed in a metal container with detonators and a barrel-reinforcing tube.)

fig. 18 ③). The grenade is a long cylinder, partly steel and partly aluminum, with a black rounded-metal nose cap and a base plate slotted to facilitate removal. The forward half of the cylinder is constructed of steel and contains the bursting charge, a light metal diaphragm shaping the hollow charge. The rear aluminum half of the cylinder, which carries an interrupted collar with eight right-hand grooves to fit the rifling of the launcher cup, contains a fuze and detonator. The weight of the bursting charge is exceedingly small compared with the total weight of the projectile, and the general design is unnecessarily complicated, with considerable waste of efficiency. There is no provision for use as a hand grenade.

(c) *Practice projectile (Gewehr Sprengranate, Übungsmunition, G. Sprgr., Üb.).*—This round is fitted with a smoke generator, six holes for smoke emission being drilled in the side of the body.

(d) *Cartridge and packing.*—Each rifle grenade is packed with bulletless blank rifle cartridge in a cardboard container, which may be marked with the German nomenclature. The cartridges are not interchangeable between rounds of different types. The containers are black, with a white spot on the end for armor-piercing grenades and gray for the high-explosive grenades.

(e) *Range.*—The high-explosive grenade has a maximum range of about 250 yards. The armor-piercing grenade probably has a maximum range of about 100 yards.

5. Pz.B.[9] 39 (ANTITANK RIFLE)

a. General

Antitank rifles are issued to the German Army on a scale of one for each platoon (or equivalent unit). There are at least two types of antitank rifles in use by the Germans: the Polish antitank rifle (model 35), which has been renamed the *Tankbüchse,* and the

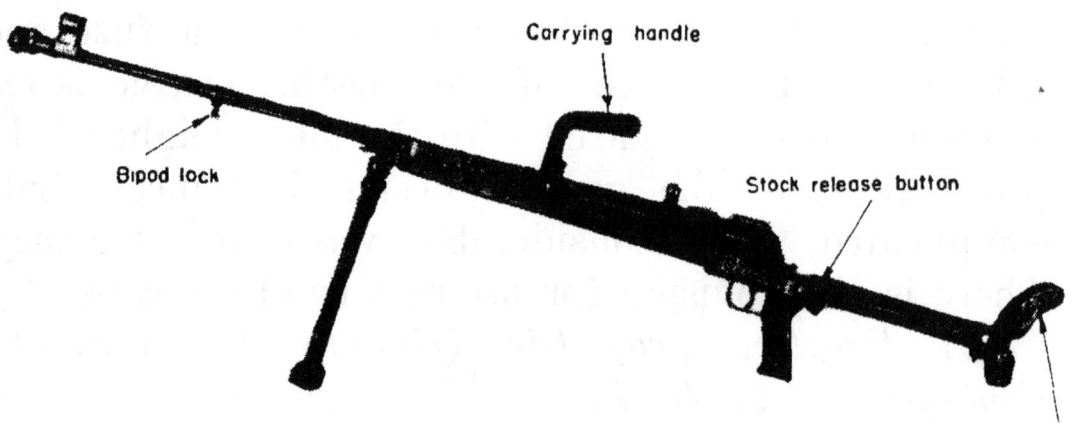

Figure 21.—Pz.B. 39 (antitank rifle).

Pz.B. 39, a later model of the *Pz.B. 38*. (See figs. 21 and 22.)

b. How to Identify

Both the *Pz.B. 38* and *Pz.B. 39* may be identified by—

(1) Folding shoulder stocks with a rubber shock absorber.
(2) Bipod mount and carrying handle.
(3) Muzzle brake.
(4) Single-shot, falling-block action worked by a moving pistol grip in the *Pz.B. 39* and by recoil in the *Pz.B. 38*.

---

[9] *Pz.B.* is the German abbreviation for *Panzerbüchse,* which means "antitank rifle." The German tactical symbol for antitank rifle is

c. Characteristics

(1) *General.*—The *Pz.B. 38* and *Pz.B. 39* are light antitank weapons carried by infantry. They are single-shot rifles fired from a bipod mount. The bullet is an armor-piercing projectile with tracer compound and sometimes with a tear-gas powder in the base. The *Pz.B. 38* and *Pz.B. 39* are basically the same and differ only slightly in appearance and com-

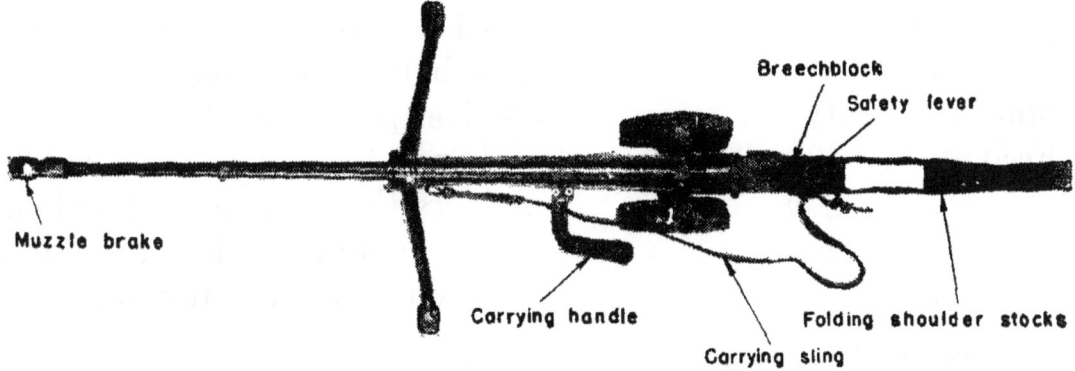

Figure 22.—Overhead view of *Pz.B. 39*, illustrating cutout folding shoulder stock.

ponent parts. The description of the *Pz.B. 39* which follows will also serve for the *Pz.B. 38*.

(2) *Table of characteristics.*—

Principle of operation	Single-shot, falling-block action.
Caliber	7.92 mm (.312 inch).
Ammunition	Caliber .50 case, necked down to take a caliber .312 bullet.
Sights:	
Front	Inverted V blade, with hood for shade and protection.
Rear	Open V notch, nonadjustable, sighted 300 meters (328 yards).

Over-all length:
  With shoulder stock in
    place_____ 62¼ inches.
  With shoulder stock
    folded_____ 50¾ inches.
Range:
  Effective_____ 250 to 300 yards.
  Penetration _____ At 300 yards, ¾-inch (20° impact) and 1-inch (normal impact) face-hardened plate; at 100 yards, 1¼-inch (normal impact) face-hardened plate.
Muzzle velocity_____ 3,540 feet per second.
Feed_____ By hand from two ammunition holders that clip on each side of stock forearm, each box holding 10 rounds of ammunition.

d. How to Operate

(1) *Safety.*—The safety lever is located on the tang of the receiver just to the rear of the breechblock. To put the rifle on "safe," move the safety lever until the letter "S" (*sicher*—"safe") is exposed. To unlock, move the safety lever until the letter "F" (*Feuer*—"fire") is exposed.

(2) *To load and fire.*—Press the bipod lock (see fig. 21), and adjust the height of the bipod by turning the adjusting screw located underneath the pivot point of the bipod. Press the stock release button and snap the shoulder stock into place. Move the safety lever to the "fire" position. Push the pistol grip forward and downward, thus depressing the breechblock. In-

PISTOLS, RIFLES, AND GRENADES   37

sert one round into the chamber, which is exposed by lowering the breechblock (see fig. 24). Close the breechblock by pulling back and up on the pistol grip. The piece is now ready to fire.[10] The safety lever

Figure 23.—Pz.B. 39 in position on edge of road. (The rifle is fired from the prone position.)

should be kept in the "safe" position until ready to fire.

(3) *To unload.*—Move the safety lever to the "fire" position. Being careful to keep the finger out of the trigger guard, open the breech by pushing the pistol grip forward and downward. This will eject the cartridge from the chamber. The rifle is now unloaded.

---

[10] See fig. 5, p. 8, above, for the method of aligning German sights.

e. Ammunition

The ammunition used has a rimless case the approximate size of the U. S. caliber .50 case, but the projectile is approximately the size of the U. S. caliber .30 projectile. The German nomenclature [11] for this ammunition is *Patr. 318 S.m.K.* for the pointed bullet with steel core, and *Patr. 318 S.m.K.(H)* for the pointed bullet with hardened-steel core. The ammunition for the *Pz.B. 38* and the *Pz.B. 39*, though of the same caliber as the rifle and machine-gun ammunition, will not function in either rifle or machine gun, as the dimensions of the cartridge case are much larger.

The Polish antitank rifle (model 35), the *Tankbüchse* (see **a**, above), uses a similar cartridge, but this cartridge will not function in either the *Pz.B. 38* or the *Pz.B. 39*. It is known as *Patr. 318 (P)*, or Polish cartridge No. 318, and is packed in boxes with green labels printed in Polish and overprinted "Patr. 318."

f. Maintenance

(1) *Oiling and cleaning.*—The rifle should be given the usual care with respect to cleaning and lubricating. Oil should be used sparingly or not at all in hot, sandy, or dusty country.

(2) *Stripping.*—Remove the pistol-grip pivot pin by compressing its spring lock and pushing it out from left to right. Remove the trigger pistol-grip group and

---

[11] See fig. 93, p. 167, below, for one type of label used to identify ammunition for the antitank rifle.

breechblock from the receiver by pulling downward on the pistol grip. Disengage the breechblock from the trigger pistol-grip by sliding the breech out along the grooves in its sides. The breechblock can be stripped by pressing on the spring-loaded button and sliding the plate upward. Removing the two pins

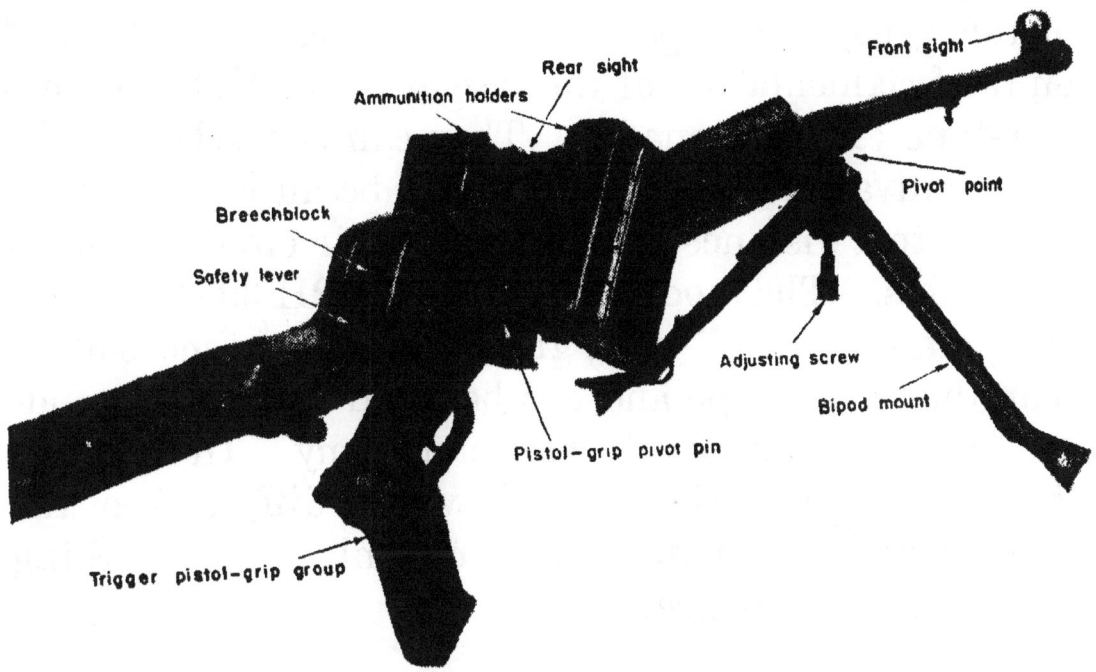

Figure 24.—Close-up of breech of *Pz.B. 39.*

from the side of the breechblock will release the trigger bar and hammer.

(3) *Assembly.*—Reverse the stripping procedure given in (2), on the opposite page. Be sure that the safety is on "fire" position so that the breechblock can be replaced in its slots in the receiver walls.

g. Accessories

The accessories for these guns are a carrying sling and two ammunition holders that clip on the wooden forearm. A small cleaning kit similar to the rifle cleaning kit is carried by the antitank rifleman.

6. HAND GRENADES

The hand grenades used by the German Army are all of the "offensive" type: that is, they have a thin metal casing with a high proportion of explosive filler. Being of this type, they depend on the blast effect, instead of on the fragmentation of the case as in the U. S. "defensive-type" Mills grenades. They can be used safely by troops advancing erect in the open, because they can be thrown to a distance greater than their effective bursting radius. The model 24 and model PH 39 stick-type, or "potato masher"-type, grenades are used more often than the "egg"-type and can be regarded as the standard hand grenades of the German Army. In addition, there is a smoke stick grenade which differs from the regular stick, or "potato masher," only in the marking on the head of the grenade.

7. STICK HAND GRENADE, MODEL 24 (STIELHANDGRANATE 24)

a. How to Identify

The stick hand grenade, model 24, may be identified by—

(1) Metal casing or body screwed onto a wooden handle with a metal cap.

(2) Model marking on the casing or body of the grenade.

(3) Porcelain ball attached to a cord in the exposed cavity after the metal cap is unscrewed.

b. Characteristics

(1) *General.*—This grenade consists of a thin iron or steel casing, or head, containing the explosive filler and screwed onto a hollow wooden handle, through the center of which runs a double length of cord (see fig. 25). This cord is attached at one end to a lead ball which is part of the friction-igniter-detonator system, and at the other end of a procelain ball. The cavity in which the porcelain ball rests is closed by a metal cap that screws on. Inside the cap is a spring-actuated metal disk that prevents movement of the porcelain ball.

(2) *Table of characteristics.*—

Over-all length	1 foot 2 inches.
Weight	1 pound 5 ounces.
Weight of explosive filler	6 ounces.
Time of delay fuze	4 to 5 seconds.
Effective blast radius	12 to 14 yards.

c. How to Operate

(1) *Safety.*—(a) The detonator is not assembled to the grenade until it is carried into combat.

(b) The metal cap on the end of the handle holds the porcelain ball in place and is not removed until the grenade is to be thrown.

(2) *To arm and throw.*—(a) *To arm grenade.*—The wooden handle is unscrewed from the head, and the metal end of the delay fuze is exposed in the interior of the handle. Insert a detonator into the open end of the delay fuze. The head and the handle are screwed together again.

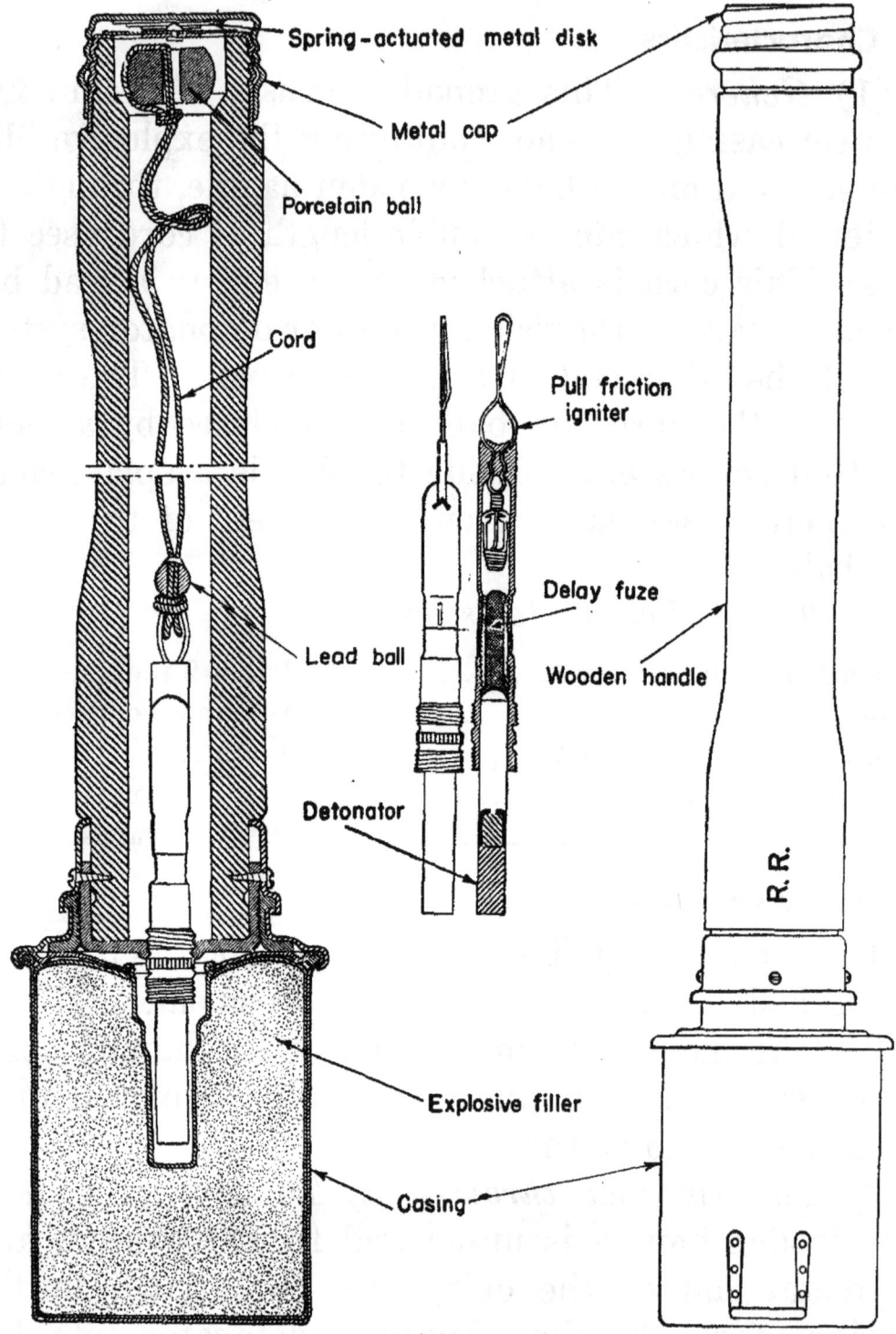

Figure 25.—Sketch of *Stielhandgranate 24* (stick hand grenade, model 24), showing outside and cross section of grenade and fuze. (The cross section of the grenade is drawn to a larger scale than the scale of the sketch of the outside view.)

(b) *To throw grenade.*—Unscrew the metal cap, pull out the porcelain ball as far as it will go, and throw. Do not throw too soon, as there is a 4- to 5-second delay.

(3) *To disarm grenade.*—(a) Unscrew the handle from the head; (b) remove the detonator from the open end of the delay fuze; (c) replace the handle.

d. Method of Carrying

Stick hand grenades, model 24, are carried in—

(1) A metal case holding 15 grenades and 15 detonators (see fig. 26);

(2) A sleeveless jacket fitting over the blouse. (In this jacket there are 10 pockets, 5 in front and 5 in the back, in which the grenades are carried with the heads down.)

(3) The belt with the grenades stuck in, handle first.

e. Use as a Booby Trap

This grenade may be made into a booby trap by removing the delay fuze. (See fig. 25.) When troops attempt to use the captured grenades, pulling the friction wire causes the grenades to explode immediately without the usual 4- to 5-second delay.

To see whether or not the delaying device has been removed from the grenade, it may be tested as follows: (1) unscrew the head (explosive cylinder) from the wooden handle; (2) remove the detonator and the fuze which project from the handle; (3) unscrew the cap at the end of the handle and let the porcelain ring hang down; (4) unscrew the delayed-action device in the top of the handle to make sure whether the delayed-action cylinder actually contains the column of compressed black gunpowder.

To reassemble the grenade, carry out the above operations in the reverse order.

If time is short, it may be sufficient to take one from each batch of suspected grenades, unscrew the

Figure 26.—Method of carrying and packing stick-type grenades.

handle from it, and operate the fuze by pulling the cord from a distance. It will then be obvious whether the explosion takes place immediately or after an interval of 4 to 5 seconds.

8. STICK HAND GRENADE, MODEL PH 39 (STIELHAND-GRANATE PH 39)

a. How to Identify

The stick hand grenade, model PH 39, may be identified by—

(1) Metal casing or body screwed to a wooden handle with a metal cap.

(2) Model marking on the casing or body of the grenade.

(3) Cord attached to the friction igniter being also attached to the metal cap (this being observed on unscrewing the metal cap on the handle).

b. Characteristics

(1) *General.*—Like the model 24 stick grenade, the model PH 39 consists of a thin iron or steel casing, or head, containing the explosive filler. This head is screwed onto a hollow wooden handle, through the center of which runs a double length of cord. At one end, this cord is attached to a lead ball which is part of the friction-igniter-detonator system, and at the other end to the metal cap which screws onto the end of the handle.

(2) *Table of characteristics.*—

Over-all length	1 foot 4 inches.
Weight	1 pound 6 ounces.
Weight of explosive filler	7 ounces.
Time of delay fuze	4 to 5 seconds.
Effective blast radius	16 yards.

c. How to Operate

(1) *Safety.*—(a) The detonator is not assembled to the grenade until it is carried into combat.

(b) The metal cap on the end of the handle is not unscrewed until the grenade is to be thrown. The cap may be unscrewed carefully and lifted slightly to be sure that the grenade is a model PH 39, as the cord that starts the delay fuze is attached to the metal cap on the model PH 39 grenade.[12] However, the cap should not be pulled away from the handle, as this action would start the fuze burning.

(2) *To arm and throw.*—(a) *To arm grenade.*—Before use in action, the grenade is ordinarily carried without the detonator assembled. To arm the grenade, the wooden handle is unscrewed from the grenade head, and the hollow end of the delay fuze is exposed; a detonator is inserted into the hollow end of the delay fuze; and the casing and the handle are screwed together again.

(b) *To throw grenade.*—Unscrew the metal cap and pull it away from the grenade handle to the full length of the cord. This ignites the 4- to 5-second delay fuze, and the grenade should then be thrown with an overarm motion.

(3) *To disarm grenade.*—The grenade is disarmed by unscrewing the handle from the head, removing the detonator from the open end of the delay fuze, and then replacing the handle.

d. Method of Carrying

Like the model 24, the PH 39 grenades are carried in—

(1) A metal case holding 15 grenades and 15 detonators.

---

[12] In this respect it differs from the model 24.

(2) A sleeveless jacket fitting over the blouse. (In this jacket there are 10 pockets, 5 in front and 5 in back, in which the grenades are carried with the heads down.)

(3) The belt with the grenades stuck in, handle first.

e. Use as a Booby Trap

The removal of the delay element in the fuze of this grenade will cause the grenade to explode at once without the usual 4- to 5-second delay. The grenade may be examined in the same manner as is described for the model 24 grenade (see par. 7e, p. 43, above).

9. SMOKE HAND GRENADE, MODEL 34 (NEBELHAND-GRANATE 34)

The smoke grenade, model 34, which is a standard stick grenade with the explosive filler replaced by smoke composition, is handled in the same manner as the other stick grenades and is identified only by a broken white line painted around the head of the grenade near its base.

10. EGG-TYPE HAND GRENADE, MODEL 39 (EIERHAND-GRANATE 39)

a. How to Identify

The egg-type hand grenade may be identified by—

(1) Egg shape, of gray-green painted metal with a raised rib around the middle.

(2) Blue knob protruding from one end.

b. Characteristics

(1) *General.*—This is a small thin-cased "offensive"-type grenade with a high proportion of a low-grade high explosive (see fig. 27). It is ignited by a friction-type igniter and a 4- to 5-second delay fuze.

(Fig. 28 illustrates the shaving-stick grenade, which has the same type of detonator as the egg-type.)

(2) *Table of characteristics.*—

Over-all length	3 inches (approximately).
Weight	12 ounces.
Maximum diameter	2 inches.
Time of delay fuze	4 to 5 seconds.
Thickness of casing	.02 inch.

c. How to Operate

(1) *Safety.*—The detonator is not assembled to the grenade until it is carried into combat.

(2) *To arm and throw.*—(a) *To arm grenade.*—Unscrew the knob from the grenade; be sure that the exposed pocket is clean; unscrew the protective cap from the detonator end of the knob; draw a detonator (standard No. 8) from its box and check the open end to see that it is dust free and not distorted (do not use a dusty or distorted detonator); carefully slip the detonator onto the detonator end of the knob, screw the armed fuze by hand, and then use the key supplied to tighten the fuze.

(b) *To throw grenade.*—Unscrew the blue [13] knob, and pull. Throw the grenade, remembering that it has a 4- to 5-second delay.

(3) *To disarm grenade.*—(a) Unscrew the knob from the grenade; (b) remove the detonator from the end of the knob; and (c) replace the knob. To render the igniter inoperative, carefully unscrew the knob,

---

[13] It has been reported that a red knob is used for those igniters having no delay element. Blue knobs have been reported on igniters having a 4- to 5-second delay. (See e, on the opposite page.)

PISTOLS, RIFLES, AND GRENADES 49

taking care not to exert any pull on the cord. Then cut the cord with scissors and replace the knob with the cord inside.

d. Method of Carrying

The egg-type grenades are carried in—

(1) The pockets.
(2) Any convenient container.

e. Use as a Booby Trap

Like all other matériel, these egg-shaped grenades can be used as booby traps. It has been reported that

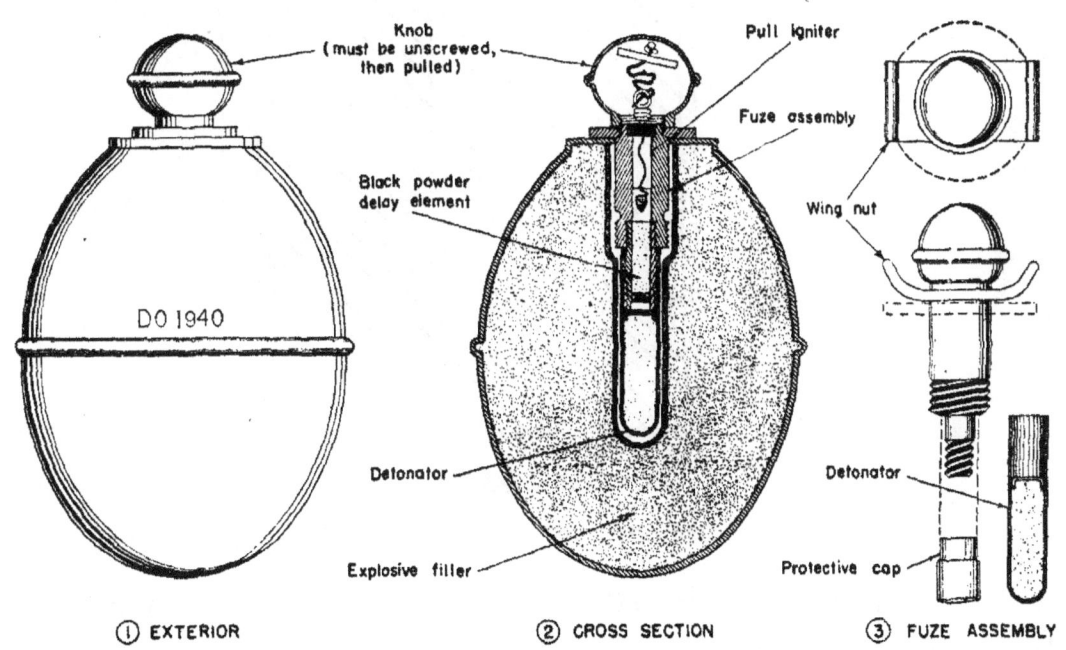

Figure 27.—Sketch of Eierhandgranate 39 (egg-type hand grenade, model 39).

the Germans in Africa have put red primer caps on the grenades which are used as traps. If the red primer cap is unscrewed and the firing string pulled, the explosion occurs instantaneously rather than after

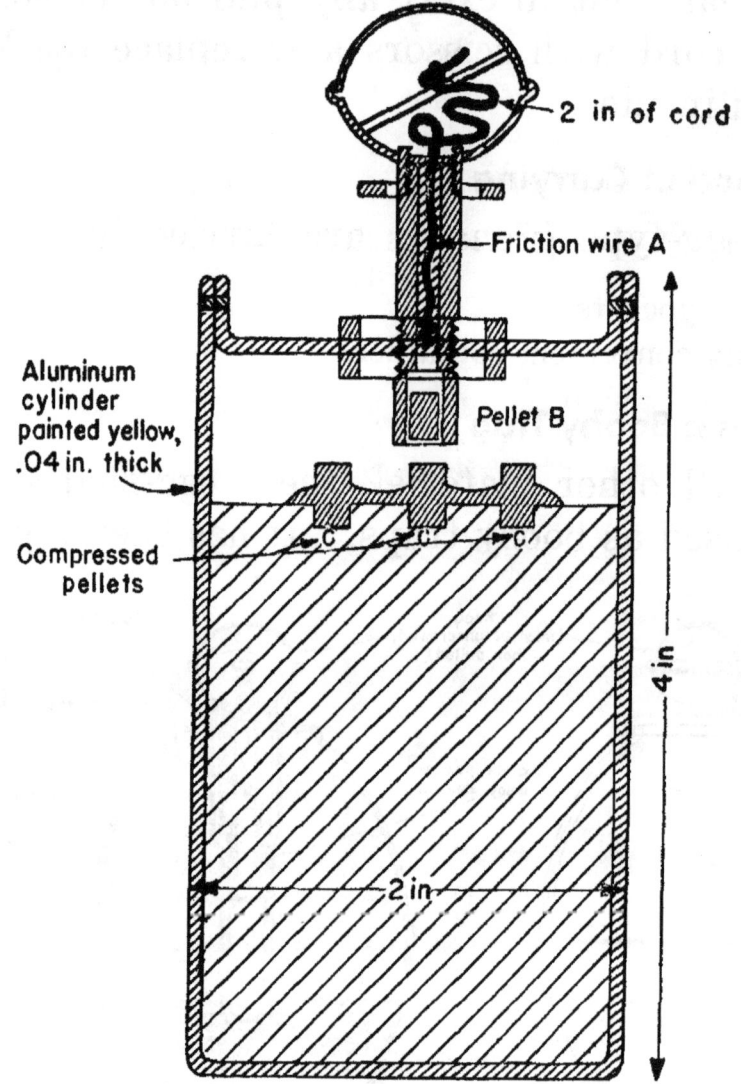

Figure 28.—Cross section of shaving-stick grenade.

a 4- to 5-second delay—the standard delay with the blue cap.

11. SPECIAL USES OF STICK GRENADES [14]

For special demolition, antitank, and antipillbox work, the heads of six model 24 or model PH 39 stick

---

[14] See TM 5-325, "Enemy Land Mines and Booby Traps" (April 19, 1943), pp. 1-96, for detailed information on the construction of German land mines and booby traps, many of which are made from grenades.

grenades can be removed from their handles and fastened securely around a seventh stick grenade from which the handle is not removed (see figs. 29 and 30). The whole can then be used as a convenient

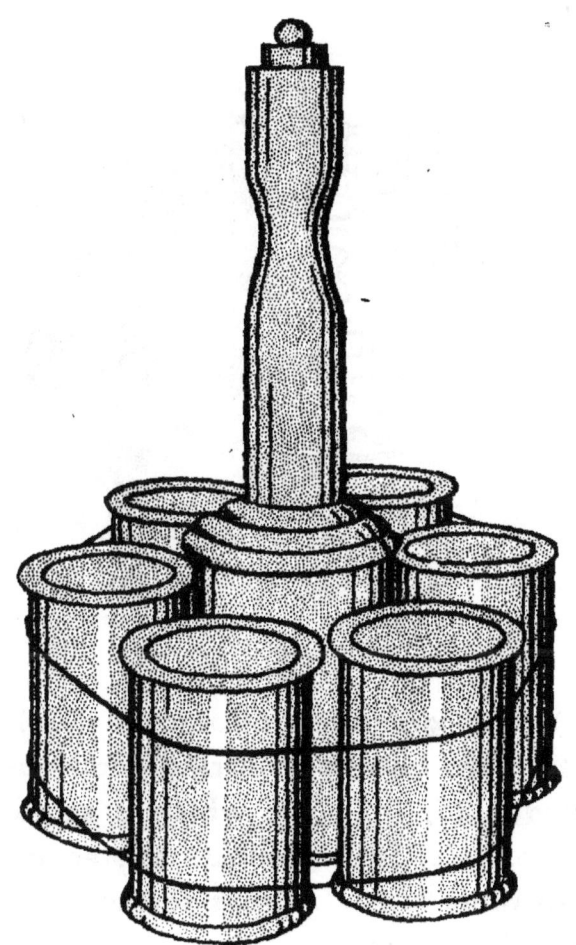

Figure 29.—Concentrated charge (geballte Ladung) made from several stick grenades. (This charge is used for demolition purposes.)

concentrated charge (*geballte Ladung*) for the above purposes.

Bangalore torpedoes for blowing paths through barbed wire can also be made by binding the desired number of grenade heads behind one another on a long stick or board (see fig. 31); the grenade nearest the operator is complete with handle and detonator, and to it is attached a long wire or cord.

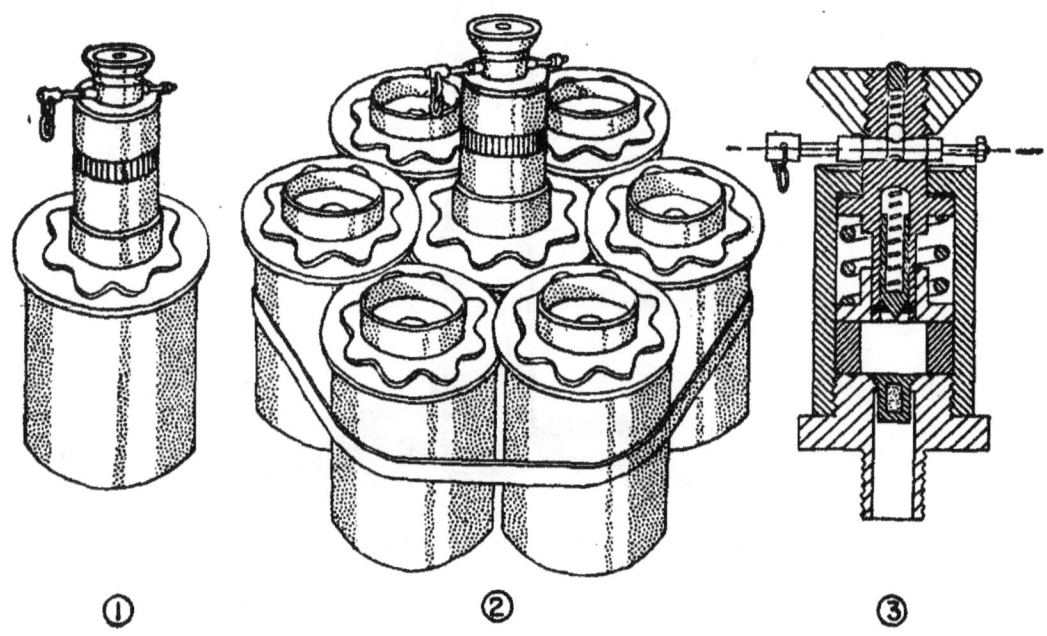

Figure 30.—① Stick grenade antipersonnel mine. (This mine is improvised from the head of a stick grenade and pressure igniter 35 (Druckzünder 35, D.Z. 35), which is screwed into the head of the grenade.) ② Stick grenade cluster mine. (This mine is a variation of mine ①.) ③ Cross section of pressure igniter 35 (Druckzünder 35, D.Z. 35).

Figure 31.—Stick grenades used as Bangalore torpedo.

Section III. MACHINE GUNS AND MORTARS[1]

12. M.G. 34 [2]

a. General

The *M.G. 34,* machine gun, model 34, is not directly comparable to any U. S. weapon. It can be fired without a mount (fig. 32), or it can be mounted on a bipod (fig. 33) for use as a light machine gun,[3] on a tripod (figs. 34 and 35) for use as a heavy machine gun,[4] and on a special antiaircraft mount (fig. 36) or on the standard tripod mount with adapter and special sight (fig. 37) for use as an antiaircraft gun, as well as on numerous other types of mounts on tanks and other vehicles (fig. 38). Consequently, this all-purpose gun is the most common German automatic weapon in use by the German armed forces. Every infantry squad,[5] and many other types of small German units, can be expected to be armed with the *M.G. 34.*

---

[1] The weapons discussed in this section are operated by more than one man.

[2] *M.G.* is the German abbreviation for *Maschinengewehr*, which means "machine gun."

[3] The German tactical symbol for a light machine gun is

[4] The German tactical symbol for a heavy machine gun is

[5] See "The German Squad in Combat," MIS *Special Series*, No. 9 (Jan. 25, 1943), for detailed descriptions of the tactical employment of the machine gun in the German squad.

b. How to Identify

The *M.G. 34* may be identified by—

(1) Air-cooled jacket.
(2) Shape of plastic shoulder stock.
(3) Plastic pistol grips and double trigger.
(4) Folding front and rear sights. (An auxiliary antiaircraft ring sight that fits on the barrel jacket may also be found.)
(5) Operating handle on the right side.

Figure 32.—M.G. 34 in action without bipod or tripod.

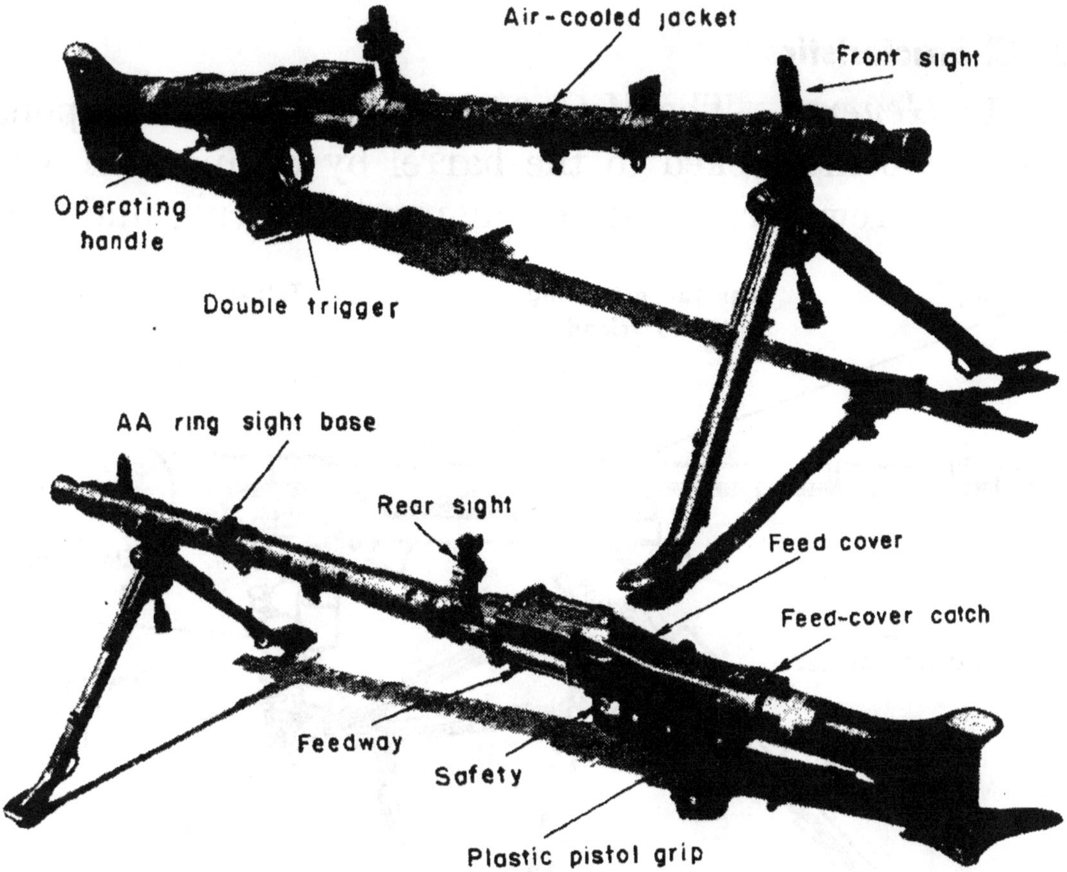

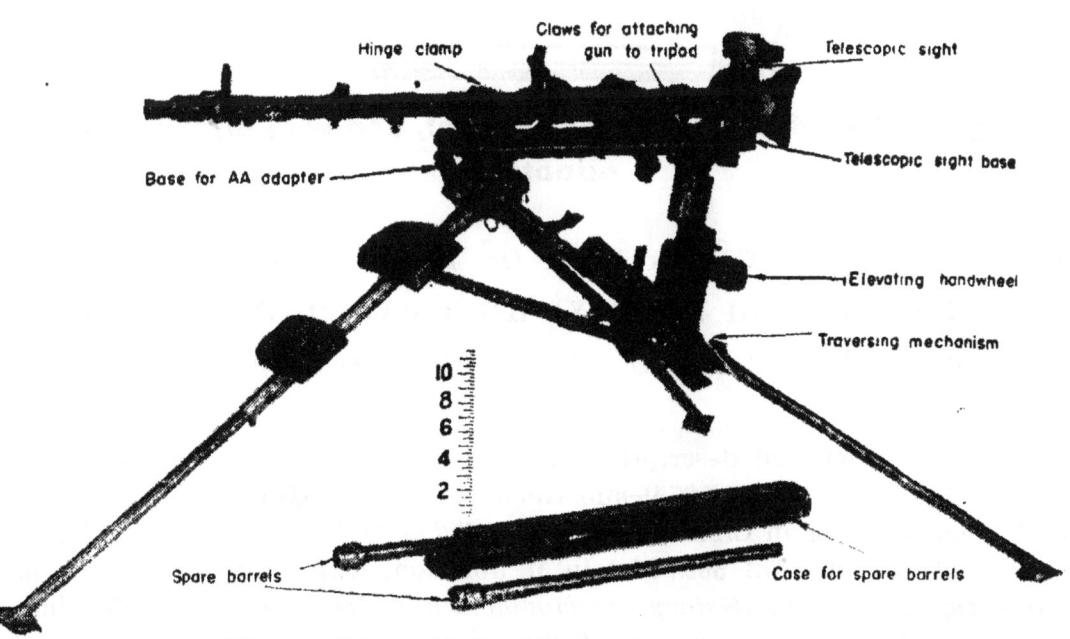

Figure 33.—Two views of M.G. 34 on bipod mount.

Figure 34.—M.G. 34 on tripod mount.

c. Characteristics[6]

(1) *General.*—The *M.G. 34* is a short-recoil weapon, the bolt being locked to the barrel by means of interrupted screw threads at the moment of firing and for

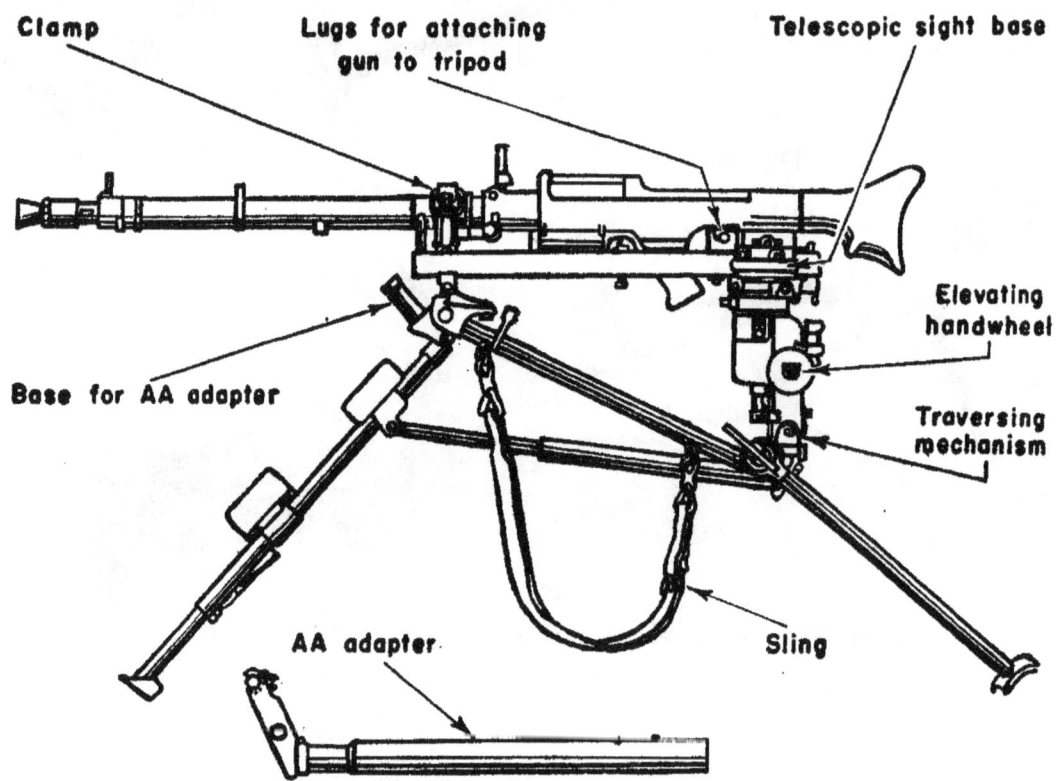

Figure 35.—*M.G. 34 on tripod mount, and with antiaircraft adapter.*

three-sixteenths of an inch of recoil, unlocking itself from the barrel in the next nine-sixteenths of an inch in travel. There is no accelerator to assist the back-

---

[6] For a more detailed description of the characteristics and operation of *M.G. 34*, see TM-E9-206A, "7.9-mm German Machine Gun, M. G. 34." Cf. M. F. Medlin, "German Light Machine Gun," *The Ordnance Sergeant*, Vol. 4, (Sept. 1942), pp. 260–273, 309; Melvin M. Johnson, Jr. and Charles T. Haven, *Automatic Arms, Their History, Development and Use* (New York: William Morrow and Co., 1941), pp. 70–77, 239–241.

ward movement of the recoiling parts, but a recoil assister on the muzzle helps to move the recoiling parts to the rear by gas pressure on the front face of the barrel. The same purpose is served by a similar part

Figure 36.—M.G. 34 on antiaircraft mount, using drum feed.

on the U. S. Browning caliber .30 M2 aircraft machine gun.

Although the rate of fire is probably too high for the weight, the gun is a handy air-cooled automatic weapon. A simple mechanism makes it easy to exchange a cool barrel for a heated one. The gun is belt- or magazine-fed, the feed usually coming from the left. However, by substituting a special feed arm in the feed cover, it can be made to feed from the right side.

(2) *Table of Characteristics.*—

Principle of operation	Short recoil on the Solothurn [7] principle.
Caliber	7.92 mm (.312 inch).
Ammunition	All 7.92 ammunition not expressly forbidden for use in the machine gun (for example, the *Patr. 318* manufactured for the *Pz.B. 39* antitank rifle is unsuitable, because it will not fit in the chamber).
Type of feed	1. Nondisintegrating metallic-link belts, which hold 50 rounds and may be connected together to make longer belts.
	2. 75-round double, or saddle-type, drums used in antiaircraft or light ground versions of the gun.
	3. 50-round belts contained in a metal drum attached to the feed block of the gun in tank or antiaircraft versions of the gun.
	4. Canvas containers holding 100-round belts are also used in tanks.

---

[7] The barrel-locking ring revolves while sliding in the supporting jacket, so that the bolt and main spring recoil in an absolutely straight line, the whole assembly being made of very simple round parts. Compare the action in the *M.G. 42* (par. 13c, p. 85, below).

Figure 37.—M.G. 34 in action on tripod mount, with antiaircraft and telescopic sights.

Figure 38.—M.G. 34 in action on boat, showing protective shield and drum feed.

Weight:
  As light machine gun (bipod) _____ 26½ pounds.
  As heavy machine gun (tripod) _____ 68½ pounds.
Sights:
  Standard sights _____ Rear vertical leaf sight with open V notch, graduated from 200 to 2,000 meters (219 to 2,187 yards). There is a folding peep sight on the rear sight that is used with the antiaircraft ring sight.
  Auxiliary _____ The antiaircraft ring sight, kept in the maintenance kit, fits its base on the barrel jacket. When used on the tripod as a heavy machine gun, a telescopic sight is mounted on the tripod. This telescopic sight is graduated up to an effective range of 3,500 meters (3,827 yards).
Muzzle velocity _____ 2,500 to 3,000 feet per second, depending on the type of ammunition used.
Range:
  Maximum _____ 5,000 yards (heavy or light).
  Effective _____ 3,827 yards (heavy, with tripod and telescopic sight), 2,000 yards (light).

d. How to Operate

(1) *Safety.*—A manual safety is located on the left side of the receiver, just above the trigger and in front of the sear. To prevent the safety lever from jumping from either the "safe" or the "fire" position, a

spring-actuated catch is assembled to the safety lever. This catch engages in notches cut in the receiver at the "S" (*sicher*—"safe") and "F" (*Feuer*—"fire") positions and holds the safety in the position where it is set. This gun cannot be cocked with the safety lever

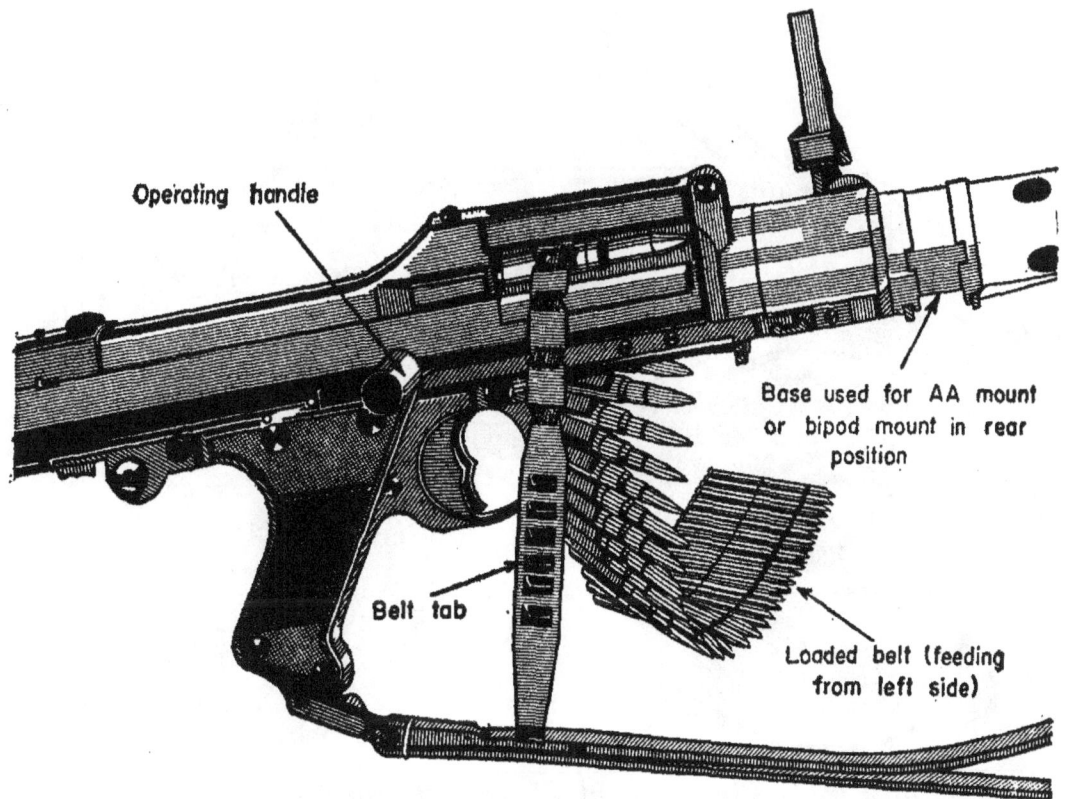

Figure 39.—Sketch showing method of inserting loaded belt in feedway of M.G. 34.

in the "safe" position, that is, when the letter "S" is exposed. When the letter "F" is exposed, the gun is ready to fire.

(2) *To load and fire.*—(a) *Using belt from belt box.*—Insert the tab of the belt (see fig. 39), with the open ends of the links down, in the feedway on the left side of the receiver (if you have no tab on the belt,

take two cartridges from the end of the belt and use the empty links as a tab). This may be done with the feed cover either open or closed. Close the cover plate, and pull the belt through until the first round is stopped by the three cartridge-holding pawls on the

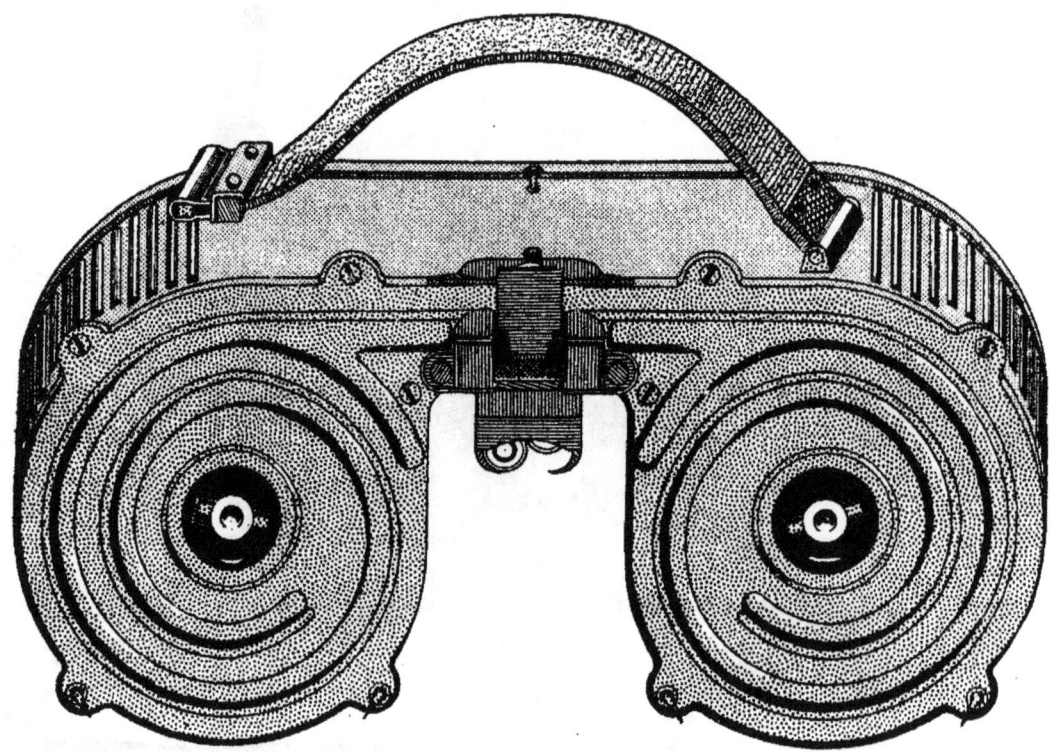

Figure 40.—Close-up of 75-round saddle-type drum.

underside of the feed block. Now cock the gun by pulling the operating handle, on the right side of the receiver, to the rear as far as it will go. The bolt now catches in its rearward position, and can be released only by squeezing the trigger. The operating handle must be returned to the forward position before firing the gun, since otherwise injury may result from the handle moving forward when the trigger is pulled. Check the safety lever to be sure that it is in the "fire" position, that is, with the letter "F" exposed.

(b) *For semi-automatic fire.*—Check the sights to see that both the front and rear sights are in position. Press the top part of the double trigger which is marked "E" (*Einzelschussfeuer*—"single-shot fire").

(c) *For full-automatic fire.*—Press the bottom part of the double trigger which is marked "D" (*Dauerfeuer*—"continuous fire"). The assistant should hold down the bipod legs, as this gun, in full-automatic fire, has a marked tendency to jump.

(d) *Using 50-round belt from drum.*—Press the catch on the sliding lever of the drum, and move the cover to the open position so that the tab end of the belt can be pulled from the drum. Insert the tab in the feedway, with the open end of the links down. Engage the hook which is on the front (narrow) end of the drum onto the lug on the front end of the feed-plate lower assembly. Turn the rear end of the drum toward the gun until the spring catch on the drum engages the lug on the rear end of the feedway. Now proceed as in belt loading from a belt box (see **d**(2)(a), p. 61, above).

(e) *Using 75-round double drum.*—If this type of drum (fig. 40) is found with the gun, more than likely the gun will be set up to take these drums without any changes, that is, with a special feed-cover (see fig. 41). This special feed-cover has an opening to take the 75-round drum, and it also has a folding dust cover to protect the breech mechanism when the drum is not in place on the gun. No belt is used in this type of drum. Place the drum in position, straddling the feed opening and thereby depressing the dust cover. Pull the operating handle to the rear and then push it forward, thus cocking the gun and placing the operating handle in a position where it will not fly forward when the trigger is squeezed. Use the trigger for semi- or full-automatic fire in the same manner as in firing belted ammunition from a belt box or drum.

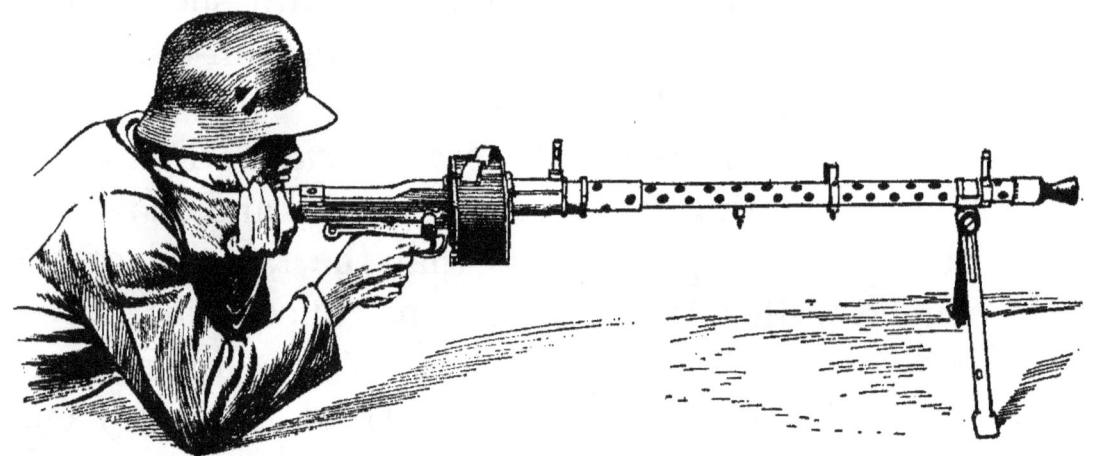

Figure 41.—German method of firing M.G. 34 from bipod mount.

(3) *Sights*—(a) *Rear sight.*—The rear sight is divided into meters. (For a conversion of the meters into yards, see fig. 42.[8])

(b) *Telescopic sight.*—The telescopic sight is used with the tripod mount for aiming the machine gun in either direct or indirect fire (see figs. 43 and 44). When direct fire is being employed the shutter is set to *direkt* ("direct"), thus exposing the meter graduations of the elevation drum. The required range is then set, in meters, on the elevation drum by turning the elevating knob.

---
[8] See fig. 5, p. 8, above, for the method of aligning German sights.

In indirect fire the shutter is usually turned to *indirekt* ("indirect"), thus covering the elevation drum and bringing into position an index for reading the elevation micrometer. The required elevation is

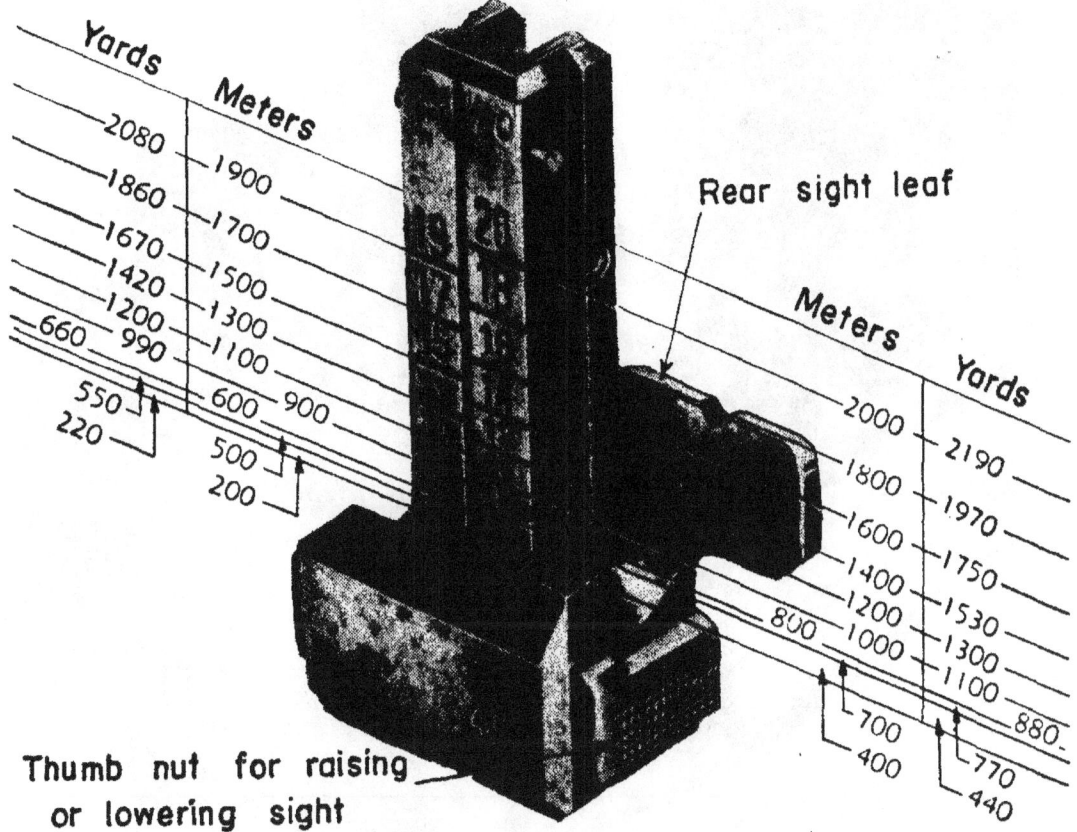

Figure 42.—Rear sight of M.G. 34, showing relation between yards and meters.

then set, in mils, on the elevation scale and elevation micrometer.[9]

A collimator (see fig. 44) is provided for use in establishing the safety point of minimum eleva-

---

[9] Elevation in mils is read on the elevation scale (coarse, 100-mil divisions) and elevation micrometer (fine, 1-mil divisions). The 300-mil setting corresponds to 0 elevation. The elevation scale graduations read from 0 to 10 (0 to 1,000 mils) for actual elevations of from minus 300 to plus 700 mils.

A—Longitudinal level.
B—Azimuth knob.
C—Azimuth micrometer.
D—Throwout lever.
E—Micrometer index.
F—Azimuth scale.
G—Scale index.
H—Light window.
J—Collimator.
K—Collimator clamping screw.
L—Eyepiece.
M—Cross level.
N—Elevation drum (direct fire).
P—Shutter.
Q—Elevating knob.
R—Wing nut.

Figure 43.—Telescopic sight on M.G. 34.

tion for firing over the crest or over the heads of friendly troops. The collimator traverses with the telescope, but can be elevated or depressed. As one looks into the collimator, a cross may be seen which remains stationary as though it were at an infinite

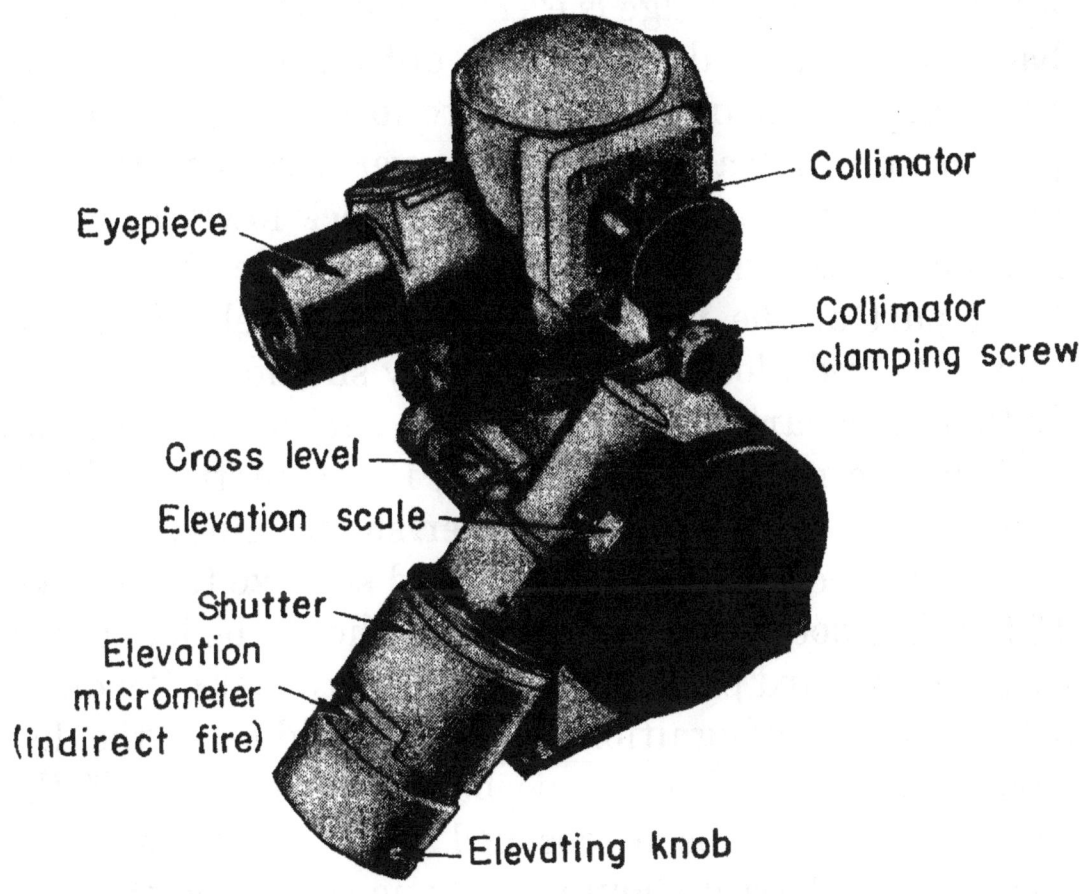

Figure 44.—Telescopic sight for M.G. 34 (rear view).

distance. Aiming is accomplished by lining up this cross with the target.

(4) *Immediate action.*—(a) *General.*—If the gun fails to fire, cock it by pulling the operating handle to the rear, and then squeeze the trigger. *In drawing back the operating handle, the gunner must know by the*

feel whether the bolt was in the extreme forward position or whether it was halfway forward. If the bolt was already in the extreme forward position and the cartridge was not fired, the gunner may, after he has made sure that the dud cartridge has been ejected, try to fire again. If no cartridge is ejected when the bolt is drawn back, or if a cartridge case falls out of the ejection port, the gunner must in no case try to fire again, but should put the gun on "safe," open the cover with the left hand, and remove the belt from the feed-block lower assembly in order to see whether a cartridge has been left in the front part of the receiver or in the barrel. If necessary, the feed-block lower assembly should be removed. If there is a cartridge in the front part of the receiver, it should be removed. However, if the cartridge is already in the chamber, the gunner should close the feed cover, put the safety on "fire," and squeeze the trigger. If the shot does not go off, the bolt should be left in the extreme forward position in order to prevent a "cooked-off round" (self-ignition of the cartridge in the hot barrel) when the breech mechanism is open. If the cartridge has not been loosened within 5 minutes, the lock and the barrel should be changed. Then the cartridge in the chamber can be removed by the gunner at his leisure. When heated by firing, a barrel which has a live cartridge in the chamber must never be changed immediately. In case another cartridge becomes stuck in the same chamber after a short time, a thorough cleaning of the chamber is recommended.

If the bolt pulls the base off a cartridge case in extracting it, and then jams a new round into that part of the empty case remaining in the chamber, first remove the new round and change the barrel. When time permits, extract the cartridge-case remnant from the barrel, using the extractor for ruptured cartridges which may be found in the *M.G. 34* tool kit.

(b) *Stoppages.*—The following chart may be helpful in curing stoppages:

Symptom	Cause	Remedy
1. The cartridge does not center the feedway. The barrel is free; the bolt is in order and in the proper forward position. *(When belt feed is used)*	a. The cartridge is too far back in the belt (belt improperly filled; belt link bent or too wide).	a. Draw back the lock, open the cover, and push the cartridge into the proper position in the link of the belt.
	b. The belt-feed (lever) is worn.	b. Load and try to fire again. If the gun does not fire, replace the worn belt-feed lever.
	c. The spring of the belt-feed lever or spring of the compressing lever is broken.	c. Put in a new spring.
	d. The feed-plate lower assembly is broken.	d. Put in a new feed-plate lower assembly.

Symptom	Cause	Remedy
1. The cartridge does not center the feedway. The barrel is free; the bolt is in order and in the proper forward position. (*When drum feed is used, for example, with the 75-round saddle-type drum*)	a. The drum is improperly filled. b. The spring in the drum is too weak.	a. Take the drum off and try by shaking to bring the cartridge into the right position. If this does not work, put on a new drum. Empty the improperly filled drum later and fill it again. b. Put on another drum and retighten the slack spring in the drum.
2. The cartridge is not pushed out of the belt or out of the drum. The bolt is obstructed in its forward movement. It is caught on the cartridge (*in the belt or the drum*).	a. The reaction of the bolt is insufficient because the recoil is too weak; movable parts are dirty or not oiled. b. The contact surfaces of bolt are too rough. c. The camming ways on the locking piece are too rough or the lock is jammed in the cartridge chamber. d. The recoil booster is loose. e. The cartridge sticks too tightly in the belt (bent belt-link).	a. Clean and oil the dirty parts. b. Change the bolt. c. Change the barrel. d. Screw the recoil booster tighter. e. Remove the cartridge from the belt link.

Symptom	Cause	Remedy
2. The cartridge is not pushed out of the belt or out of the drum. The bolt is obstructed in its forward movement. It is caught on the cartridge *(in the belt or the drum)*.	*f.* The safety grip-spring is too weak. *g.* In drum feeding, the cartridge is pressed too hard against the bolt.	*f.* Change the safety grip-spring. *g.* Put on another drum; loosen the tension on the spring in the drum.
3. The feed pawl does not take hold of the cartridge *(in the belt or the drum)*, in spite of sufficient recoil and forward movement of the lock.	*a.* The ejector is worn out or broken. *b.* The ejector spring is weak or broken. *c.* The feed pawl spring is weak or broken.	*a* and *b.* Change the bolt. *c.* Replace the feed pawl spring.
4. A round is not fired. The bolt is in its extreme forward position. In reloading, a live cartridge is ejected.	*a.* The firing-pin spring is broken or too short. *b.* The firing pin spring is weak or broken. *c.* The sear is worn or broken. *d.* The bolt is broken or the return spring is weak or broken. *e.* A deformed cartridge is in the barrel. *f.* The return-spring rod is jammed in its rear position. *g.* There are dirty or rough locking lugs.	*a* and *b.* Change the bolt and replace the firing pin (new spring). *c.* Replace the sear. *d.* Replace the bolt or return spring. *e.* Reload and fire again. *f.* Remove burrs or rough places on the receiver. *g.* Clean and oil the dirty parts.

Symptom	Cause	Remedy
5. Cartridge case is not extracted. The bullet of the new round has struck the cartridge case still sticking in the chamber.	a. The extractor is worn or broken. b. The extractor spring is weak or broken. c. A cartridge case is jammed in the chamber. d. A cartridge case is torn off (ruptured case).	a. Change the bolt. b. Repair the extractor spring. c. Change the belt or drum. Let the bolt spring forward once more, and pull it back again. If this does not help, change the barrel. d. Change the barrel; later remove the cartridge case from the barrel.
6. A cartridge case is not ejected. The cartridge is jammed in the ejector opening by the closing bolt.	a. The ejector is worn. b. The ejector stud is loose or worn. c. The recoil is insufficient. d. A cartridge has bounced outside of the gun and sprung back into the gun through the ejection port.	a. Change the bolt. b. Insert a new ejector stud. c. See under 2, above, especially *a* and *d*. d. Change the position of the gun.

(5) *To unload.*—To unload (*using the belt drum or belt*), cock the gun by pulling the operating handle to the rear, and set the safety lever to the "safe" position. Raise the feed cover by pushing forward the feed-cover catch (at the rear end of the feed cover). Remove the belt from the gun. After checking to be sure that the chamber is empty, close the feed cover,

move the safety lever to the "fire" position, and ease the bolt forward by holding the operating handle and squeezing the trigger.

To unload when using the 75-round double drum, proceed as in unloading with the belt or belt drum, except that the double drum must be removed before the feed cover is opened.

(6) *To change barrels.*—(a) *General.*—The barrels on this gun should be changed after firing 250 rounds

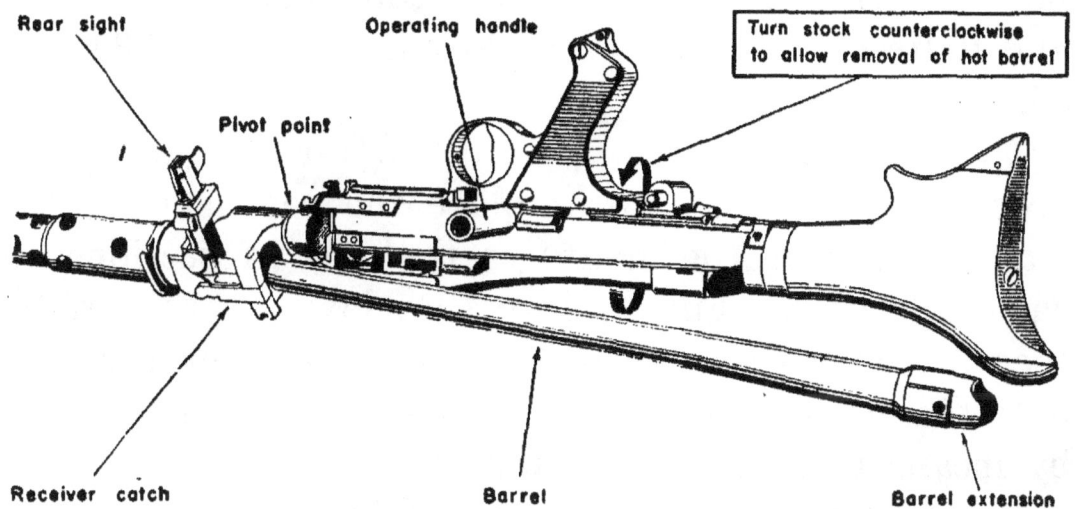

Figure 45.—Removal of barrel of M.G. 34

in full-automatic fire, or, in cases of emergency, after firing 400 rounds. Spare barrels are regular equipment with the *M.G. 34* and are carried in either single- or double-barreled containers by the gun crew.

(b) *Procedure.*—Cock the gun and set the safety lever to the "safe" position. Push in the receiver catch (located just below the rear sight base on the left side of the barrel jacket) and turn the receiver almost a half turn in a counterclockwise direction (see fig. 45). Lower the shoulder stock until the barrel slides out of the barrel jacket. Remove the hot barrel, using an asbestos hand pad which is furnished with the spare-parts kit. Now level the piece and insert a cool barrel into the barrel jacket. Turn the receiver back to the right until the receiver catch again locks together the barrel jacket and the receiver. Set the safety lever to the "fire" position and commence firing.

(7) *Tripod mount.*—(a) *General.*—When the *M.G. 34* is employed on its tripod mount, it is considered to be a heavy machine gun. On this mount, overhead and indirect fire may be employed. (See figs. 34 and 35.)

(b) *Mounting gun on tripod.*—After unfolding and erecting the mount,[10] first place the rear end of the machine gun on the mount so that the projections on each side of the gun fit into the claws on the cradle (see fig. 34); then lower the muzzle end of the gun onto the cradle. The front part of the gun is secured by means of the hinge clamp.

(c) *Elevation and traverse.*—The elevating handwheel is on the left of the elevating gear (see fig. 46).

---

[10] If the tripod mount is folded, it should be unfolded and erected as follows:

(a) Release the clamping lever on the front leg, extend the front leg to the required position, and then lock the clamping lever.

(b) Loosen the wing nuts on the rear legs and push the rear legs back. Raise the mount to the required height and tighten the wing nuts.

(c) With one hand, grasp the handle; with the other hand, grasp the cradle. Push the press lever forward and raise the cradle, drawing the elevating gear smartly back (fig. 46) until it stands erect and engages the upper part of the mount.

(d) Adjust the legs, so that the cradle is horizontal when the elevating gear is adjusted to its old position. The machine gun can now be mounted on the mount.

A wing nut is furnished for clamping the elevating gear, and adjustable elevating stops are provided to enable the gun to be elevated gradually.

Adjustments for direction are made by shifting the traversing slide along the traversing arc by means of

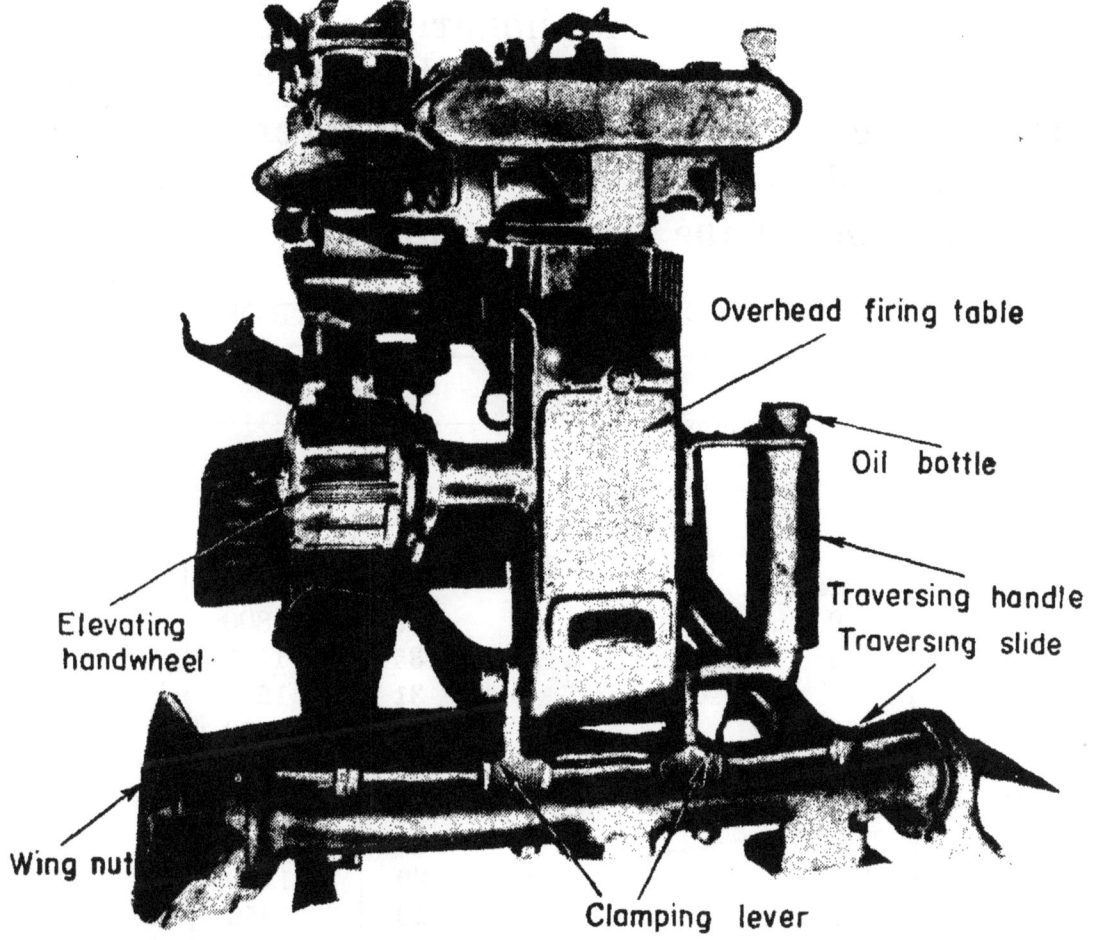

Figure 46.—Rear view of tripod mount for M.G. 34. (See tables 1 and 2, pp. 76–77, below, for a translation of the plate containing overhead firing data.)

a handle on the right in which an oil bottle is fitted. There is a clamping lever for locking the traversing slide. Traversing stops are arranged for the traversing arc, which is graduated to facilitate adjustment of the stops (see fig. 46).

In front of the elevating gear is an automatic searching-fire device, operated by the recoil of the gun in the cradle, which causes a projection on the cradle slide to strike a roller on the device. Actuated in this manner, the device alternately elevates the cradle step by step and depresses it similarly each time a shot is fired. The limits of the searching fire, and consequently the distance on the ground covered by it, can be increased or reduced by means of two levers at the inner end of the elevating handwheel.

OVERHEAD FIRING TABLE (IN YARDS)

Distance to own troops	Safety	
	Divisions	Sight
55	61	2250
80	49	2030
110	39	1800
140	35	1730
165	31	1550
190	29	1500
220	27	1450
250	23	1350
280	23	1350
330	20	1250
440	20	1250
550	20	1250
660	22	1300
770	23	1350
880	27	1450
990	29	1500
1100	21	1550
1200	35	1730
1300	37	1750
1400	41	1860
1500	44	1920

Table 1

OVERHEAD FIRING TABLE (IN YARDS)—Continued

Distance to own troops	Safety	
	Divisions	Sight
1670	49	2030
1750	55	2130
1860	60	----
1970	66	----
2080	73	----
2190	81	----
2300	90	----
2400	99	----
2520	109	----
2620	119	----
2730	131	----
2840	143	----
2950	156	----
3060	170	----
3170	184	----
3280	199	----
3390	215	----

Table 1—Continued

TABLE OF MINIMUM CLEARANCE

Target	Depth	Double depth
1300	1	2
2190	2	4
2840	3	6
3280	4	8
3600	5	10

Table 2

e. Ammunition

(1) *Belts.*—The belts used in this gun are of the non-disintegrating metallic-link type. Each length holds 50 rounds. Lengths may be joined together to give a belt

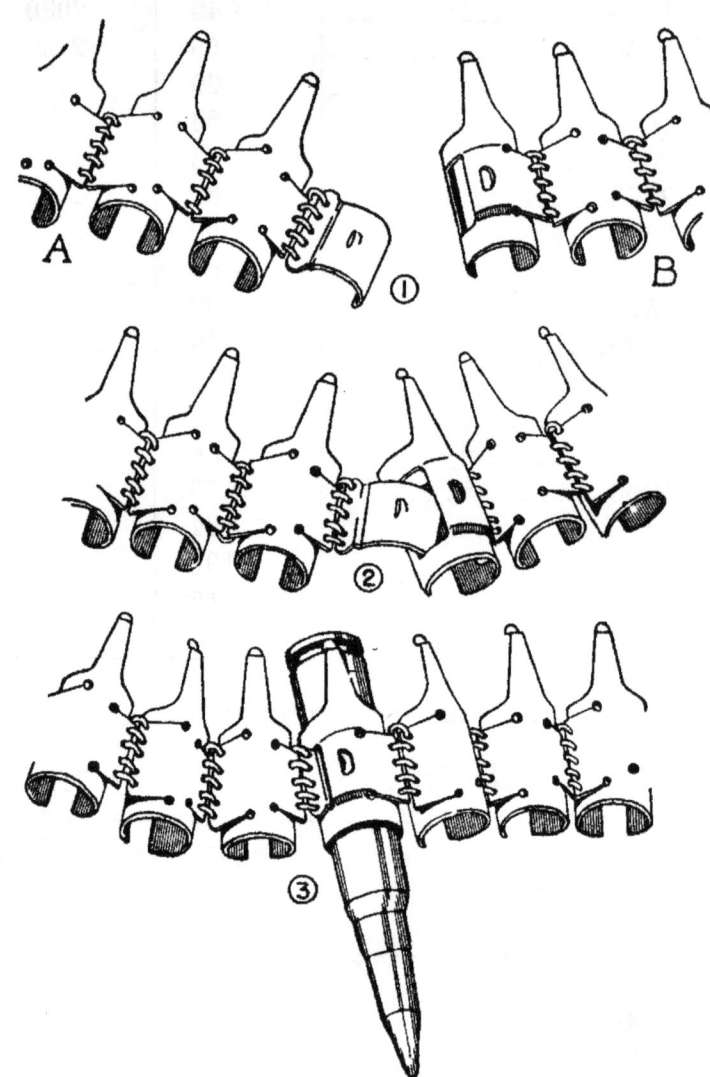

Figure 47.—Method of joining metallic-link ammunition belt.

of any length, but lengths of 250 rounds are usually the longest used. When the gun is moved frequently, and when it is used for antiaircraft purposes, the 50-round belt in the belt drum is employed (see fig. 47).

(2) *To join belts.*—At one end of a belt there is a link with a small semicircular tongue (fig. 47 ① B) and at the other end of the belt (fig. 47 ① B) there is a link with a small rectangular hole in the side of the curved body of the link. To join one belt to another, the tongue on the last link of one belt is slipped through the hole on the first link of the second belt until the small projection on the tongue is over the small D-shaped hole in the center of the curved body of the link (fig. 47 ②). Now place a round in the link and the belts will be locked together (fig. 47 ③). This can be done while the gun is firing.

(3) *Types of ammunition.*—

Type	German Name	Identification
Ball	*Patrone schweres Spitzgeschoss (Patr. s.S.)*, cartridge with heavy, pointed bullet.	Green lacquer coloring around the primer seat.
AP	*Patrone mit Spitzgeschoss mit Stahlkern (Patr. S.m.K.)*, cartridge with steel-core pointed bullet.	Red lacquer coloring around the primer seat.
AP tracer	*Patrone mit Spitzgeschoss mit Stahlkern and Leuchtspur (Patr. S.m. K.L'Spur)*, cartridges with steel-core pointed bullet with tracer.	Red lacquer coloring around the primer seat, and black tip on the bullet.

Ammunition is usually packed 1,500 rounds to a case. A case weighs about 113 pounds. Ammunition cartons holding 5-round clips have their identification labels overprinted with **I.L.** in red ink. Ammunition is not packed in belts; it is loaded into the nondisintegrating metallic link belts with the aid of a belt-loading machine. These belts are not expendable.

(4) *Hand-loading belt.*—When there is no belt-loading machine available, the belts may be loaded by hand. Insert rounds in the belt from the end with the projection until the cannelure of the cartridge case is stopped by the tit on the end of the projection. This will correctly place the round in the belt. Belts are connected as stated in **e** (2), p. 79, above.

(5) *Lubrication of belt.*—The belts should be lubricated with heavy oil if the cartridges are kept in them for any purpose other than immediate use. One application of heavy oil will last for 10 usings of the belt in the gun.

f. Maintenance

(1) *Oiling and cleaning.*—The *M.G. 34* is sensitive to dirt, dust, and sand. To function well, it must be kept cleaned and oiled at all times. The ejection-port cover should be kept closed whenever the gun is not firing. This ejection-port cover will automatically open whenever either of the double triggers is pulled. The belts should be kept oiled. The same type of care and cleaning given to similar U. S. weapons will suffice.

(2) *Stripping.*—(a) *To remove bipod.*—Raise the front sight. Press the leaf spring catch of the bipod (located underneath the barrel jacket behind the bipod guide). Rotate the bipod until it is on top of the barrel, and then remove it from the gun.

(b) *Feed cover and feed block.*—Release the feed-cover catch (at the back end of the feed cover) by pushing it forward, and raise the feed cover. Press the feed-cover hinge pin (see fig. 48) from right to left and remove the feed cover. Center the belt feed slide in the feed block and pull the feed block off the feed cover.

(c) *Shoulder stock.*—Press the catch located on the underside of the plastic shoulder stock. Give the

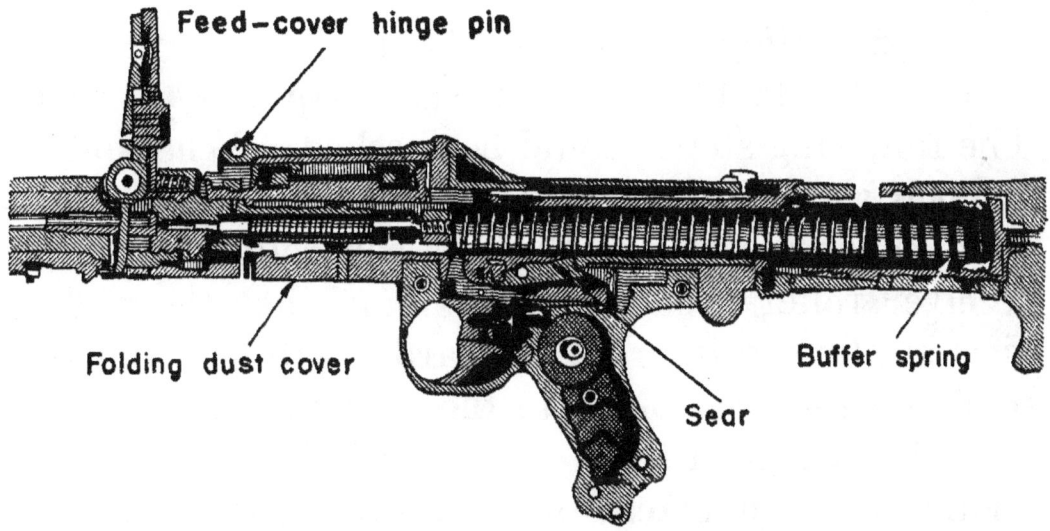

Figure 48.—Cross section of trigger, recoil, and feed mechanism of M.G. 34.

shoulder stock a quarter turn (in either direction) and then remove it.

(d) *Buffer housing and return spring.*—In removing the buffer housing, the large return spring will be released. Therefore, care should be taken to maintain pressure on the buffer housing while removing it. Press the buffer-housing catch, which is located beneath the rear end of the receiver back of the pistol grip, turn the buffer housing a quarter turn counterclockwise, and allow the tension on the return spring to be gradually relieved.

(e) *Bolt.*—Strike the operating handle toward the rear with the palm of the hand, bringing the bolt back. Withdraw the bolt from the open rear end of the receiver, pushing with the finger if necessary.

(f) *Barrel.*—Proceed as stated in *d* (6), page 73, above.

(3) *Assembly.*—Assembly is carried out in the reverse order to that used in the stripping procedure. The following steps should be checked. When putting the bolt assembly back into the receiver, insert the bolt head in the receiver so that the bolt rollers fit into the receiver roller grooves. Make sure that the nail-like ejector plunger is in its forward position. When assembling the feed block to the feed cover, first center the belt-feed pawl slide on the feed block. Next, center the feed arm extension on the feed cover. Finally, slide the feed block onto the feed cover so that the belt pawls will be on the left side of the gun. The raised rib on the feed arm should match the grooves on the stud on the top rear end of the bolt carrier.

g. Accessories

Several accessories go with the gun itself. These are—

(1) Spare barrels, usually three, in a single- and a double-barreled holder;
(2) Tripod for using the weapon as a heavy machine gun (this may have an antiaircraft mount adapter);
(3) Antiaircraft tripod;
(4) Belts and belt boxes;
(5) Belt drums and belt-drum holders;

(6) Tool kit, containing

1 spare bolt,
1 ruptured-cartridge extractor,
1 antiaircraft auxiliary ring sight,
1 open-end wrench,
1 cartridge-extractor tool,
1 oil container,
1 plastic case containing sulphur (used with oil as a lubricant);

(7) Canvas or leatheroid breech cover;

(8) Spare parts (in the belt box marked with a yellow "E" (*Ersatzstücke*—"replacements"):

1 brush,
1 screw-top metal container,
1 oil container with bristle brush on cap,
1 open-end wrench,
2 complete bolt assemblies,
1 bolt carrier,
1 firing pin,
1 firing-pin retainer,
1 firing-pin lock;

(9) Asbestos hand pad (for handling hot barrels);
(10) Package of rubber muzzle caps;
(11) 1 belt-feed pawl-slide housing;
(12) 1 belt-feed pawl assembly;
(13) 1 feed-plate lower assembly.

13. M.G. 42 [11]

a. General

Recently a new dual-purpose machine gun has appeared which may eventually replace the *M.G. 34* in the German Army. Like the *M.G. 34*, it can be used on a bipod (see fig. 49) as a light machine gun, on a tripod as a heavy machine gun, as an antiaircraft machine gun (on a special tripod), and for numerous other special purposes on special mounts. Because of the wide use of stamping, welding, and riveting, this

---

[11] *M.G.* is the German abbreviation for *Maschinengewehr*, which means "machine gun."

gun is far easier to manufacture and less smooth in finished appearance than the *M.G. 34*. It is, however, equally as serviceable as the older model, which is still the main armament of all types of German units. A new and faster method of barrel change is another outstanding characteristic of this new model. The rate of

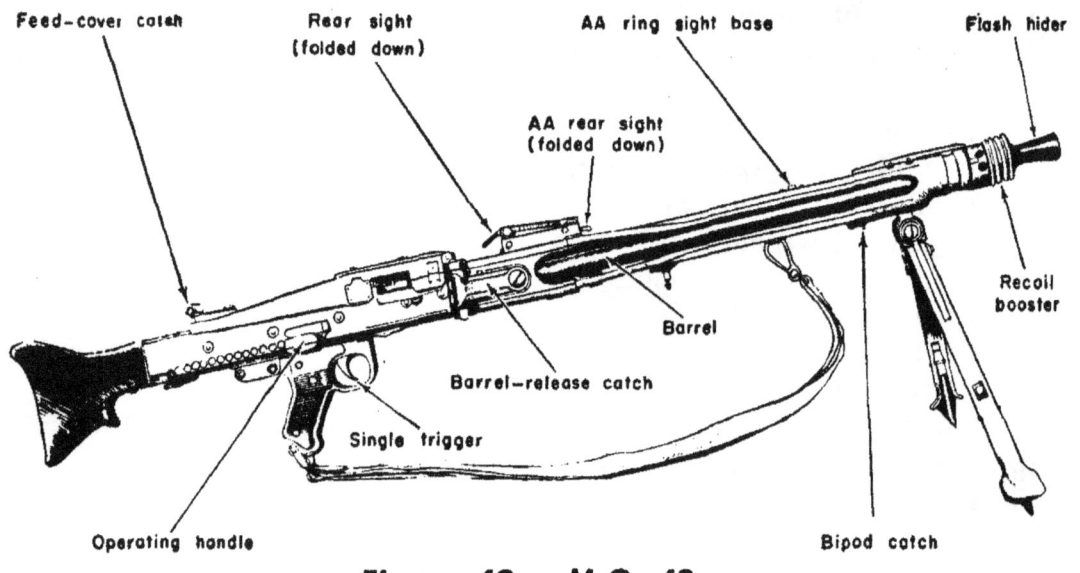

Figure 49.—M.G. 42.

fire has been increased over that of the *M. G. 34*, but a certain decrease in accuracy has resulted.

b. How to Identify

The *M.G. 42* may be identified by—

(1) Rectangular shape of receiver and barrel jacket.
(2) Barrel jacket opening on the right side to allow change of barrel. (This change is effected by a handle, also on the right side.)
(3) Operating handle much larger than that of the *M.G. 34* and grooved for the fingers.
(4) Leaf rear sight sliding on ramp (unlike the *M.G. 34* rear sight, which is of the upright leaf type).

(5) Separate antiaircraft rear sight hinged on the right sight base.

(6) Bolt of a different pattern from that of the *M.G. 34*, the body being round and having a separate bolt head of a nonrotating type.

(7) Single trigger. (The trigger mechanism is not equipped with two triggers as in the *M.G. 34*, and the gun cannot fire semi-automatically.)

c. Characteristics

(1) *General.*—The *M.G. 42* is a combination short-recoil blowback weapon. Instead of the rotating bolt action of the *M.G. 34*,[12] the bolt is locked to the barrel by means of two movable locking studs, located in the bolt head, and operating on two locking cams on the barrel extension. These locking studs resemble a wheelbarrow wheel and axle, and are placed symmetrically in slots in the sides of the bolt head with their axles vertical. The edges of the wheels are in contact with the operating surfaces of the locking cams in the barrel extension. As the bolt closes, the locking cams force the locking wheels outward, so that their axles, which project above and below the slots, enter the corresponding slots in the barrel extension. The barrel is then locked to the bolt head. On firing, the barrel extension and the bolt recoil together a half inch, and then the locking cams serve to unlock the locking wheels from the barrel extension, while the blowback pressure from the barrel drives the bolt to the rear, operating the weapon. This system gives a high rate

---

[21] See note 7, p. 58, above.

of fire, which is what the Germans seem to be seeking in this weapon.[13]

The feed is the same as for the *M.G. 34,* a belt or drum being used (fig. 50). It is not known whether

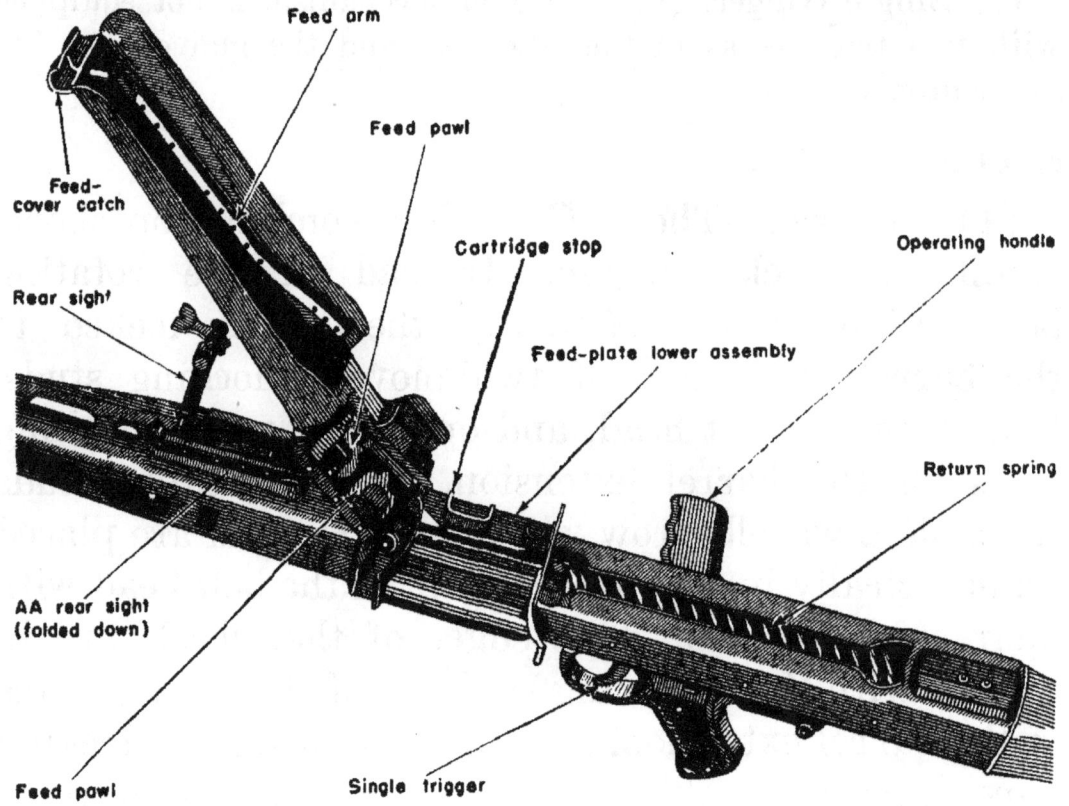

Figure 50.—M.G. 42 with feed cover raised to show feed mechanism.

a special feed cover to take a 75-round saddle-type drum is made for this gun. The tripod mount is the same as that of the *M.G. 34* except for the method of fastening the gun to the mount. No detailed information on the antiaircraft tripod is available.

---

[13] This increased rate of fire is not desirable from any point of view except that of use as an antiaircraft machine gun, because the accuracy is decreased considerably.

(2) Table of characteristics.—

Principle of operation	Combination short recoil and blowback.
Caliber	7.92-mm (.312 inch).
Rate of fire (cyclic)	1,050 to 1,350 rounds per minute.
Ammunition	All types of 7.92-mm not expressly forbidden for use in the machine gun (for example, the *Patr. 318* manufactured for the *Pz.B. 39* antitank rifle is unsuitable, because it will not fit in the chamber).
Type of feed	1. Non-disintegrating metallic-link which holds 50 rounds and may be connected to make longer belts. 2. 50-round belts, for use by the light (ground) version when the position of the gun is being changed frequently and rapidly; or, in antiaircraft versions of the gun, contained in a metal drum attached to the feedblock.
Weight as light machine gun (bipod)	25½ pounds.
Sights:	
Front	Inverted V adjustable for height, on a folding post.
Rear	Leaf with open V notch sliding on ramp, graduated from 200 to 2,000 meters (219 to 2,187 yards) (there is an antiaircraft rear peep sight hinged on the open rear sight base).

Auxiliary_____ Antiaircraft ring sight, kept in the maintenance kit, and fitting on the barrel jacket. (This is used in conjunction with the folding antiaircraft rear peep sight attached to the rear sight base.)

d. How to Operate

(1) *Safety.*—There is a plunger-type safety catch located just above the pistol grip. Unlike the *M.G. 34* safety, it works from side to side. The safety catch cannot be operated unless the gun is cocked. To put the gun on "safe," push the safety catch toward the left (facing the muzzle), until the letter "S" (*sicher*—"safe") shows on its surface. To put the gun on "fire," push the safety catch toward the right until the letter "F" (*Feuer*—"fire") is exposed.

(2) *To load and fire.*—(a) *Using belt from belt box.*—Insert the tab of the belt, with the open end of the links down, in the feedway on the left side of the receiver (if there is no tab on the belt, take two cartridges from the end of the belt and use the empty links as a tab). The feed cover may be either open or closed during this operation. Pull the belt through until the first round can be engaged by the feed pawls (a three-cartridge width). The cartridges in the belt should not be pulled so far as to cover the feed opening in the feed-plate lower assembly. Do not cock the gun until ready to fire. When ready to fire, cock by pulling the operating handle to the rear as far as it will go. The handle should then be shoved forward again until a "click" is heard. This will prevent a misfire,

since the recoil (return) spring is not powerful enough to close the bolt and at the same time to shove the operating handle forward. The safety can be put on "safe" only when the gun is cocked. To fire, move the safety to "fire," and press the single trigger.[14] There is no double trigger (to give provision for semiautomatic fire) as in the *M.G. 34*.

(b) *Using 50-round belt from drum.*—Press the catch on the sliding cover of the drum, and move the cover to the open position so that the tab end of the belt can be pulled from the drum. Insert the tab in the feedway, with the open end of the links down. Engage the hook which is on the front (narrow) end of the drum onto the lug on the front end of the feedplate lower assembly.

Turn the rear end of the drum toward the gun until the spring catch on the rear end of the drum engages the lug on the rear end of the feedway. Now proceed as in belt-loading from a belt box (see **d** (2), on the opposite page).

(c) *Using 75-round double drum (if furnished with gun).*—If this type of drum is found with the gun, more than likely the gun will be fitted to take these drums without any changes, that is, with a special feed cover. This special feed cover has an opening to take the 75-round drum, and it also has a folding dust cover to protect the breech mechanism when the drum is not in place on the gun. No belt is used in

---

[14] See fig. 5, p. 8, above, for the method of aligning German sights. See par. 12**d** (3) (b), p. 64, above, for a description of the telescopic sight which may also be used with the *M.G. 42*.

this type of drum. Place the drum in position, straddling the feed opening and thereby depressing the dust cover. Pull the operating handle to the rear and then push it forward, thus charging the gun and placing the operating handle in a position where it will not fly forward when the trigger is squeezed. Use the trigger for semi- or full-automatic fire in the same manner as in firing belted ammunition from a belt box or drum.

(d) *Immediate action.*—If the gun fails to fire, pull the operating handle to the rear and return it to its forward position. Then pull the trigger. About the only types of stoppage that will occur in the *M.G. 42* are caused as follows: (1) by empty cases jamming in the catch between the bolt and the operating handle, or (2) by empty cases jamming between the bolt head and the barrel extension. To clear the first type of stoppage, the bolt must be drawn back a little by pulling back on the operating handle, holding the bolt level with the feed-arm roller, and moving the operating handle back and forth. To clear the second type of stoppage, merely hold the bolt back and shake the gun several times. This stoppage cannot be cleared by pushing in the end of the bolt or by using a stick or other object to remove the jammed case.

(3) *To unload.*—To unload (using the belt drum or belt), cock the gun by pulling the operating handle to the rear, and set the safety lever to the "safe" position. Raise the feed cover by pushing forward the feed-cover catch (at the rear end of the feed cover).

Remove the belt from the gun. After checking to be sure that the chamber is empty, close the feed cover, move the safety lever to the "fire" position, and ease the bolt forward by holding the operating handle and squeezing the trigger.

To unload when using the 75-round double drum, proceed as in unloading with the belt or belt drum, except that the double drum must be removed before the feed cover is opened.

(4) *To change barrels.*—(a) *General.*—The barrel on this gun should be changed after firing 250 rounds in full-automatic fire, or, in cases of emergency, after firing 400 rounds. Spare barrels are regular equipment with the *M.G. 42* and are carried in either single- or double-barreled containers by the gun crew. The single-barreled container opens up so that the hot barrel can be laid on it and exposed to the air to facilitate cooling.

(b) *Procedure.*—Cock the gun and set the safety catch to the "safe" position. Push the barrel-change lever forward, and rotate the rear end to the right and forward (see fig. 51). This will bring the rear end of the barrel clear of the barrel jacket, and it can be withdrawn by grasping it with the asbestos hand pad furnished with maintenance kit. Place the cool barrel in the loop of the barrel-change lever, and seat the muzzle of the barrel in the front end of the barrel jacket; then swing the barrel-change lever toward the barrel jacket until it locks in place. Set the safety catch to "fire" and recommence firing.

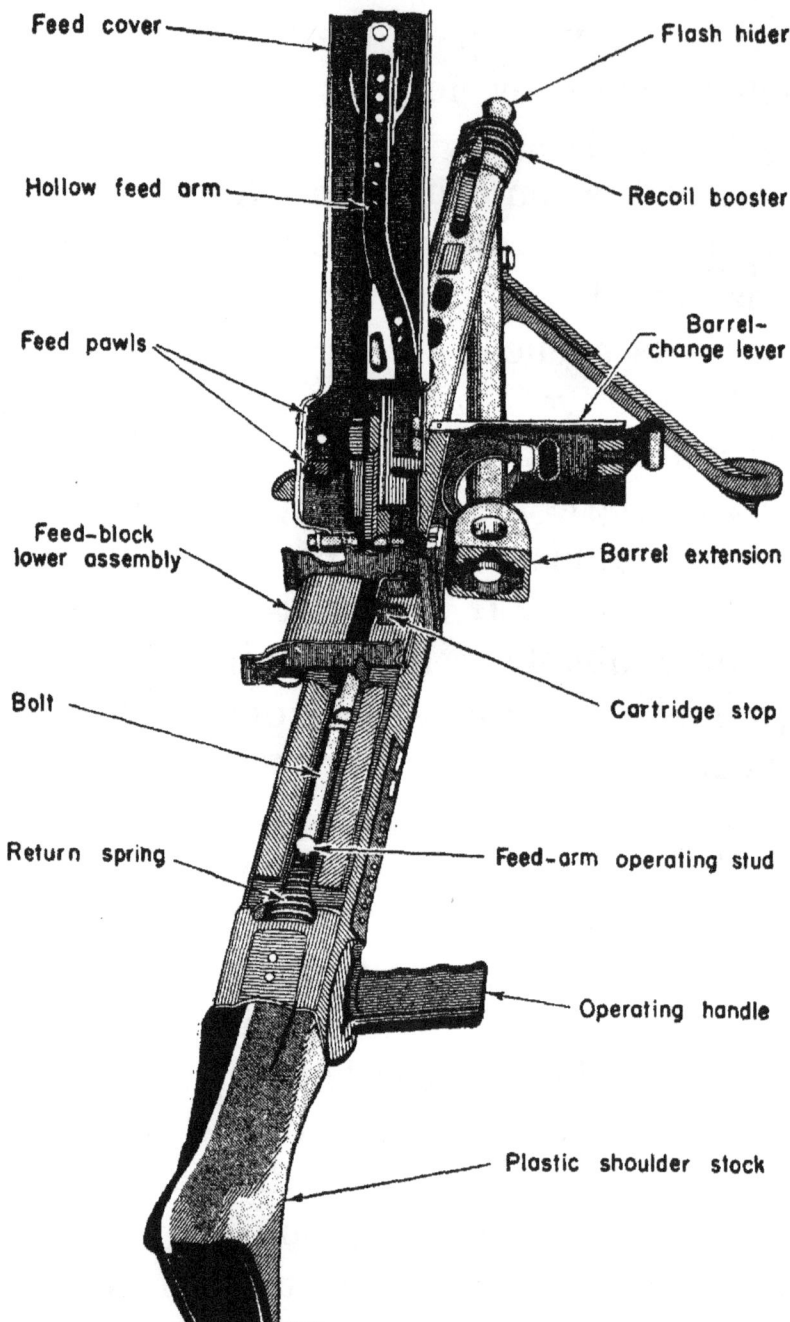

Figure 51.—M.G. 42, showing method of operating barrel extension.

e. Ammunition

The same type of ammunition may be used in both the *M.G. 42* and the *M.G. 34*. (See par. 12**e**, p. 78, above.)

f. Maintenance

(1) *Oiling and cleaning.*—Like the *M.G. 34*, the *M.G. 42* is sensitive to dust, dirt, and sand. To function well, this weapon must be kept cleaned and oiled at all times. The ejection port should be kept closed whenever the gun is not actually firing. The ejection-port cover will open automatically whenever the trigger is pulled back. The tracks on which the bolt slides should be oiled carefully. The bolt head and bolt parts should be oiled lightly. Otherwise, normal care, such as given U. S. automatic weapons, will suffice.

(2) *Stripping.*—(a) *To remove bipod.*—Compress the spring catch on the bipod. Rotate the bipod forward, and remove it from the gun.

(b) *Feed cover and feed block.*—Release the feed-cover catch (located at the back end of the feed cover) by pushing it forward. Raise the feed cover to a 45-degree angle (halfway). The feed-cover hinge pin may now be removed, and the feed-cover assembly removed from the gun. To remove the feed mechanism, push back the spring-loaded cover over the pawls to the rear. At the same time, compress the spring clip on the feed arm and lift out the feed mechanism.

(c) *Shoulder stock.*—Press the catch located on the underside of the plastic shoulder stock. Give the shoulder stock a quarter turn (in either direction) and then remove.

(d) *Buffer housing and return spring.*—In removing the buffer housing, the large recoil, or return, spring will be released. Therefore, care should be taken to maintain pressure on the buffer housing while removing it. Press the buffer-housing catch, which is located beneath the rear end of the receiver just back of the pistol grip, turn the buffer housing clockwise 180 degrees (one-half turn), and ease the buffer housing away from the receiver, releasing gradually the tension on the return (recoil) spring.

(e) *Bolt.*—First, press the trigger; then strike the operating handle toward the rear with the palm of the hand, thus bringing the bolt to the rear. Withdraw the bolt from the open rear end of the receiver, if necessary, by pushing with the finger.

(f) *Barrel.*—Proceed as stated in **d** (4), p. 91, above.

(3) *Assembly.*—Assembly is carried out in the reverse order of that used in the stripping process. The following steps should be checked when putting the bolt assembly back into the receiver. Insert the bolt head, being sure that the heel of the firing pin (which is on the bolt housing) is on top. The feed-arm operating stud should also be upward, and the extractor should be on the bottom side of the bolt.

g. Accessories

Not all the accessories of the *M.G. 42* are known, but they are probably similar to those of the *M.G. 34*.

14. 5–CM[15] LIGHT MORTAR, MODEL 36[16]
a. General

This 5-cm weapon, which is comparable to the U. S. 60-mm mortar, is the standard light mortar[17] of the German Army. It is a small light weapon, easy to carry but somewhat slow to set up.

b. How to Identify

The *l.Gr.W. 36* is identified by—

(1) Rectangular base plate (no bipod legs).
(2) Position of the traversing and elevating mechanisms.
(3) Cleaning rod clipped to the base plate.

c. Characteristics

(1) *General.*—Like U. S. mortars, this German weapon is a muzzle loader, but unlike the U. S. models it is fired by a trigger arrangement. The 5-cm is designed for high-angle fire and cannot be depressed below a 45-degree elevation. It is a two-man load,[17] the base plate and the traversing and cross-leveling gear being carried by one man, and the barrel and elevating screw by another. A third man carries ammunition.

---

[15] Note that the German practice is to designate in centimeters weapons with calibers of 20 mm and higher. (See par. 21, p. 161, below). The German style will be followed in the descriptions of German weapons in order to avoid confusion with similar U. S. weapons.

[16] *Leichter Granatwerfer 36 (l.Gr.W. 36).*

[17] The German tactical symbol for a light mortar is ⟂ or ⌐.

[18] In combat this weapon could be carried complete by one man; a second man would then carry the ammunition.

(2) Table of characteristics.—

	German 5-cm	U. S. 60-mm
Principle of operation.	Muzzle loader, trigger.	Muzzle loader, not trigger fired.
Weight in action	31 pounds	42 pounds.
Caliber	50 mm (1.97 inches)	60 mm (2.4 inches).
Length of barrel	18 inches	28.6 inches.
Maximum range	568 yards	1,935 yards.
Minimum range	55 yards	100 yards.
Type of shell	HE	HE.
Over-all length	8.5 inches	9.54 inches.
Maximum diameter	50 mm	60 mm.
Weight	2 pounds	2.96 pounds.
HE filling	TNT	TNT.
No. of charges, or zones	1	4.
Propellant	Nitrocellulose	Nitrocellulose.
Markings	Bomb painted maroon, stenciled in black.	HE, dull olive drab; practice, blue.
Fuze	Percussion	Superquick.
Sights	Early models have a telescopic sight. Later ones are laid by means of a white line on the barrel. Elevation is established by a quadrant.	
Traverse	600 mils (change in deflection).	140 mils (70 either way).
Elevation	45 degrees to 90 degrees	
Rate of fire	6 rounds in 8 seconds (but this rate cannot be maintained).	Maximum: 1 round in 2 seconds; normal: 1 round in 4 seconds (this rate can be maintained).

MACHINE GUNS AND MORTARS

d. How to Operate (Figs. 52 and 53)

(1) *Safety.*—After releasing the mortar shell, the loader and pointer lower their faces to the ground.

If a misfire occurs, the trigger lever should be immediately pulled several times. If this fails, wait at least 1 minute before unloading.

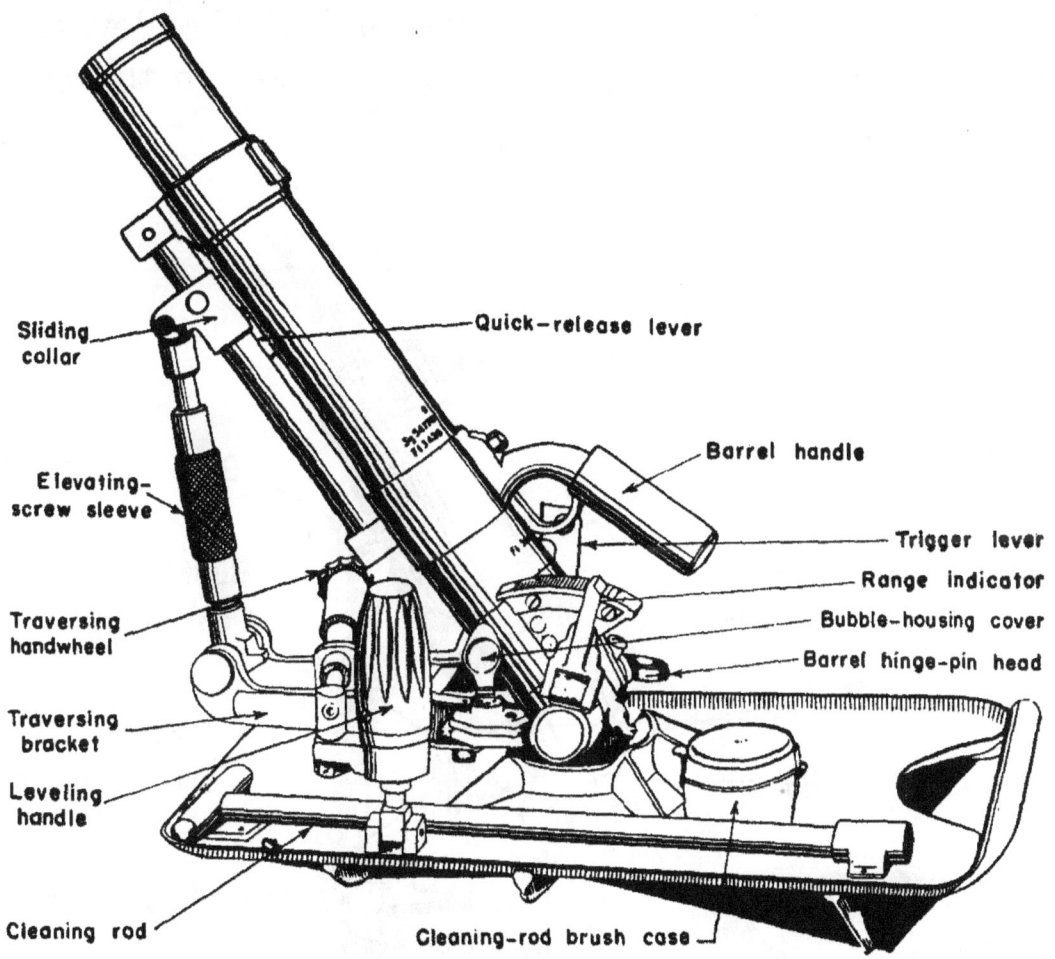

Figure 52.—Left side of 5-cm mortar.

(2) *To unload.*—Pull out the barrel hinge pin, lower the elevation indicator, and gently raise the bottom of the barrel until the shell slides into the hands of the man waiting to receive it.

(3) *Preparation for action.*—(a) Adjust the traversing handwheel to zero. Pull out the hinge pin connecting the barrel to the base plate. Be sure that the range indicator is folded down.

(b) Hold the barrel by its handle and adjust the elevating screw to its minimum elevation.

(c) Insert the barrel in the base-plate socket. Squeeze the catches at the lower end of the elevating-screw pillar, and engage them in recesses in the front end of the traversing bracket.

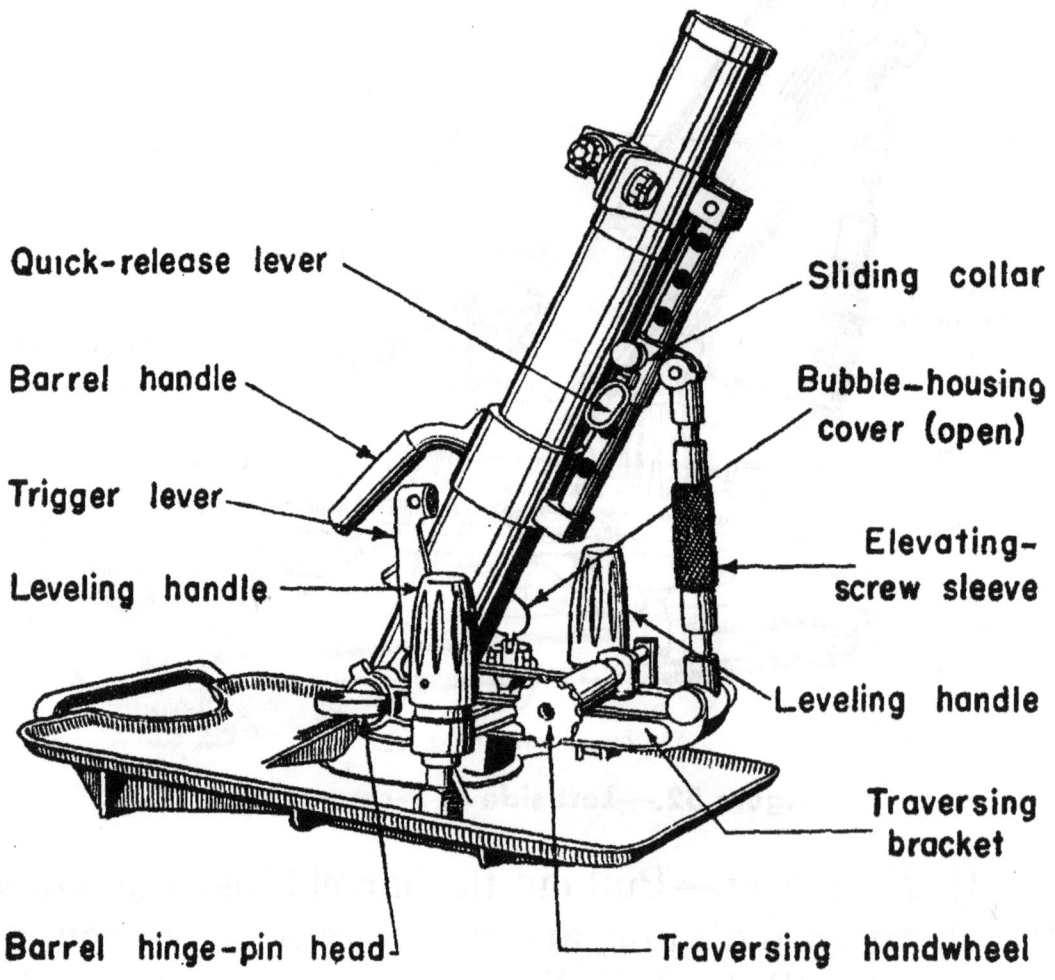

Figure 53.—Right side of 5-cm mortar.

(d) Push in the hinge pin and raise the range indicator.

(e) If time permits, loosen the ground on which the base plate is placed.

(f) Place the mortar in position, and lay it roughly on the target by moving the base plate and by using the white line on the barrel. Bed the base plate into the ground by pressing down on the barrel-plate handles so that the base plate will slope slightly in the direction of the target.

(4) *Leveling.*—The mortar is leveled by means of the two leveling handles situated on each side of the base plate and connected by a cross bar. A leveling bubble is mounted on the traversing bracket on the left side of the barrel socket.

To center the bubble: (a) to move the bubble toward the firer, turn both handles to the right; (b) to move the bubble toward the target, turn both handles to the left; (c) to move the bubble to the right, turn both handles inward; (d) to move the bubble to the left, turn both handles outward.

(5) *Elevation.*—Range is shown on an arc fixed on the left side of the barrel by the rear edge of an indicator hinged on the traversing bracket. The arc is graduated from 60 to 520 meters (65.4 to 568.8 yards), and the indicator can be folded down when the mortar is dismantled.

A rough adjustment of elevation can be effected in the following manner: pressing a quick-release lever unlocks the catch of the sliding collar connected to the upper end of the elevating screw pillar; the collar is then free to slide along its guide, and the barrel can be elevated by means of the barrel handle.

As soon as the range ordered is indicated approximately on the range scale, the sliding collar is locked in its guide by the release of the quick-release lever. Fine adjustments are effected by rotation of the sleeve of the elevating-screw pillar.

(6) *Laying for line.*—The mortar can be laid direct or by means of aiming stakes. Rough adjustments for line are effected by moving the base plate with the traverse set at zero.

A deflection scale consisting of two rows of graduations is marked on the cross bar which connects the two leveling handles. The distance between the graduations in each row is 20 mils, but the rows are offset so that graduations on one row are halfway between those on the other. This permits measurement of deflection to the nearest 10 mils.

The total traverse—300 mils right and 300 left—is 600 mils (33°45′). Fine adjustments are made by rotating the traversing knob until the desired deflection is shown on the traverse scale.

(7) *To load and fire.*—The layer's position during loading and firing is on the left behind the mortar. He lies on his stomach, holding the leveling handles and steadying the base plate with his forearms.

The loader, lying on the right of the layer, loads by inserting the shell in the muzzle, tail first. The loader then grasps the trigger, and both he and the layer lower their faces to the ground, the layer still steadying the base plate by resting his weight on it. To fire, the loader pulls the trigger slowly and evenly.

e. Ammunition

(1) *Shell.*—The 5-cm mortar shell, model 36 (*5-cm Wgr. 36*),[19] has a cast-steel shell casing with a fin assembly screwed into the base and is fired by a propellant charge contained in a shot-gun cartridge-type container, which fits into the hollow-fin assembly and is held there by a set screw.

(2) *Fuze.*—The fuze (*Wgr. Z. 38*)[20] is a nose-percussion type fitted for graze, and becomes armed when approximately 60 yards from the muzzle of the mortar barrel.

Ammunition is carried in a steel container that holds 10 rounds and has handles for carrying.

f. Maintenance

This mortar requires no more maintenance than the U. S. 60-mm mortar. Bearing surfaces are well protected from the entrance of dust, and the threaded sections of the elevating and traversing mechanisms are completely enclosed in tubes or long nuts. A cleaning rod and brush are attached to the base plate.

---

[19] *5-cm Werfergranate 36* (50-mm mortar shell 36).
[20] *Werfergranatzünder 38* (mortar shell fuze 38).

15. 8-CM [21] HEAVY MORTAR, MODEL 34 [22]

a. General

The 8-cm model 34 mortar (see figs. 54 and 55) is the standard heavy infantry mortar of the German Army and like the U. S. 81-mm M1 mortar it is a smoothbore, muzzle-loading weapon for high-angle fire. For manhandling it is broken down into three parts: (1) the

Figure 54.—8-cm mortar, model 34, in action.

base plate, (2) the tube, and (3) the bipod with the traversing, elevation, and cross-leveling mechanisms. It is basically similar to the U. S. 81-mm mortar, except

---

[21] Actually this is an 8.1-cm mortar, but it is called an 8-cm by the Germans.

[22] *Schwerer Granatwerfer 34* (*s.Gr.W.34*). The German tactical symbol for a heavy mortar is s ∠ or ⊓.

that the cross-leveling mechanism is not connected with the bipod leg, as in the U. S. 81-mm mortar, but is controlled by a handwheel located underneath the elevating mechanism between the bipod legs.

This weapon is so similar to the U. S. heavy mortar that anyone who has used the latter can handle this

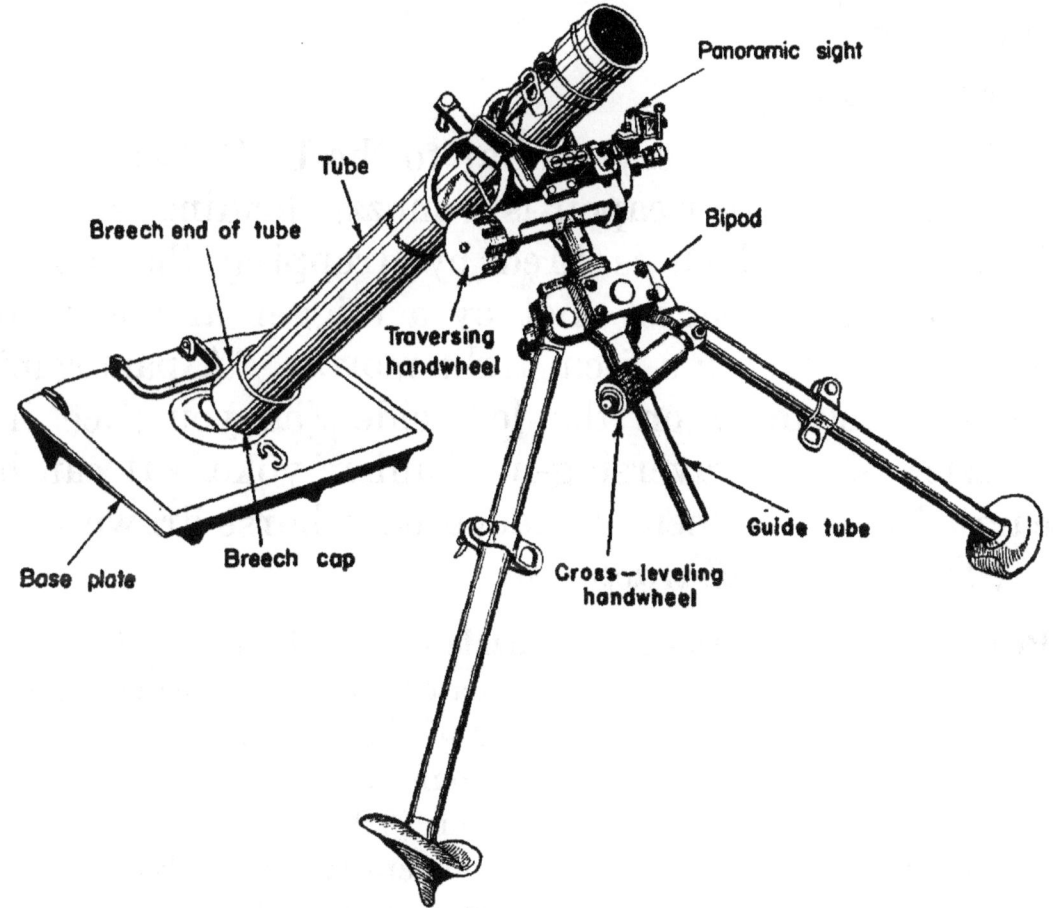

Figure 55.—Right view of 8-cm mortar, model 34.

German weapon effectively after a little practice. The German sights are graduated in mils, are basically the same as the U. S. mortar sight, and so will not cause any difficulty. This weapon is a serviceable mortar and should give a good account of itself in American hands.

b. How to Identify

The 81-mm heavy mortar, model 34, may be identified by—

(1) Rectangular base plate with only one socket to take the ballshaped section (the spherical projection) on the breech (or base) end of the tube.

(2) Bipod with cross-leveling handwheel located between the bipod legs.

c. Characteristics

(1) *General.*—Very similar to the U. S. heavy mortar, this German weapon is a muzzle-loading, smoothbore mortar which is fired by dropping the mortar shell down the barrel—not by a trigger arrangement as with the German 5-cm light mortar. A panoramic sight is mounted on the left side (as you face the muzzle) of the traversing-mechanism yoke. It can be carried by three men or loaded on a horse-drawn cart.

(2) *Table of characteristics.*—

Principle of operation	Muzzle loader, fired by a firing pin situated at the inside breech end of the barrel.
Weight in action	125 pounds.
Caliber	81.4 mm (3.2 inches).
Maximum range	1,900 meters (2,078 yards).
Minimum range	60 meters (66 yards).
Effective range	400 to 1,200 meters (437 to 1,312 yards).
Weight of shell, model 34	3.5 kilograms, or 7¾ pounds.
Rate of fire	6 rounds in 8 to 9 seconds (but this rate cannot be maintained).
Sights	Line on tube for rough laying; panoramic sight for fine adjustments.

MACHINE GUNS AND MORTARS 105

d. How to Operate (Figs. 55 and 56)

(1) *Safety.*—In the event of a misfire, wait one minute; put on "safe" by pressing in the spring-actuated bolt, which is located on the ball-shaped section of the breech (or base) cap, and then turning the bolt in a clockwise direction until the arrow on the bolt

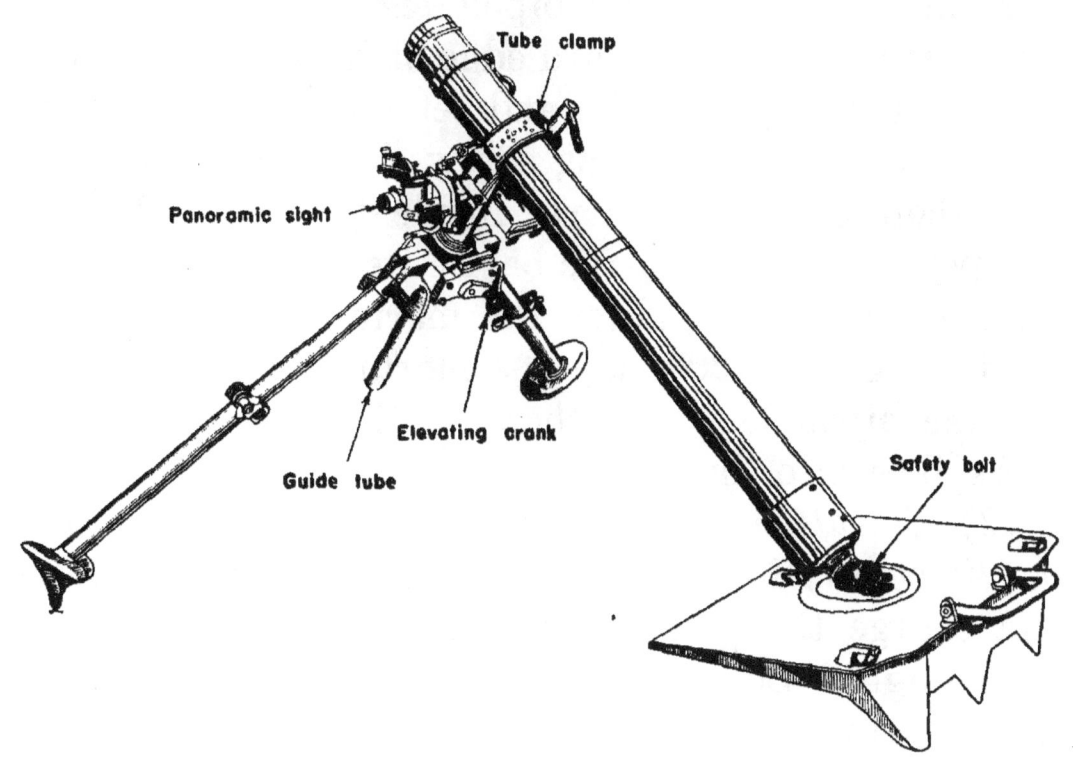

Figure 56.—Left view of 8-cm mortar, model 34.

points to the letter "S" (*sicher*—"*safe*") (about 90 degrees); loosen the mortar barrel clamp, rotate the tube 90 degrees, and tighten the mortar barrel clamp again; and finally gently raise the breech end of the barrel until the shell slides out into an operator's hands. Be sure that the bore of the barrel is kept clean, in order to prevent shells from sticking.

(2) *Preparation for action.*—(a) Set the base plate and bed it into the ground; set the ball-shaped section of the breech cap of the tube into the base-plate socket, with the flat section to the side. Turn the tube in the socket until the spring-actuated bolt is on top; spread the bipod legs, put the bipod in position with the elevating handwheel toward the tube, and see that the line formed by the bipod legs is parallel to the line formed by the forward edge of the base plate; open the mortar barrel clamp and set the elevation so that one-third of the elevating screw shows above its tube, and then place the barrel inside the clamp between the position marks on the barrel itself; place the sight on the sight base, tighten the mortar tube clamp, and set the sight to 1200; lay the mortar roughly by moving the bipod legs and then set the legs by pressing the spikes into the ground.

(3) *Elevation.*—Check the firing table (see table 3, p. 110, below) for the elevation necessary for the range and charge that you are using, and adjust the sight accordingly. Set the elevation clinometer by moving the elevating crank.

(4) *To zero mortar.*—Sight the upper part of the sight on your aiming point or stake, and lay the mortar for direction by using the deflection adjustment on the sight. Note the angle shown on the deflection scale of the sight.

(5) *Determination of direction of fire.*—Set up an aiming stake or select an aiming point in line with the target (see fig. 57). With the deflection scale on the sight at zero degrees if the aiming point or stake is

in front, or at 180 degrees if the aiming point or stake is in back of the mortar, lay accurately for line. Be sure the cross-level bubble is kept centered while you are determining the direction of fire.

Figure 57.—Laying 8-cm heavy mortar for direction during training.

(6) *Corrections for direction.*—Corrections are made by adding or subtracting the required deflection (positive or negative) on the deflection scale of the sight, and then relaying the mortar by using the traversing handwheel.

To correct for direction to the *left,* the extra deflection must be *added* to the angle on the deflection scale; to correct to the *right,* it must be *subtracted* from that angle. For example, if a round falls to the right of the target and the estimated correction for direction is 30 mils to the left, the setting on the deflection scale should be increased by 30 mils.

(7) *To load and fire.*—When the order to load is given, take the shell in the right hand and insert it, fins first, into the muzzle of the mortar, guiding it in with the left hand. On the order "Fire," allow the shell to slide down the barrel and remove the left hand from the muzzle. At this point all members of the crew should lie flat on the ground.

(8) *Immediate action.*—In case of misfires, follow the safety precautions listed under **d** (1), page 105, above. If the primer has been struck, insert another propelling cartridge into the base of the shell. If the primer has not been struck, a new firing pin may be needed, or the inside of the barrel may require cleaning.

e. Ammunition

The model 34 mortar shell is of conventional type with a percussion fuze. Charge 1, containing 154 grains of powder and giving a muzzle velocity of 246 feet per second, is fitted to the shell. Charge II, containing 293 grains of powder and giving a muzzle velocity of 344 feet per second, Charge III, having 432 grains of powder and giving a muzzle velocity of 427 feet per second, or Charge IV, containing 570 grains of powder and giving a muzzle velocity of 499 feet per second, are used as additional increments and fit between the tail fins.

Ammunition is carried in steel cases, each case holding 4 complete rounds. Twenty-four rounds are usually carried by a mortar crew in action. (See the firing table on p. 110, below, for elevation and charge information.)

f. Maintenance

The mortar requires the usual care and cleaning given to U. S. mortars. Cleaning materials will be found with the equipment or can be improvised from materials at hand.

FIRING TABLE
8-Cm Heavy Mortar, Model 34 (German)
8-Cm Shell No. 34
WEIGHT OF SHELL NO. 34—3.5 KILOGRAMS (7.75 POUNDS)

Range		Elevation	Charge	Elevation	Charge
Meters	Yards	Mils		Mils	
60	65.4	1,545	1	-----	-----
80	87.2	1,526	1	-----	-----
100	109.0	1,507	1	-----	-----
120	130.8	1,488	1	-----	-----
140	152.6	1,469	1	-----	-----
160	174.4	1,450	1	-----	-----
180	196.2	1,430	1	-----	-----
200	218.0	1,410	1	-----	-----
220	239.8	1,390	1	-----	-----
240	261.6	1,370	1	-----	-----
260	283.4	1,349	1	-----	-----
280	305.2	1,327	1	-----	-----
300	327.0	1,305	1	1,447	2
320	348.8	1,283	1	1,437	2
340	370.6	1,259	1	1,426	2
360	392.4	1,235	1	1,415	2
380	414.2	1,210	1	1,404	2
400	436.0	1,185	1	1,393	2
420	457.8	1,157	1	1,382	2
440	479.6	1,127	1	1,371	2
460	501.4	1,094	1	1,360	2
480	523.2	1,058	1	1,348	2
500	545.0	1,016	1	1,337	2
520	566.8	1,325	2	-----	-----
540	588.6	1,313	2	-----	-----
560	610.4	1,301	2	-----	-----
580	632.2	1,289	2	-----	-----
600	654.0	1,276	2	1,383	3
620	675.8	1,263	2	1,380	3
640	697.6	1,250	2	1,372	3
660	719.4	1,237	2	1,365	3
680	741.2	1,224	2	1,357	3

Table 3

FIRING TABLE—Continued

Range		Elevation	Charge	Elevation	Charge
Meters	Yards	Mils		Mils	
700	763.0	1,210	2	1,349	3
720	784.8	1,196	2	1,341	3
740	806.6	1,182	2	1,333	3
760	828.4	1,167	2	1,325	3
780	850.2	1,152	2	1,317	3
800	872.0	1,135	2	1,309	3
820	893.8	1,118	2	1,301	3
840	915.6	1,101	2	1,292	3
860	937.4	1,082	2	1,284	3
880	959.2	1,062	2	1,275	3
900	981.0	1,040	2	1,267	3
920	1,002.8	1,017	2	1,258	3
940	1,024.6	991	2	1,249	3
960	1,046.4	962	2	1,240	3
980	1,068.2	926	2	1,231	3
1,000	1,090.0	874	2	1,222	3
1,020	1,111.8	1,212	3	------	------
1,040	1,133.6	1,203	3	------	------
1,060	1,155.4	1,193	3	------	------
1,080	1,177.2	1,183	3	------	------
1,100	1,199.0	1,173	3	1,289	4
1,120	1,220.8	1,163	3	1,282	4
1,140	1,242.6	1,152	3	1,276	4
1,160	1,264.4	1,141	3	1,269	4
1,180	1,286.2	1,130	3	1,262	4
1,200	1,308.0	1,118	3	1,256	4
1,220	1,329.8	1,106	3	1,249	4
1,240	1,351.6	1,094	3	1,242	4
1,260	1,273.4	1,081	3	1,235	4
1,280	1,395.2	1,067	3	1,228	4
1,300	1,417.0	1,052	3	1,221	4
1,320	1,438.8	1,038	3	1,214	4
1,340	1,460.6	1,021	3	1,206	4
1,360	1,482.4	1,005	3	1,199	4
1,380	1,504.2	987	3	1,191	4
1,400	1,526.0	968	3	1,184	4

Table 3—Continued

FIRING TABLE—Continued

Range		Elevation	Charge	Elevation	Charge
Meters	Yards	Mils		Mils	
1,420	1,547.8	945	3	1,176	4
1,440	1,569.6	917	3	1,168	4
1,460	1,591.4	881	3	1,160	4
1,480	1,613.2	1,152	4		
1,500	1,635.0	1,143	4		
1,520	1,656.8	1,135	4		
1,540	1,678.6	1,126	4		
1,560	1,700.4	1,116	4		
1,580	1,722.2	1,107	4		
1,600	1,744.0	1,097	4		
1,620	1,765.8	1,087	4		
1,640	1,787.6	1,077	4		
1,660	1,809.4	1,067	4		
1,680	1,831.2	1,056	4		
1,700	1,853.0	1,045	4		
1,720	1,874.8	1,033	4		
1,740	1,896.6	1,021	4		
1,760	1,918.4	1,008	4		
1,780	1,940.2	994	4		
1,800	1,962.0	980	4		
1,820	1,983.8	963	4		
1,840	2,005.6	946	4		
1,860	2,027.4	925	4		
1,880	2,049.2	901	4		
1,900	2,071.0	869	4		

Table 3—Continued

Section IV. ANTITANK GUNS AND INFANTRY HOWITZERS[1]

16. 3.7-CM PAK[2]

a. General

The *3.7-cm Pak* (1.45-inch antitank gun) formerly the chief German antitank gun, has been largely replaced by the *5-cm Pak 38*, but the *3.7-cm Pak* is still likely to be encountered (see figs. 58 and 59). It has recently been provided with the AP 40 type of ammunition, which has a good penetration performance at ranges up to 400 yards. A stick bomb 5.7 inches in diameter and 11 inches long, with a rod which fits into the bore, has also recently been introduced (see fig. 62). Its use is likely to be restricted to short ranges. The bomb is the hollow-charge type. The gun is also in service with the Italian Army.

This gun, which is organic equipment of the German infantry regiment,[3] is normally towed on its own

---

[1] The information in this section is mainly based on reports; facilities have not been available to make an actual examination of the pieces. The German Army provides infantry howitzers and antitank guns as accompanying weapons of the infantry. These weapons are also equipment of German artillery units. For a description of their employment under desert conditions see "Artillery in the Desert," MIS *Special Series*, No. 6 (Nov. 25, 1942).

[2] *Pak* is the German abbreviation for *Panzerabwehrkanone* which means "antitank gun." *Pak* has gained currency as a word. Note that the German practice is to designate artillery calibers in terms of centimeters rather than millimeters (see par. 21, p. 161, below). The German tactical symbol for *3.7-cm Pak* is ⫯ or ⫯

[3] See fig. 1, p. xii, above.

wheels by a prime mover, but may also be carried in a truck. Weighing only about 880 pounds, it is a suitable weapon for use by airborne troops.

b. Table of Characteristics

Muzzle velocity:
    AP _____ 2,625 feet per second.
    AP 40 _____ 3,450 feet per second.
Effective range _____ 600 yards.
Rate of fire _____ 8 to 10 rounds per minute.
Length of gun _____ 65.52 inches.
Elevation _____ 25 degrees.
Depression _____ 8 degrees.
Traverse _____ 60 degrees (6 degrees with trails closed).

c. How to Operate

(1) *Safety.*—There are three safety arrangements:

(a) Before the breech can be opened after a misfire, the hand-operated block stop must be released by pressing the plunger (see fig. 59).

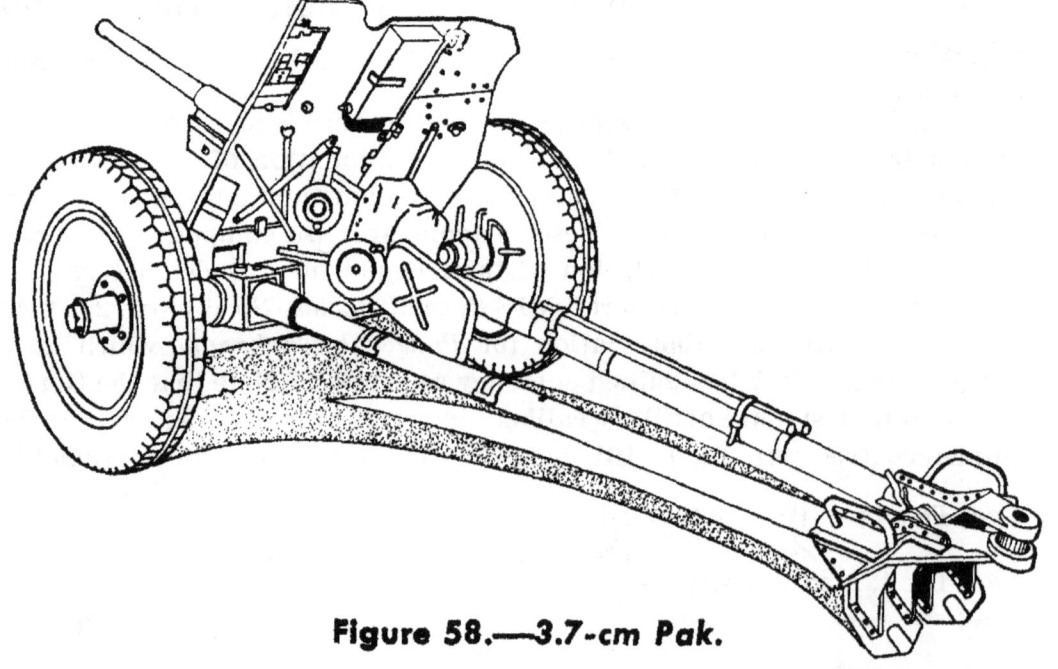

Figure 58.—*3.7-cm Pak.*

ANTITANK GUNS AND INFANTRY HOWITZERS   115

Figure 59.—3.7-cm Pak in action.

(b) When turned to *sicher* ("safe"), the safety catch on the left prevents the sear from releasing the firing pin, and also prevents the breech from opening.

(c) The gun cannot be fired when the buffer cylinder is not correctly assembled, as a spring-loaded plunger prevents the actuation of the sear.

(2) *To load and fire.*—To open the breech, set the safety catch at *Feuer* ("fire"), press the hand-operated block-stop plunger (top left of the rear face of the breech ring) and turn the breech-mechanism lever clockwise (see figs. 60 and 61). The plunger is pressed back automatically by inertia when the gun is fired.

To load the gun, insert a round and give it a final impetus in order to cause the breech to close automatically.

To fire the gun, press the push button in the center of the elevating handwheel. Firing may also be accomplished by pulling outward the trigger lever located on the right of the breech. The firing mechanism is recocked automatically during recoil.

To recock after a misfire, push the right-hand firing lever toward the piece, and start opening the breech until resistance is felt. The hand-operated block-stop plunger must not be pressed in, or the breech might open completely. The breechblock is automatically unlocked after firing, and the block stop goes forward by inertia. Movement of the breech-mechanism lever then extracts the cartridge case.

(3) *To open trails.*—With the trails closed, the traverse is only 106 mils (6 degrees), but with the

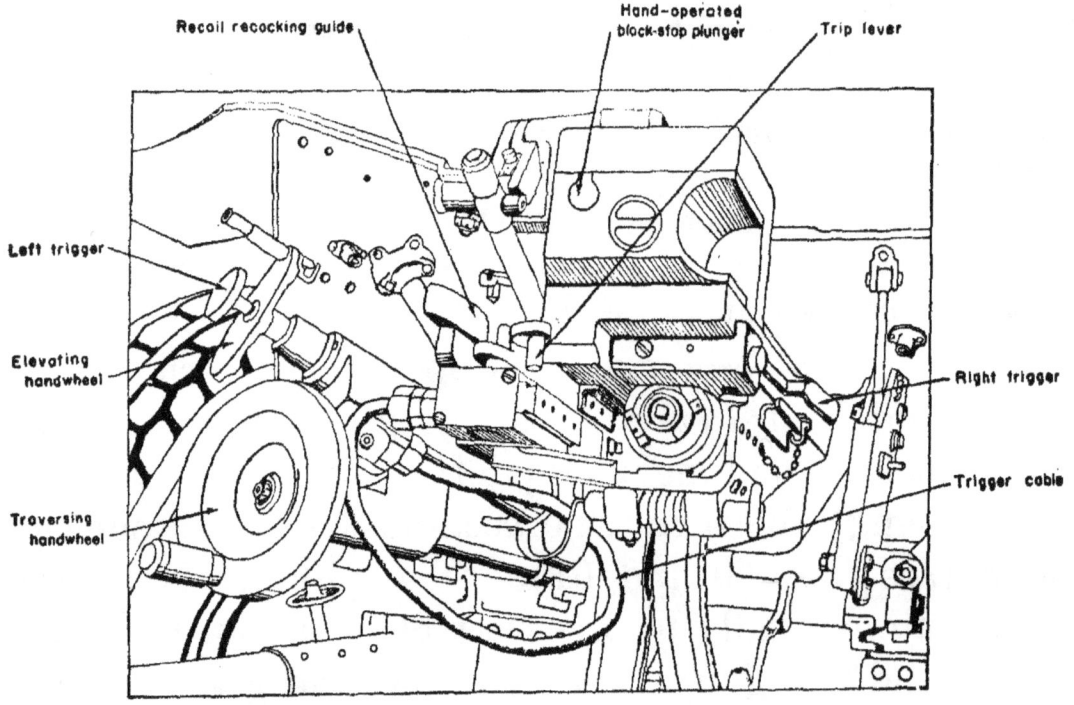

Figure 60.—Close-up of rear of 3.7-cm Pak

ANTITANK GUNS AND INFANTRY HOWITZERS 117

trails open it is 1,062 mils (60 degrees). To open the trails, lift the locking lever at the trail end. Press down the locking levers of the trail hinges. Lock the trails in the open position by pushing up the hinge locking levers.

(4) *Sights.*—The sights are mounted on an upright bracket carried on the top of the carriage. Adjustment of the sights is obtained by two pairs of adjusting screws (one pair for vertical adjustment, the other for horizontal).

(5) *Gun crew.*—The German gun crew numbers six, with duties as follows:

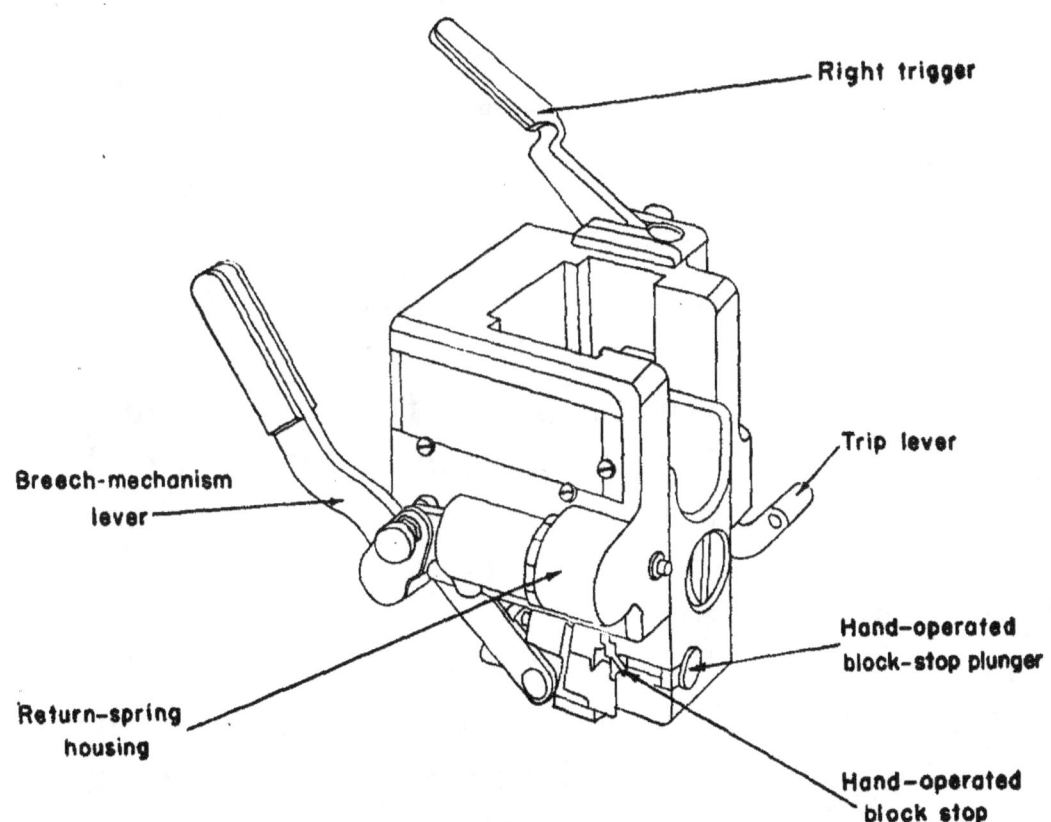

Figure 61.—Breech mechanism of 3.7-cm Pak (viewed from top, rear).

(a) The chief of section is responsible for seeing that all duties are properly performed, all commands executed, and all safety precautions observed.
(b) The gunner lays the piece.
(c) No. 1 loads and fires the piece.
(d) Nos. 2 and 3 handle the ammunition.
(e) No. 4 drives the prime mover.

d. Ammunition

The following three types of ammunition (carried in 12-round metal containers) are fired:

Type	Weight of complete round	Weight of projectile	Fuze	Marking
AP tracer shell	3 lbs 2 oz	1 lb 8 oz	Base (*Bd. Z.* (5103))	Black shell marked *3.7-cm Pak Pzgr.*
AP 40 shot [1]	2 lbs	12.5 oz	None	Black shell marked *3.7-cm Pak Pzgr. 40.*
HE tracer shell	2 lbs 10 oz	1 lb 6 oz	Delayed action (either *A. Z. 39 Rh S274* or *Rh S222*).	Gray shell marked *3.7-cm Spgr.*

[1] This projectile consists of a mild steel body, an aluminum-alloy windshield (ballistic) cap, and tungsten carbide armor-piercing core.

In addition to the ordinary types of ammunition listed above the Germans have developed a stick bomb for use with the *3.7-cm Pak* (see fig. 62). The stick bomb consists of a hollow-charge projectile attached to a perforated sleeve within which there is a rod. The rod fits into the muzzle end of the bore; the concentric perforated sleeve fits over the muzzle end of the barrel. The standard 3.7-cm shell case and primer are used with a propellant charge of 216 grams of nitrocellulose. There are two fuzes, one in the nose and another in the base.

ANTITANK GUNS AND INFANTRY HOWITZERS

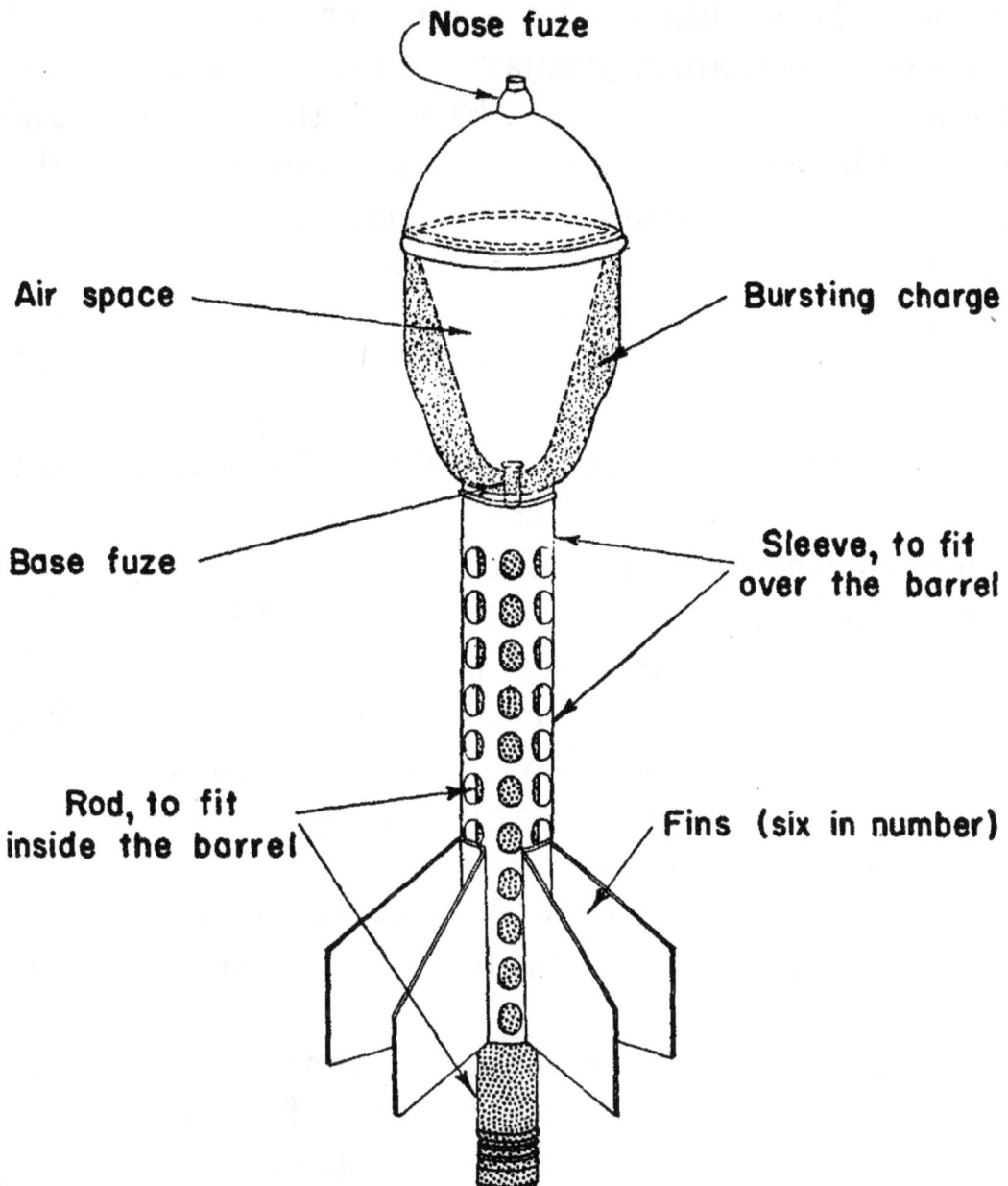

Figure 62.—Stick bomb for use with 3.7-cm Pak.

e. Maintenance

(1) *Stripping.*—(a) *To disassemble breech mechanism.*—Press the hand-operated block stop, and open the breech all the way by pulling the breech-mechanism lever to the right rear. Insert an artillery tool

between the shoulder of the plunger and the link of the breech-mechanism actuating shaft in order to take the weight off the spring. Remove the axis pin and the spring case by turning 40 degrees to the right. Release the extractors, slightly closing the block to remove the axis pin. Remove the extractors. Open the breech fully and remove the actuating spindle and the breech-mechanism lever. Remove the breech-block.

(b) *Recoil.*—The recoil cylinder is hydraulic, being filled from the center of the piston shaft at the rear by using a screw pump. The liquid is of the glycerine type. The cylinder contains 2 pints when full. To disconnect the gun from the recoil system, use a small flat bar to turn the connecting ring counterclockwise, about one-half turn. This presses back a safety plunger at the lower forward face of the breech ring and locks the firing mechanism.

If, during recoil, the recoil indicator on the right of the cradle reaches graduation 595, further firing is unsafe.

German handbooks recommend that no one shall stand within 35 feet directly in rear of the gun when it is being fired, as the piece may become separated from the cradle.

The recuperator is of the double-banked spring type.

(2) *Assembly of breech mechanism.*—Insert the hand-operated block-stop spring and retaining bush. Place the breechblock in the breech ring in the fully open position, insert the actuating shaft of the con-

necting arm into the breech ring, and connect the breech-mechanism lever. Insert the actuating spindle. Insert the extractors by slightly closing the breech to admit the extractor axis pin, and then close the breech. Next, insert the return spring and plunger, placing the flats of the plunger into a link of the breech-mechanism actuating spindle. Insert the axis pin as far as possible. Then release the hand-operated block stop and open the breech until it is held by the extractor claws, and press home the axis pin. Insert the firing pin and release the sear. Replace the main spring and cover plate, giving the cover plate a quarter turn, and release it.

f. Carriage

(1) *Axle.*—The axle incorporates an independent suspension, which is, however, locked when firing. The releasing and locking are controlled by the opening and closing of the trail legs.

(2) *Lower carriage.*—The lower carriage has a pivot housing and bearing face for the top carriage. It also houses the axle and carries the traversing rack, the traveling clamp, and the locking gear for the trail legs.

(3) *Traversing mechanism.*—The gunner is on the left side of the weapon and operates the traverse with his right hand by a small handwheel (clockwise to the right, counterclockwise to the left). (See fig. 63.) The traverse is 60 degrees (1,062 mils), and is completed by 30½ turns of the handwheel.

(4) *Elevating mechanism.*—The arc of 21 degrees (372 mils) elevation and 13 degrees (229 mils) depression is completed by 33½ turns of the handwheel, which the gunner operates with his left hand. (See fig. 63.)

(5) *Cradle.*—A locking device for use when traveling is mounted at the rear end and mates with the upper carriage when fully elevated. A leather buffer is fitted to the rear end and forms a stop for the gun on counterrecoil.

(6) *Shield.*—The shield is composed of the gun shield and the leg shield. The leg shield folds under

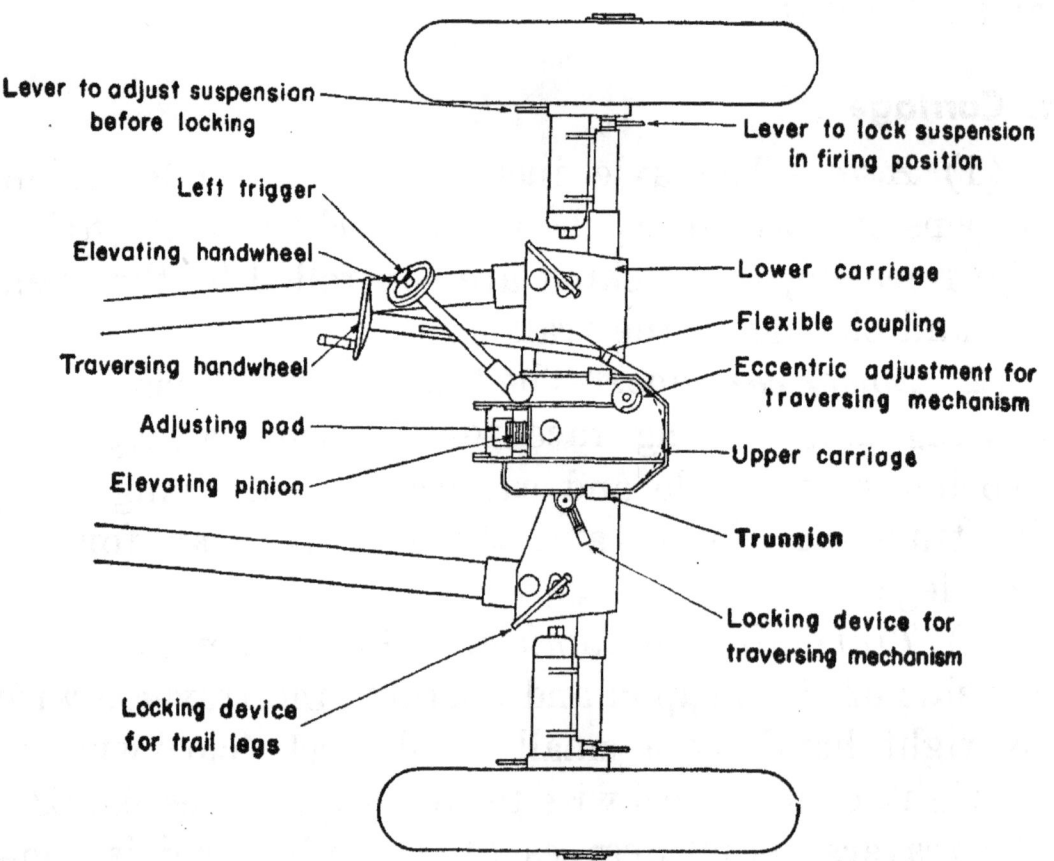

Figure 63.—Carriage of 3.7-cm Pak, showing traversing and elevating mechanisms.

the lower carriage when traveling, and folds down to the ground level when in action. The gun shield has a slope of approximately 45 degrees when in action, the upper half being hinged and folded forward as required.

17. 5–CM PAK [4] 38

a. General

This 50-mm (1.97-inch) antitank weapon [5] (figs. 64 and 65) was introduced in the spring of 1941 to replace the *3.7-cm Pak*. Mounted on a split-trail carriage and

Figure 64.—5-cm Pak 38.

normally towed by a half-track prime mover, it is one of the most effective German antitank guns at present in service and is part of the equipment of the German infantry regiment.[6]

The gun fires armor-piercing shell, high-explosive shell, and armor-piercing shot (AP 40).[7] The latter,

---

[4] *Panzerabwehrkanone* ("antitank gun"); see par. 16a, p. 113, note 2, above.

[5] The German tactical symbol for the *5-cm Pak* is ⍓ or ⍓.

[6] See fig. 1, p. xii, above.

[7] See paragraph 16d, p. 118, note 1.

a light shot with a "windshield" nose[8] and tungsten carbide core, has a good performance at ranges under 500 yards. The latest type of armor-piercing shell has a piercing cap.

b. Characteristics

(1) *General.*—The carriage is provided with a tubular split trail and an armor-plated double shield. The gun has a muzzle brake.

(2) *Table of characteristics.*—

Muzzle velocity:	
AP	2,700 feet per second.
AP 40	3,940 feet per second.
HE	1,800 feet per second.
Maximum range:	
AP	1,540 yards.
AP 40	770 yards.
HE	2,640 yards.
Effective range:	
AP	880 yards.
AP 40	500 yards.
HE	2,000 yards.
Practical rate of fire	10 to 15 rounds per minute.
Over-all length of gun (including breech ring and brake)	124.96 inches.
Depression	319 mils (18 degrees).
Elevation	478 mils (27 degrees).
Traverse	115 mils (65 degrees).
Weight (gun and mechanism)	675 pounds.
Weight of complete equipment (including extra wheel)	2,145 pounds.

---

[8] Ballistic cap.

Figure 65.—5-cm Pak 38 from rear.

c. How to Operate

(1) *Safety.*—There are three mechanical arrangements which operate as safety devices: (1) unles the breechblock is properly closed, the safety plunger will not enter its recess and the gun cannot be fired; (2) the safety plunger must be in its recess in the lower face of the breech ring before the firing shaft can be rotated; (3) the breech cannot be opened if the striker is not cocked, because the firing shaft is engaged with the safety plunger, which is in its recess.

(2) *To load and fire.*—To open the breech by hand, recock the firing mechanism by turning the safe-and-fire lever to *sicher* ("safe") (fig. 66) and pushing it for-

ward again; then turn the breech-mechanism lever in a clockwise direction. The breech will then be held in the open position by the extractors.

To load the gun, insert a round smartly. The round will then release the extractors, and the breech will close automatically.

To fire the gun, press the push button in the middle of the elevating handwheel (fig. 67). If this fails, pull the firing lever backward or lift the plunger.

A semi-automatic action operates when the plunger in the center of the front end of the spring case is

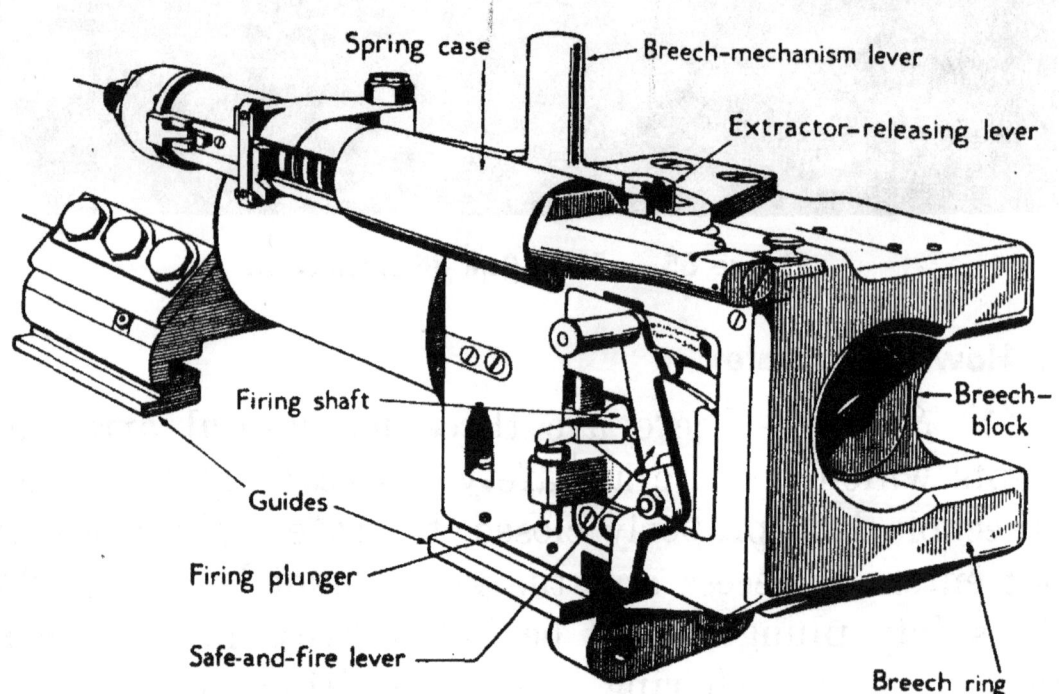

Figure 66.—Breech of 5-cm Pak.

(The spring assembly for the breech-mechanism lever consists of the spring case, which is in two parts (the front with the piston retaining cap and the rear with the piston, piston catch, and pawl), the rack-spindle retaining catch, the rack spindle, the semi-automatic and hand plunger, and the inner and outer springs. When set for hand operation, the piston catch is rotated inwards and the carriage lever does not engage it. The piston head then has the word *EIN* ("in") showing upwards.)

pressed in and turned so that the word *ein* ("in") shows upward. When the plunger is set in this position, the breech is opened automatically during the counterrecoil. The gun is always recocked automattically during recoil. The breech is ready to close automatically when a round is slammed in.

Figure 67.—Gunner's position on 5-cm Pak, showing traversing and elevating handwheels.

(3) *To open trails.*—Push to the right the cradle clamp which fixes the gun in the fully elevated position. The trails being fully open, the weight of the gun is taken off the road springs, and a catch on each side locks the trails in the open position.

(4) *Sights.*—The sighting gear is operated from the left side and is fitted to the left saddle trunnion. The sight bracket carries an open or telescopic sight, and is provided with a lateral-deflection gear, a range drum, and means of adjustment for line and elevation. Magnification of the telescopic sight is threefold. A battery for lighting the graticules for night shooting is fitted.

The range drum is graduated in black for AP (*Pz.*) and in red for HE (*Spr.*). The figures 5–8–10–12–14 on the AP scale correspond to ranges of 500, 800, 1,000, 1,200, and 1,400 meters. Ranges of 300, 700, and 1,100 meters are set on intermediate graduations, which, however, have no figures against them.

The scale for HE is marked 4–6–8–10, etc., up to 24. These figures correspond to ranges of 400, 600, 800, 1,000 meters, etc. Ranges in between are set on the intermediate graduations.

A small lever with a worm screw operates the lateral deflection gear. When a tank approaches directly from in front, the lever should be pointed towards the gunner. If the tank is moving across the line of sight, the lever should be turned two notches in the direction of travel (for example, the lever should be turned to the left for engaging a tank moving from right to left). The lever should be moved only one notch for an oblique target. Lateral deflections may be set in this way for targets traveling at less than 12 miles per hour.

For targets traveling at more than 12 miles per hour the graticules on the sight should be used. The central mark should be employed for tanks approaching from the front, and the left and right laying-off marks for targets moving to the right and left, respectively.

The Germans use the following table as a guide to avoid frequent alteration of the sight during action:

Range (yards)	Range-drum setting	Part of tank laid on
1,100 to 880	8 *Pz*	Between top and center of tank.
880 to 550	8 *Pz*	Between center and bottom of tank.
Less than 550	8 *Pz*	Center of tank.

For example, to engage a tank 770 yards away and traveling obliquely to the left at 18 miles per hour, the layer sets the range drum to 8 *Pz.*, moves the lever one notch to the left, and lays the right laying-off mark on the center of the target.

If the telescope is missing, an emergency open sight, held by a lanyard on the right of the sight bracket, can be fitted.

(5) *Gun crew.*—The Germans have a gun crew of eight, whose duties in firing are as follows:

(a) The chief of section is responsible for seeing that all duties are properly performed, all commands executed, and all safety precautions observed.

(b) The gunner sets the announced deflection, and lays for direction.

(c) No. 1 loads and fires the piece.

(d) Nos. 2, 3, 4, and 5 handle the ammunition.

(e) No. 6 drives the prime mover.

d. Ammunition

The following three types are fired:

Type	Weight of complete round	Length of complete round	Weight of projectile	Fuze	Identification
AP tracer shell	9 lbs 3 oz	21.4 in	4 lbs 9 oz	Base	Black, shell case marked *5-cm Pak 38 Pzgr.*
HE shell	7 lbs 3 oz	23.7 in	3 lbs 15 oz	Nose (A.Z. 39)	Dark green, shell case marked *5-cm Pak 38 Spgr.*
AP 40 shot [1]	6 lbs 11 oz	19.5 in	2.025 lbs	None	Black, shell case marked *5-cm Pak 38 Pzgr. 40.*

[1] See paragraph 16 **d**, p. 118, note 1, above.

e. Maintenance

(1) *Stripping.*—(a) *To disassemble the breech mechanism.*—Remove the securing pin from the spring case of the breech-mechanism lever (fig. 66), swing the case to the left and front, and remove the castellated nut and case complete.

Remove the extractor releasing lever, pulling it upwards. Rotate the breech-mechanism lever to the right and rear, thus moving the breechblock and extractors. Remove the extractors (fig. 68) from the left. Close the breech, and set the safe and fire lever to "fire". Press the striker cap in and remove with the spring and striker, which must be uncocked. Open the breech slightly until the key on the actuating shaft is in line with the keyway on the breechblock. Remove the breech-mechanism lever dust cap, pinion, and actuating shaft.

Withdraw the breechblock (fig. 69) and crank. Remove the retaining pin from the firing and recocking

ANTITANK GUNS AND INFANTRY HOWITZERS

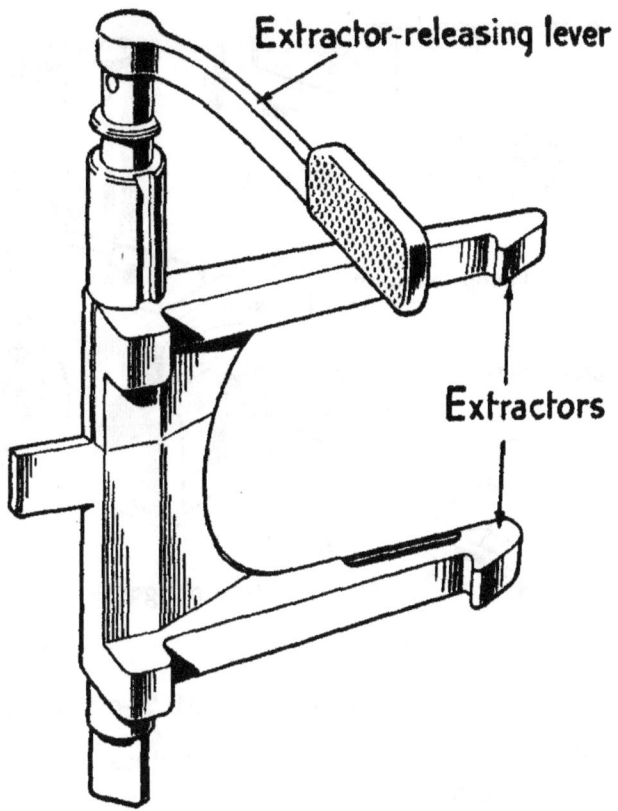

Figure 68.—Extractors of 5-cm Pak.

shafts. Remove the firing and recocking shafts with the safety plunger.

(b) *Recoil cylinder.*—The recoil cylinder is mounted in the cradle. The piston rod, which is connected to the gun lug, is hollow and fitted with a bronze piston head. Ports are drilled in the conical part of the piston; a tapered rod is screwed into the front plug of the cylinder and projects into the hollow piston rod.

Counterrecoil control is effected by a brass control plunger screwed to the end of the tapered rod. Toward the end of the run-out, this plunger enters a bore of smaller diameter in the piston rod. Tapered

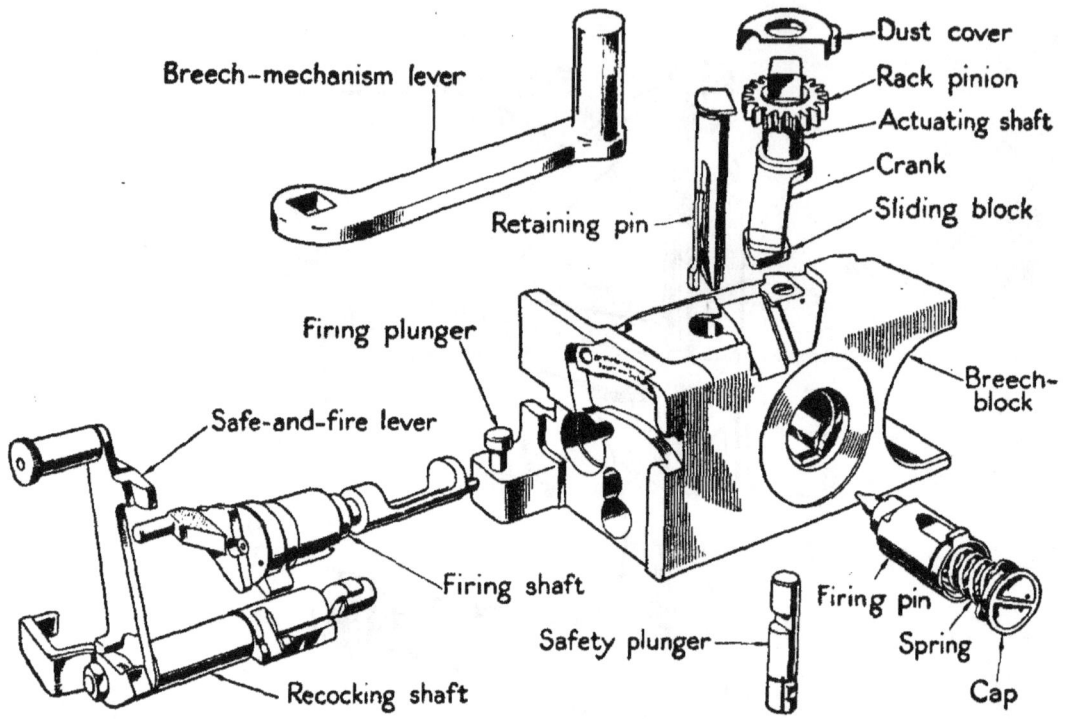

Figure 69.—Breechblock of 5-cm Pak.

(The breechblock is of the horizontal sliding-block type arranged for semi-automatic working. The firing shaft is in two parts. The front has a toe piece engaging the safety plunger, which, when the breech is properly closed, is clear of the toe piece, allowing the plunger to drop into a recess in the breech ring. The rear has a projection which engages the firing plunger. When the breech is closed, the firing shaft holds the firing pin in the cocked position. The recocking shaft has a safe-and-fire lever incorporated which can be operated independently. A recocking lever on the left engages a cam on the cradle during recoil; the right end of the shaft engages the firing pin and, rotating during recoil, it forces the firing pin to the rear. When the safe-and-fire lever is set to *sicher* ("safe"), the recocking shaft is moved so that a projection on it retains the firing pin in the cocked position, preventing it from moving forwards. At *Feuer* ("fire"), the projection is cleared, and allows the front shoulder on the firing pin to engage the firing shaft, ready to fire. The actuating shaft receives the breech mechanism lever at the top, and the crank below. The rack pinion is mounted centrally on it. The crank is fitted with a sliding block which engages a radial groove in the breechblock. The rack pinion engages the rack in the spring case when operated by hand or semi-automatically. The firing pin has a shoulder at the front and a lug at the rear to engage the firing and actuating shafts, and is held in position by a spring. The firing plunger, in the lug on the front lower end of the breech ring, engages the firing shaft when firing.

grooves, which are cut in the plunger, graduate the control.

The piston-rod stuffing box is packed with soft packings. Normal recoil is 700 mm (27.56 inches); metal to metal, 730 mm (28.74 inches). The recoil cylinder should, according to German instructions, be filled until the oil gauge on the near edge protrudes 44 mm (1¾ inches).

The safety plunger in the breechblock has a cutaway portion to engage the firing shaft. When the breech is properly closed, the plunger can enter its recess in the bottom of the breech ring.

To open the breech (by hand): First, set the semi-automatic plunger to *AUS* ("out"). The firing pin has been recocked during recoil. When the breech-mechanism lever is pulled to the right rear, the crank is actuated, forcing the sliding block to the left and thereby opening the breech. The extractors eject the cartridge case and retain the breechblock in the fully open position.

To close the breech (by hand): Release the extractors by loading a cartridge or actuating the extractor releasing lever. The breech should close automatically.

To open the breech (semi-automatic): Set the spring-plunger to semi-automatic. The word *EIN* ("in") will then show upwards. On recoil a stop fitted to the cradle overrides the piston catch. On run-out, the stop and front face of the piston catch engage, forcing the piston to the rear and compressing the inner and outer springs, until the piston catch is forced inward and the outer spring reasserts itself. The piston with the rack spindle then moves forward under the action of the outer spring, the rack engages the breech-mechanism lever pinion, revolves it, and rotates the breech-mechanism lever to the right rear, so opening the breech.

To close the breech (semi-automatic): Release the extractors by loading a cartridge. The inner spring then asserts itself, allowing the rack spindle to move forward and rotate the pinion and breech-mechanism lever to the closed position.

To fire: The firing plunger is forced upward by a lever on the carriage, which engages the firing lever and rotates it. The firing pin is held cocked by the firing shaft, and is released when the cutaway portion on it is opposite the front shoulder on the firing pin, thus firing the round. The recocking process follows on recoil.)

(c) *Recuperator.*—The recuperator is hydropneumatic. The hydropneumatic and recuperator cylinders are situated one above the other in the cradle. The recuperator piston rod is fixed to the gun lug.

(2) *Assembly.*—Assemble the breech-mechanism spring case to the breech ring (fig. 70). Insert the safety plunger in the breechblock. Insert the firing and recocking shafts, securing them by the retaining pin. Fit the crank to the breechblock and place the breechblock in the breech ring.

Assemble the pinion on the actuating shaft with the dust cap and breech-mechanism lever. Fit them to the breechblock, with the pinion engaging the assembling line on the rack, and the key on the actuating shaft in line with the keyway on the breechblock. Place the striker, spring, and cap in the breechblock.

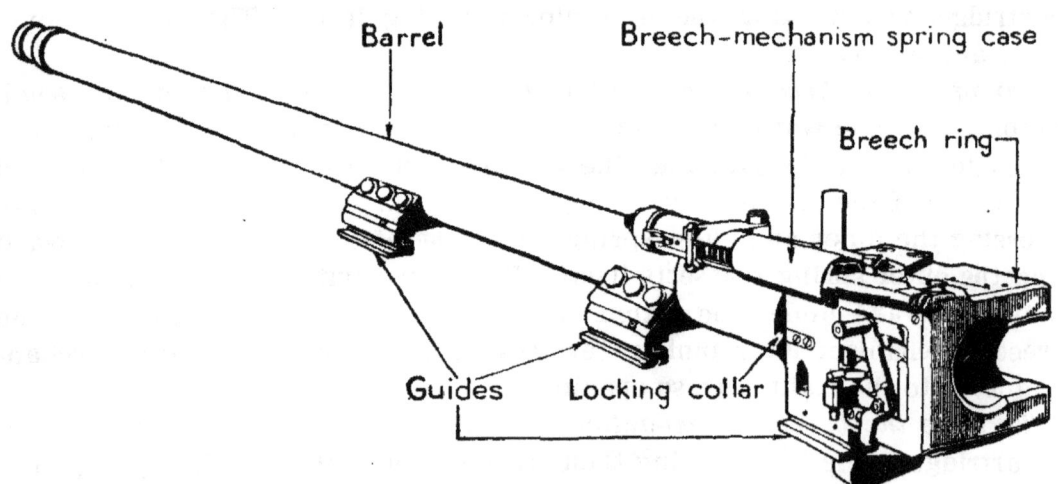

Figure 70.—Barrel and breech of 5-cm Pak.

(The barrel is of monobloc, loose barrel construction and is fitted with a muzzle brake. The breech ring is rectangular and is secured to the barrel by a locking collar. A clinometer plane is provided. The recuperator system is attached underneath the breech ring by a detachable lug. The extractors are fitted to, and kept in position by, an extractor releasing lever which passes through the breech ring.)

Assemble the extractors to the breechblock, and push the block to the closed position until the extractor releasing lever can be inserted.

f. Carriage

The carriage is of the split-trail type carried on two disk wheels, with a third detachable wheel to increase the speed of bringing the gun into action. The carriage consists mainly of the following:

(1) *Trail.*—The trail has split tubular legs. The right leg has a cradle clamp near the front and a traversing stop. The left leg is fitted with a stop for the cradle clamp and a lunette and locking bolt, so that the legs can be locked together for traveling. Each leg has a spade, lifting handle, and traversing handle.

(2) *Axle.*—The axle houses a pintle to which a traversing rack is fixed. The ends are cranked forward to take the wheels.

(3) *Saddle.*—The saddle supports the cradle and gun, and is pivoted to the axle. The sighting gear and layer's guard are mounted on the left trunnion and a hydropneumatic compensating cylinder is fitted to the right. The function of the cylinder, filled with air under pressure and a small quantity of liquid, is to balance the cradle and piece, which are muzzle-heavy.

(4) *Cradle.*—The cradle houses the recoil cylinder and recuperator. The semi-automatic cam arms which engage the recoil cylinder stop on the breech-mechanism lever are bolted to the left side.

(5) *Elevating gear.*—The elevating gear gives 27 degrees (478 mils) elevation and 18 degrees (319 mils) depression. It is operated by a handwheel on the left side of the carriage.

(6) *Traversing gear.*—The traversing gear is operated from the left side of the carriage and allows about 32½ degrees (565 mils) traverse left and right (a total of 65 degrees (1,151 mils)).

(7) *Sighting gear.*—The sighting gear is operated from the left side and is fitted to the left saddle trunnion.

(8) *Cradle firing gear.*—The cradle firing gear is operated from the elevating handwheel. A push knob, to which is attached a cable, actuates the firing mechanism.

(9) *Shield.*—The shield consists of two 4-mm sheets of armor plate spaced about 1 inch apart. The left side of the shield has a sight port.

18. 7.5-CM LIGHT INFANTRY HOWITZER [9]

a. General

The Germans introduced the *7.5-cm l.I.G. 18* [10] in 1933–34 as an infantry close-support weapon (figs. 71, 75, and 78). It is found in the cannon company of the infantry regiment.[11] There are two versions: one on steel-type artillery wheels and the other on pneu-

---

[9] *Leichtes Infanteriegeschütz 18.* The German tactical symbol for the light infantry howitzer is ⊥ or ⊥⊥⊥.

[10] *Leichtes Infanteriegeschütz* is translated literally as "light infantry weapon." Sometimes *Geschütz* is translated as "gun." But this weapon in U. S. terminology is termed a howitzer.

[11] See fig. 1. p. xii. above.

ANTITANK GUNS AND INFANTRY HOWITZERS

matic tires. The steel-wheeled carriage is also used by airborne troops, and is often referred to as the 7.5-cm mountain-infantry howitzer.[12]

b. Characteristics

(1) *General.*—The howitzer is drawn by six horses or by a motor vehicle. This weapon can be split into six loads (a maximum of 165 pounds each) for pack transport.

(2) *Table of characteristics.*—

Muzzle velocity (maximum)	730 feet per second.
Maximum range	3,870 yards.
Theoretical rate of fire	15 to 20 rounds per minute.
Length of barrel	10 calibers (10 x 7.5 cm).
Depression	177 mils (10 degrees).
Elevation	1,292 mils (73 degrees).
Traverse	212 mils (12 degrees).
Weight in action	880 pounds.

c. How to Operate

(1) *Safety.*—The gun cannot be fired until the barrel is properly closed. A projection on the firing lever must enter a recess in the breech-mechanism lever when fully closed (figs. 72 and 73).

The breech-mechanism lever and firing lever cannot be moved when the arrow on the safe and fire lever is at *sicher* ("safe") because (a) the toe on the breech-mechanism lever engages the safe-and-fire lever and prevents any movement, and (b) the toe on the safe-and-fire lever engages a cutaway portion in the firing lever and prevents any movement (fig. 74).

---

[12] The German tactical symbol for the mountain-infantry howitzer is

(2) *To load and fire.*—To open the breech, set the arrow on the safe-and-fire lever to *Feuer* ("fire"). Then disengage the retaining catch by gripping the breech-mechanism lever handle, and pull the breech-mechanism lever to the rear. This movement causes the actuating link to be revolved in the slipper block.

Figure 71.—7.5-cm infantry howitzer in action.

The inner stud of the actuating link, being displaced from the bearing center of the link, is given a circular motion, causing the slide to be raised and drawn slightly to the rear. The slide, dovetailed to the breech ring, causes the barrel to be revolved about its trunnions and the breech end to be raised to the open position.

When the round is inserted, the extractor is carried forward, the breech-mechanism lever is rotated, and the actuating link causes the slide to move down and forward in its groove, thus lowering the breech to the closed position.

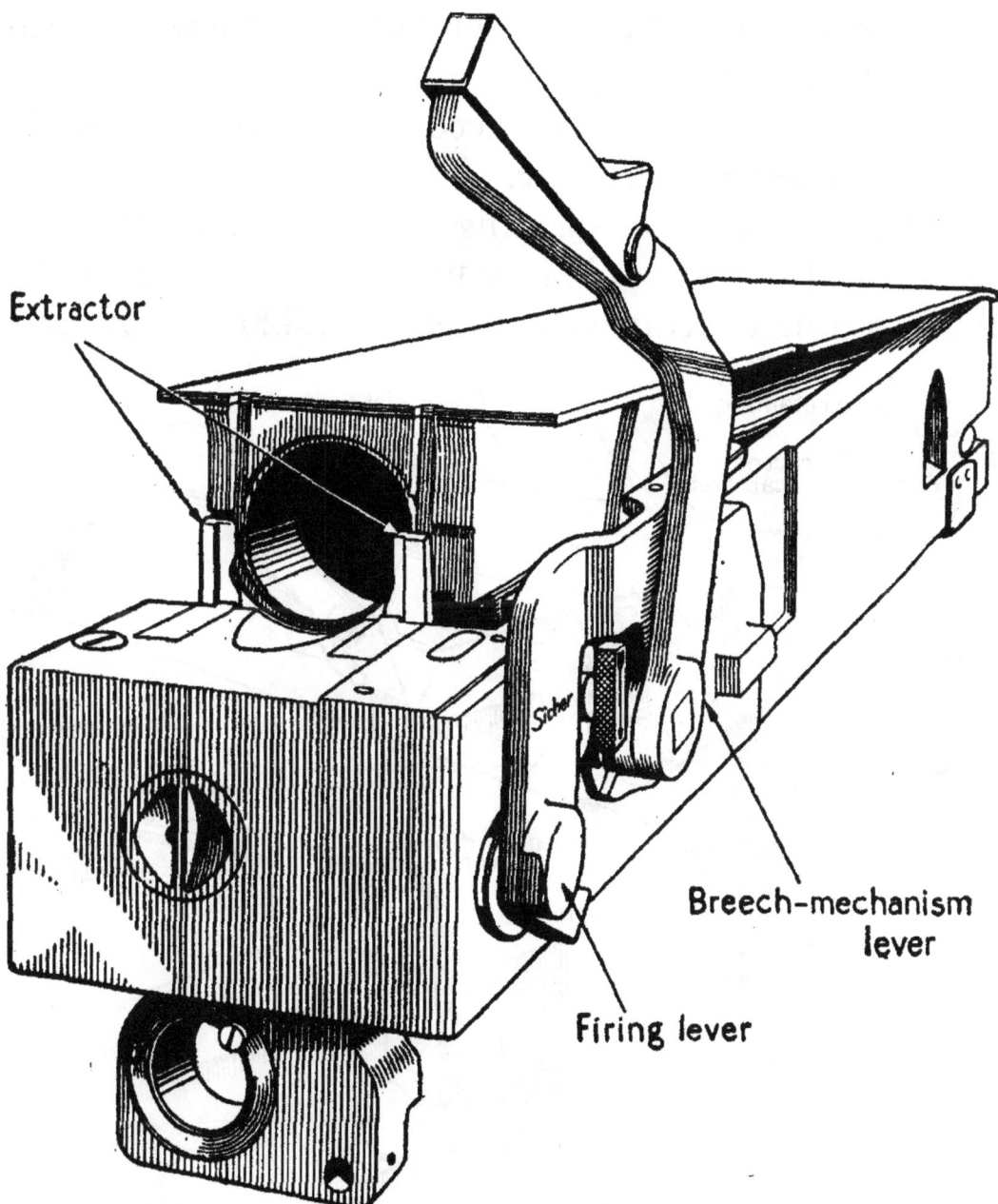

Figure 72.—Breech of 7.5-cm infantry howitzer.

To fire, pull the firing lever to the rear. On rotating the firing lever to the rear, the torsion spring is put under tension. The spring-loaded lug on the shaft engages the firing pin, forcing it to the rear against its spring and cocking it. When the lug on the shaft trips the lug on the firing pin, the latter is allowed to move forward and fire the gun.

The firing pin can be recocked and fired by pulling the firing lever to the rear.

(3) *Sights.*—The sighting mechanism works on the reciprocating principle (see figs. 76 and 77). It is fitted with a range drum graduated to 1,320 meters and a

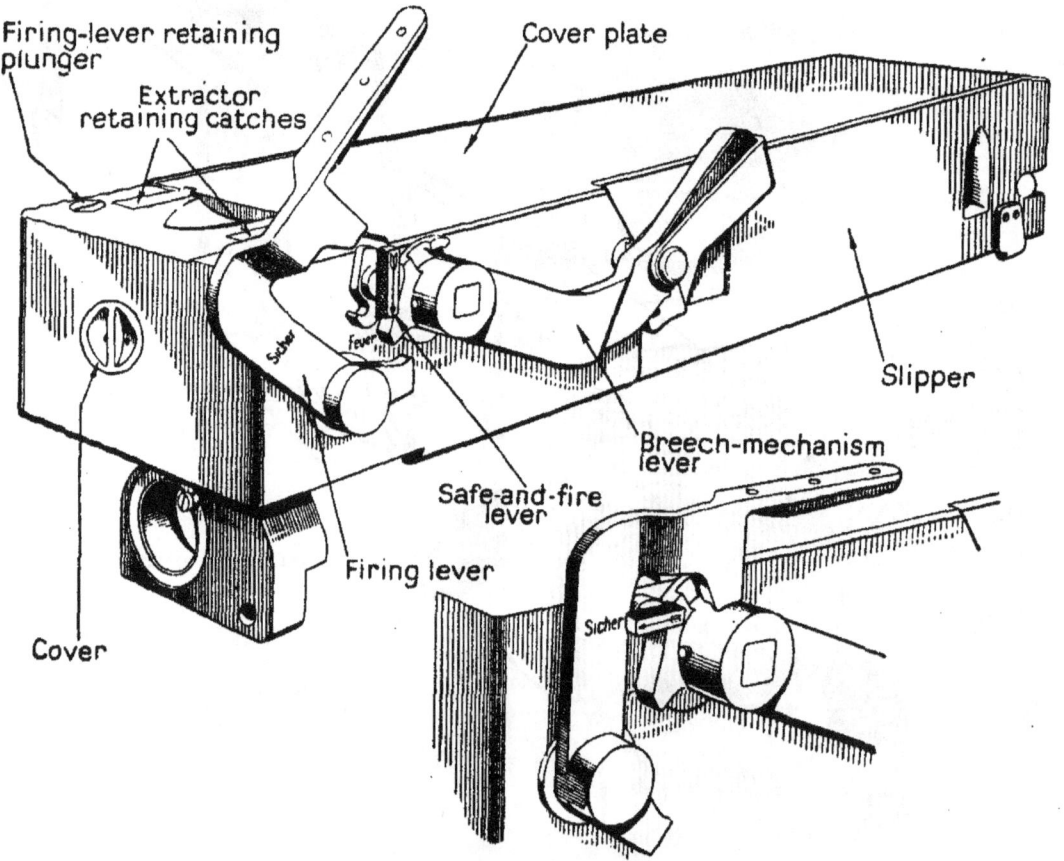

Figure 73.—Breechblock and firing mechanism of 7.5-cm infantry howitzer.

ANTITANK GUNS AND INFANTRY HOWITZERS 141

correction scale for the five charges used. A rocking platform for the sight is operated by a worm spindle and deflection nut. A clicker arrangement is also incorporated.

The dial sight is the *Rundblickfernrohr 16* (*Rbl. F. 16*) (fig. 79).[13] The *Rbl.F. 16* has a magnification of

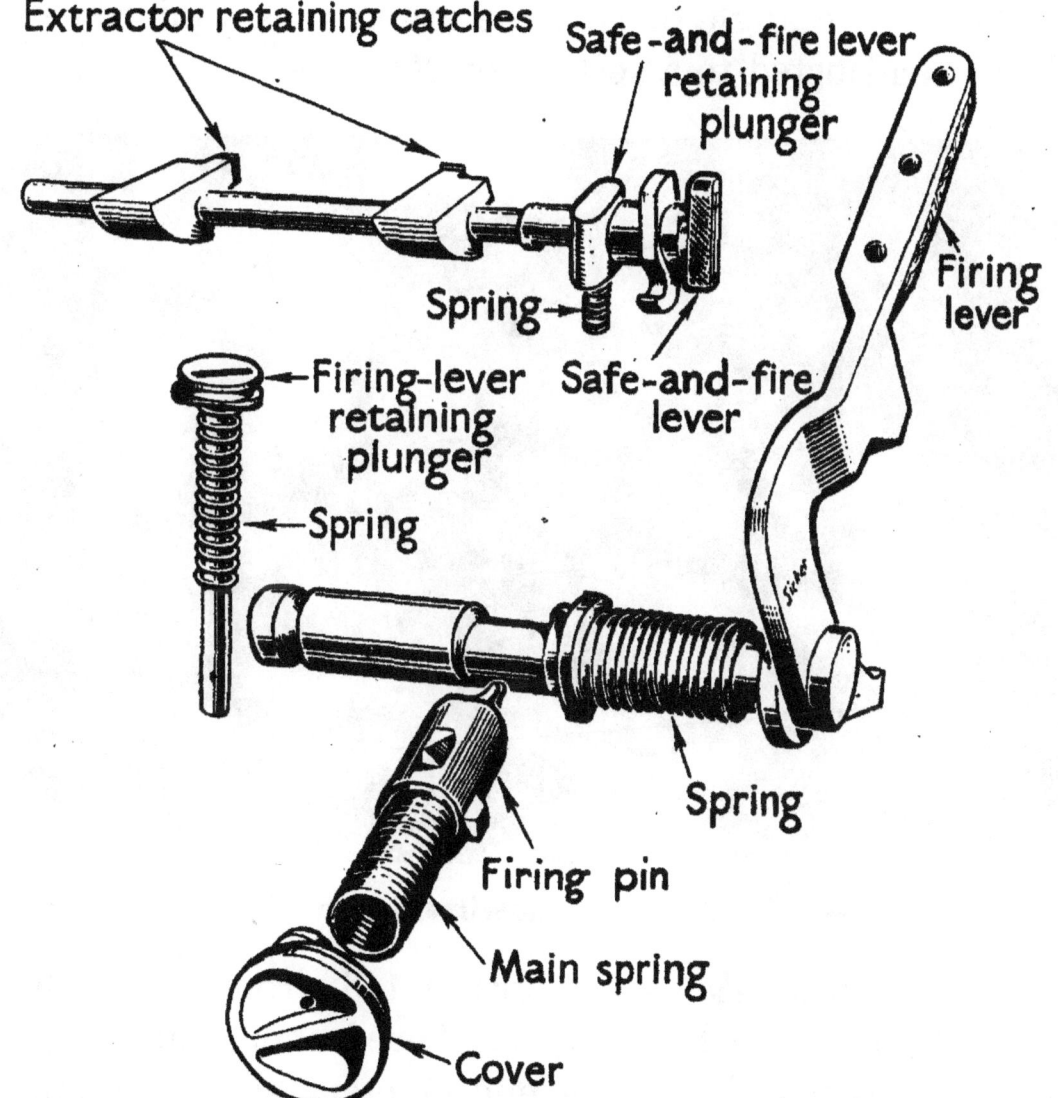

Figure 74.—Firing mechanism parts of 7.5-cm infantry howitzer.

---

[13] A more modern sight, the *Rundblickfernrohr 32* (*Rbl.F. 32*), is used on the newest equipment.

four and a 10-degree (177-mil) field of view. The graticule shows an inverted V and a broken verticle line. There is no means of focusing the eyepiece, and the gunner must keep his eye about three-fourths of an inch away. There is provision for illuminating the graticule at night.

For a zero angle of site, the upper prism micrometer head is adjusted to a setting of 300 mils.

Figure 75.—7.5-cm infantry howitzer in traveling position.

The azimuth scales are graduated from 0 to 6,400 mils, the main scale being numbered every hundredth mil from 0 to 64 and the micrometer scale every mil from 0 to 100.

d. Ammunition

Separate ammunition is used; the cartridge cases are either *6341* (brass) or *6341 St* (steel). Ammunition is carried in baskets holding three rounds, or in a

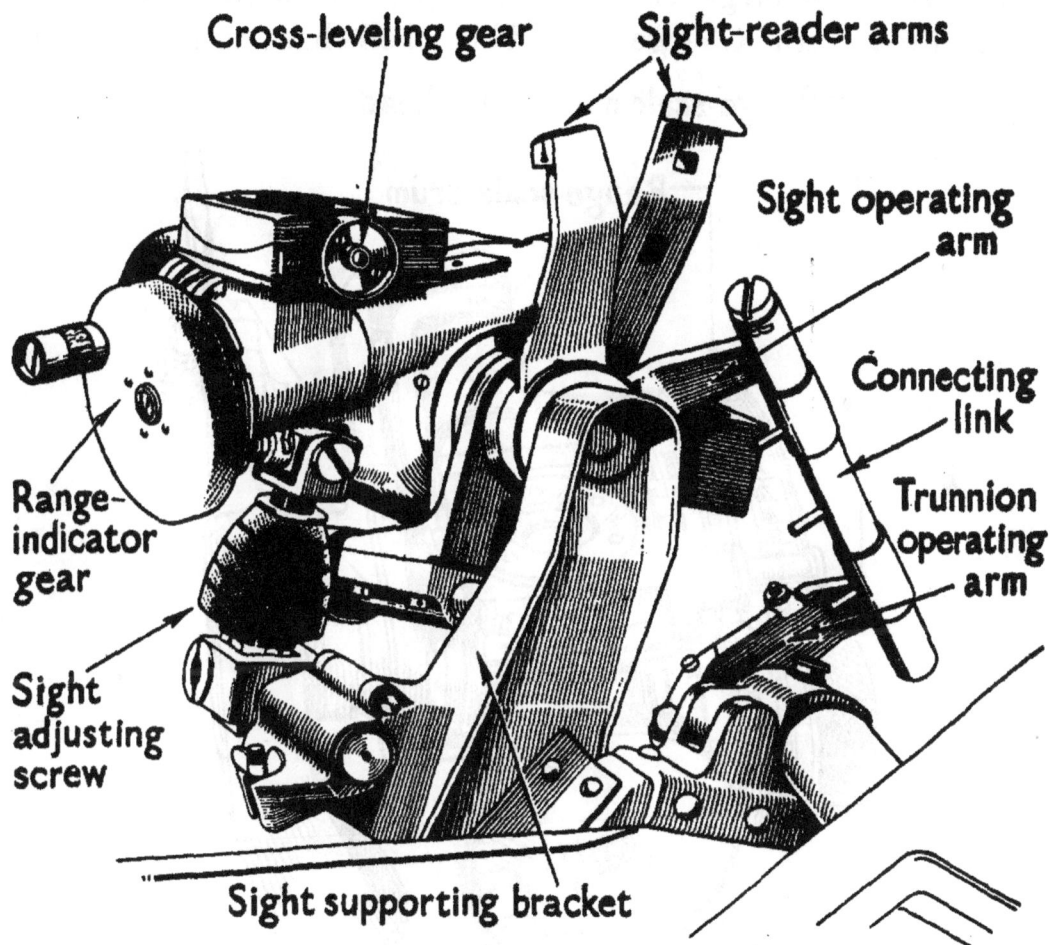

Figure 76.—Sighting mechanism (side view) of 7.5-cm infantry howitzer.

more recent type of metal container also holding three rounds. The following types of shell are used:

(1) HE shell *7.5-cm Igr. 18*, with fuze *Az. 23 n.A.* The weight is 12 pounds 2 ounces. The fuze can be set to instantaneous (*o.V.*), or to a .15-second delay (*m.V.*). This shell is not provided for the *7.5-cm l.Geb.I.G. 18*.

(2) HE shell *7.5-cm Igr. 18Al.*, with fuze *Az. 23 n.A.* The weight is 12 pounds 2 ounces. When fired by *l.Geb.I.G. 18*, a time and percussion fuze, the *Dopp. Z. (S/60) Geb.*, can also be used. The letters *Al* are understood to indicate inclusion of a granular, aluminium flash composition in the filling.

(3) Hollow-charge shell *7.5-cm Igr. 38*, with fuze *Az. 38.* It is fired with Charge V. This shell has been introduced

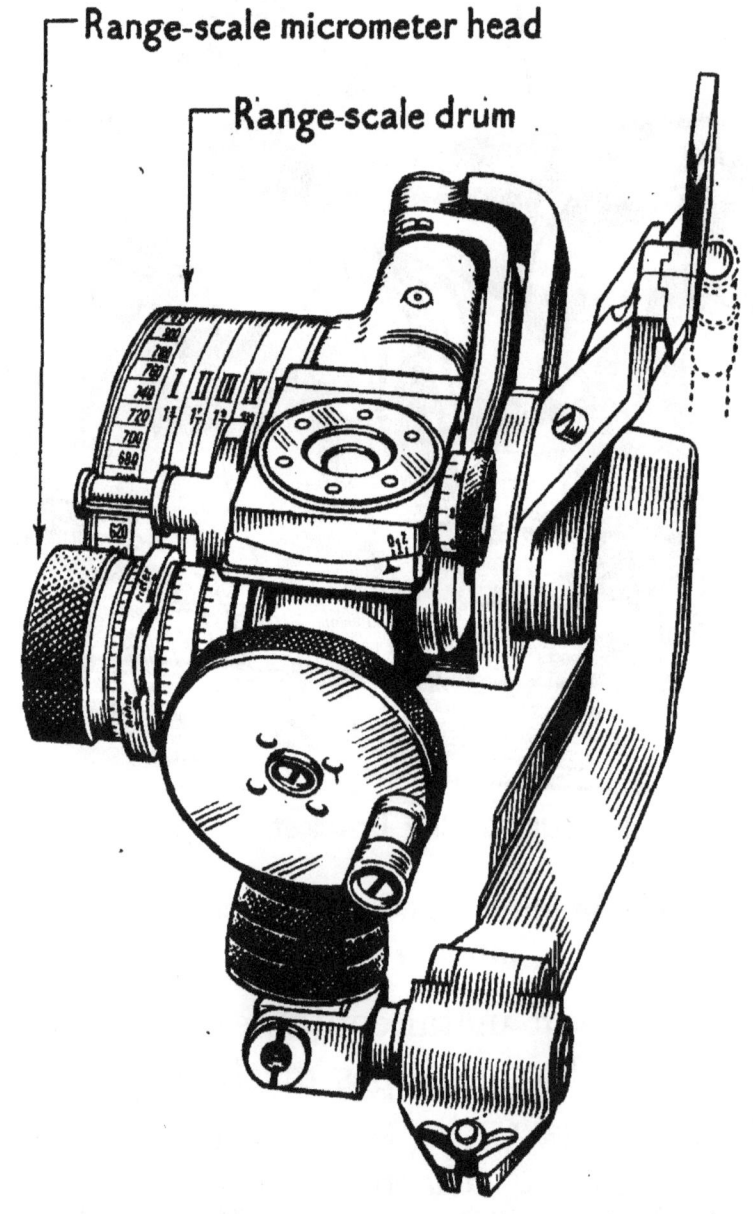

Figure 77.—Sighting mechanism of 7.5-cm infantry howitzer, showing range-scale drum.

primarily for antitank purposes, but in emergency it can also be used against personnel. Penetration is approximately 55 mm at normal, 45 mm at 30°. There are also two practice shells: *7.5-cm Igr. (Üb.)* and *7.5-cm Igr. (Üb. Al.)*.

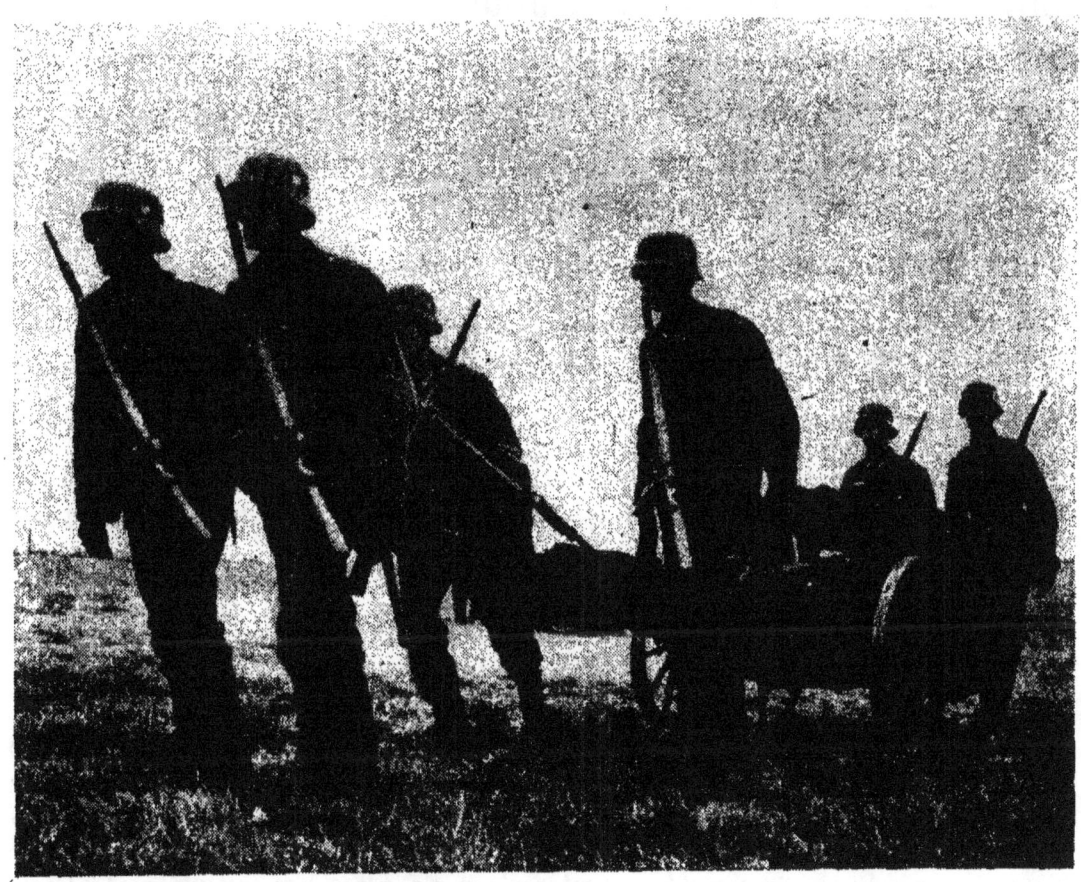

Figure 78.—Manhandling 7.5-cm infantry howitzer.

e. Maintenance

(1) *Stripping.*—(a) *To dismantle breech mechanism.*—Turn the safe-and-fire lever to *Feuer* ("fire"). Remove the firing-pin cover by pushing in and rotating through 90 degrees in a counterclockwise direction. Take out the spring and firing pin. Release the firing-lever retaining plunger by depressing and rotating the lever, and remove the firing lever with the trsion

spring and collar. Depress the retaining plunger of the safe-and-fire lever and remove the latter. Hold the breech open and remove the extractor, together with the extractor retaining catches. After taking out the taper pin, rotate the breech-mechanism lever to the fully open position and remove. Operate the actuating shaft until it disengages the actuating slide, which can then be removed. If necessary, the barrel can now be lifted out.

(b) *Recoil and recuperator system.*—The recoil system is carried in the cradle, the recoil cylinder on the left and the hydropneumatic recuperator on the right. The hydropneumatic cylinder is placed above the liquid cylinder. A communicating channel connects the cylinders and a valve is fitted to regulate the flow. The liquid cylinder has a piston and packing, and the rear end of the piston rod is secured to the breechblock lug. A spring-loaded valve is fitted to the front of the hydropneumatic cylinder. The recoil cylinder, with piston control rod with sliding valve, is closed by a stuffing box and gland at the front. The rear end has a nut to secure the cylinder to the breechblock lug.

(2) *Assembly.*—Assemble the breech mechanism by first placing the actuating slide in its groove in the barrel; then insert the actuating link in the slipper and engage it with the slide. Replace the breech-mechanism lever and taper pin. Open the barrel until the extractor and the extractor retaining catches can be placed in position. Insert the safe-and-fire plunger, and spring; pass the safe-and-fire shaft in from the

right side, when it will engage and retain the extractor retaining catches. Replace the firing shaft with the two feathers engaging the feather ways in the recess, the smaller feather uppermost. Place a slight tension on the spring and push the shaft home. Insert the retaining plunger and spring of the cocking-and-firing shaft. Finally, replace the firing pin, spring, and cover.

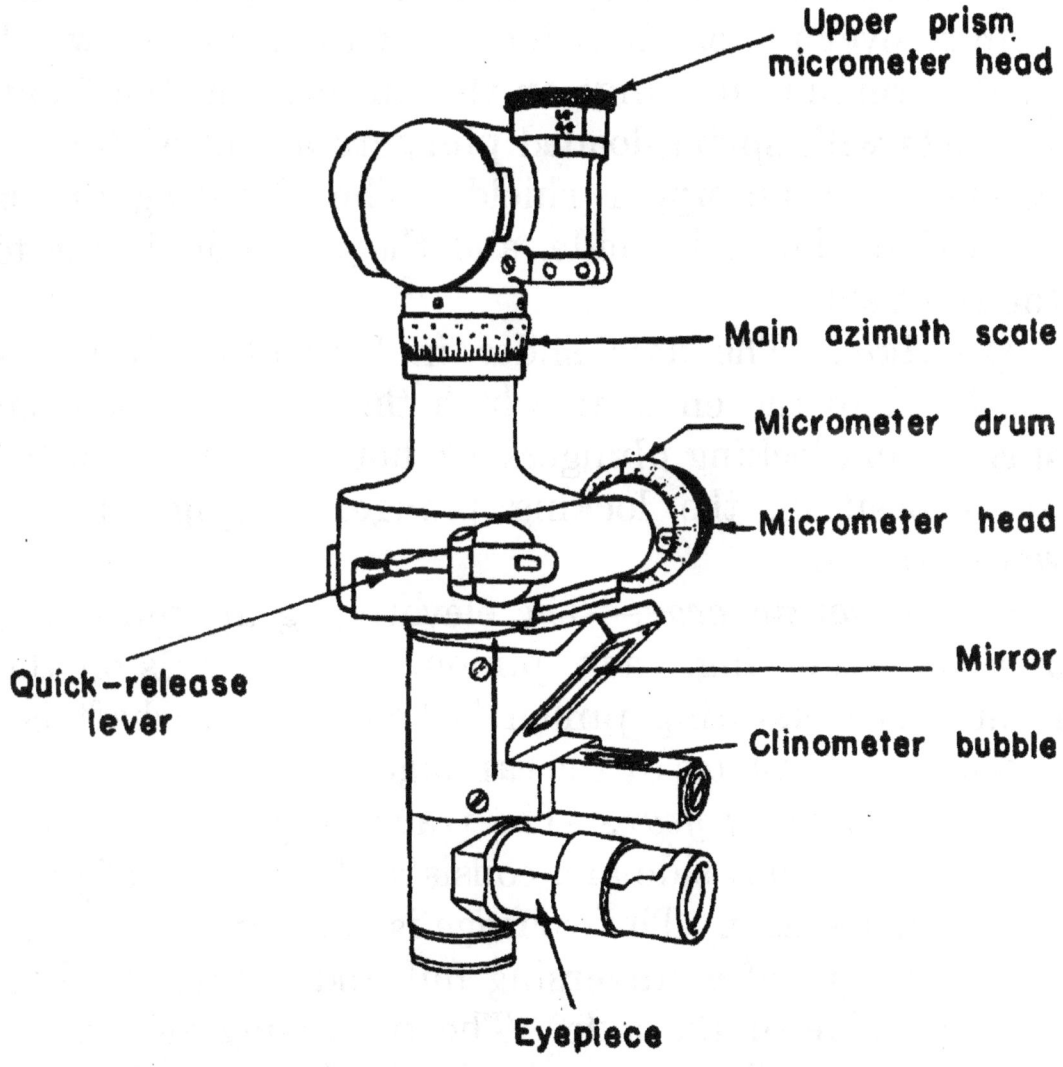

Figure 79.—Panoramic sight (*Rundblickfernrohr 16, Rbl.F. 16*) used on 7.5-cm infantry howitzer.

f. Carriage

The carriage is of the box type, supported on pneumatic tires. It consists of two side pieces supported by transoms at the front. Toward the front, it is prepared with bearings to receive the trunnions on the cradle. The rear end is fitted with a spade, a lunette, and lifting handles. Two boxes for spares are fitted, one in the center and the other at the rear.

(1) *Cradle.*—The cradle is trough-shaped and fitted with a cover plate. It is formed with trunnions which fit the trunnion bearings on the carriage; at the front, brackets with spring-loaded plungers are fitted for the reception of an upper shield. The elevating arc is secured to the under side, and the recoil indicator to the right side.

(2) *Axle.*—The axle slides in bearings. Brackets are fitted to the ends, in which the wheel suspension springs and locking plungers are housed. When in the firing position, the locking plungers engage in the wheel cranks.

(3) *Elevating gear.*—The elevating gear, consisting of a worm gearing, rack, pinion, and shaft, is on the right. The elevating pinion is housed on a shaft between the side plates of the carriage.

(4) *Traversing gear.*—The traversing gear is operated from the left side and consists of a system of gear wheels and shafts. The carriage is traversed along the axle by means of a traversing nut and screw, fitted to the right side of the axle. The traversing clamp, securing the cradle to the carriage when traveling, is fitted to the left side of the carriage.

ANTITANK GUNS AND INFANTRY HOWITZERS   149

(5) *Sight bracket.*—The sight bracket is fitted to the left side of the carriage. The lower end of its connecting rod is secured to the left cradle trunnion, and the upper end to the sight reader.

19. 15–CM HEAVY INFANTRY HOWITZER

a. General

The *15-cm s.I.G. 33* [14] is a standard German infantry support weapon found in the cannon company of the infantry regiment (see figs. 80 and 81).[15] It fires a

Figure 80.—15-cm infantry howitzer in action.

---

[14] *Schweres Infanteriegeschütz 33* (see p. 136, note 10, above). The German tactical symbol for the heavy infantry howitzer is ⊥⊥⊥ or ⊥.

[15] See fig. 1, p. xii, above.

high-explosive shell with a percussion fuze, or a smoke shell, and is used for either high- or low-trajectory shooting. The gun may be horse- or motor-drawn or self-propelled (see fig. 82).

Figure 81.—15-cm infantry howitzer (rear view).

ANTITANK GUNS AND INFANTRY HOWITZERS

b. Table of Characteristics

Caliber	149.1 mm.[16]
Length of piece	64.57 inches.[17]
Maximum elevation	1,300 mils.[18]
Maximum depression	0 mils.
Traverse	200 mils.[19]
Diameter of wheels	43.3 inches.
Muzzle velocity	790 feet per second.
Maximum range	6,000 yards.
Weight	1.5 tons.

c. How to Operate

(1) *Safety.*—The safe-and-fire shaft passes from the right face of the breechblock to the firing-pin way. Its right end is formed into a grip, marked with an arrow which may be set to *sicher* ("safe") or *Feuer* ("fire"), so marked on the breechblock. At the other end it is reduced to a semicircular section; it is so placed that the flat surface either engages a surface of the firing pin, or, if the shaft is turned through 90 degrees, is cleared by it.

The breechblock locking plunger passes from the rear face of the breechblock to the safe-and-fire shaft (see figs. 83, 84, and 85). It is held against a surface of the latter by a spring. When the safe-and-fire shaft is set to "safe," the rotation of the shaft forces the locking plunger back against its spring so that it projects beyond the breechblock and engages a recess in

---

[16] 149.1 mm equals 5.87 inches.
[17] 11 calibers.
[18] One turn of elevating handwheel equals 12 mils.
[19] One turn of traversing handwheel equals 2.2 mils.

the breechblock way, thus locking the breechblock in the closed position.

When the safe-and-fire shaft is set to fire, the locking plunger is enabled, under pressure of its spring, to re-enter the block, which is then free to move.

Figure 82.—15-cm infantry howitzer on self-propelled mount.

(2) *To load and fire.*—To open the breech, grasp the breech-mechanism lever and press the catch inward. This raises the catch clear of the stop on the breech ring, so that the breech-mechanism lever can be rotated. Then rotate the breech-mechanism lever clockwise

ANTITANK GUNS AND INFANTRY HOWITZERS 153

through 180 degrees. The rotation of the breech-mechanism lever forces the toe of the crank against the right side of the groove in the top face of the block, thrusting the block to the right into the open position.

Insert a round.

To close the breech, return the breech-mechanism lever to its original position and release the handle,

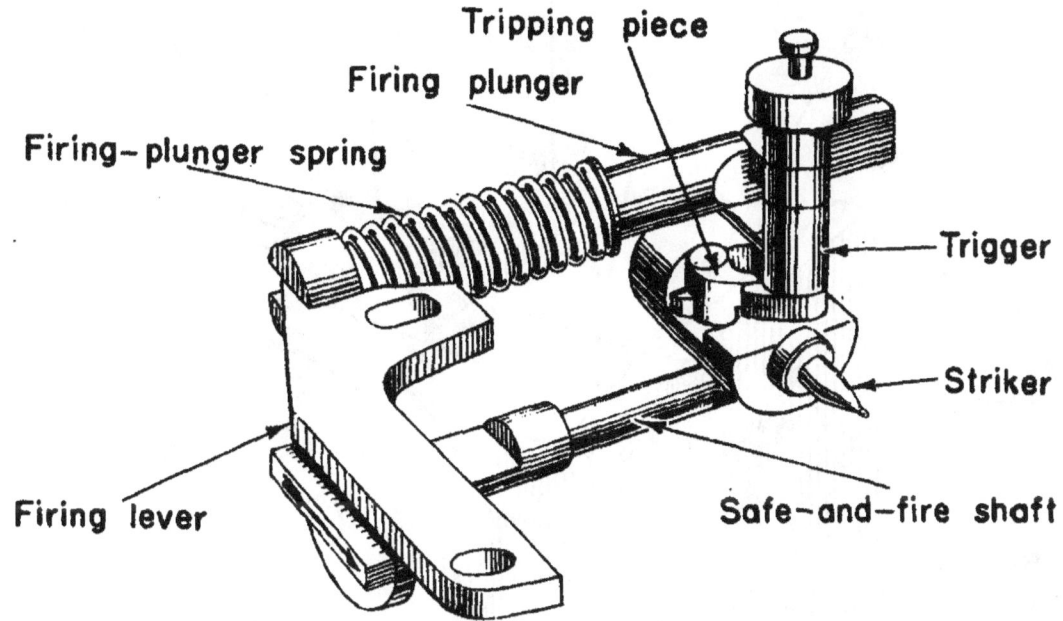

Figure 83.—Firing mechanism of 10.5-cm light field howitzer 18 (l.F.H. 18). (This firing mechanism is similar to that of the 15-cm infantry howitzer.)

so that the catch is held behind the stop on the breech ring.

The rotation of the breech-mechanism lever forces the toe of the crank against the left side of the groove in the top face of the block, thrusting it to the left into the closed position.

As the breech closes, a projection on the toe of the crank comes into position behind the cam of the crank stop so that the block is locked in the closed position.

To fire the howitzer, pull the firing lanyard to the right rear. This rotates the firing lever on its axis pin so that the angle of the former bears against the

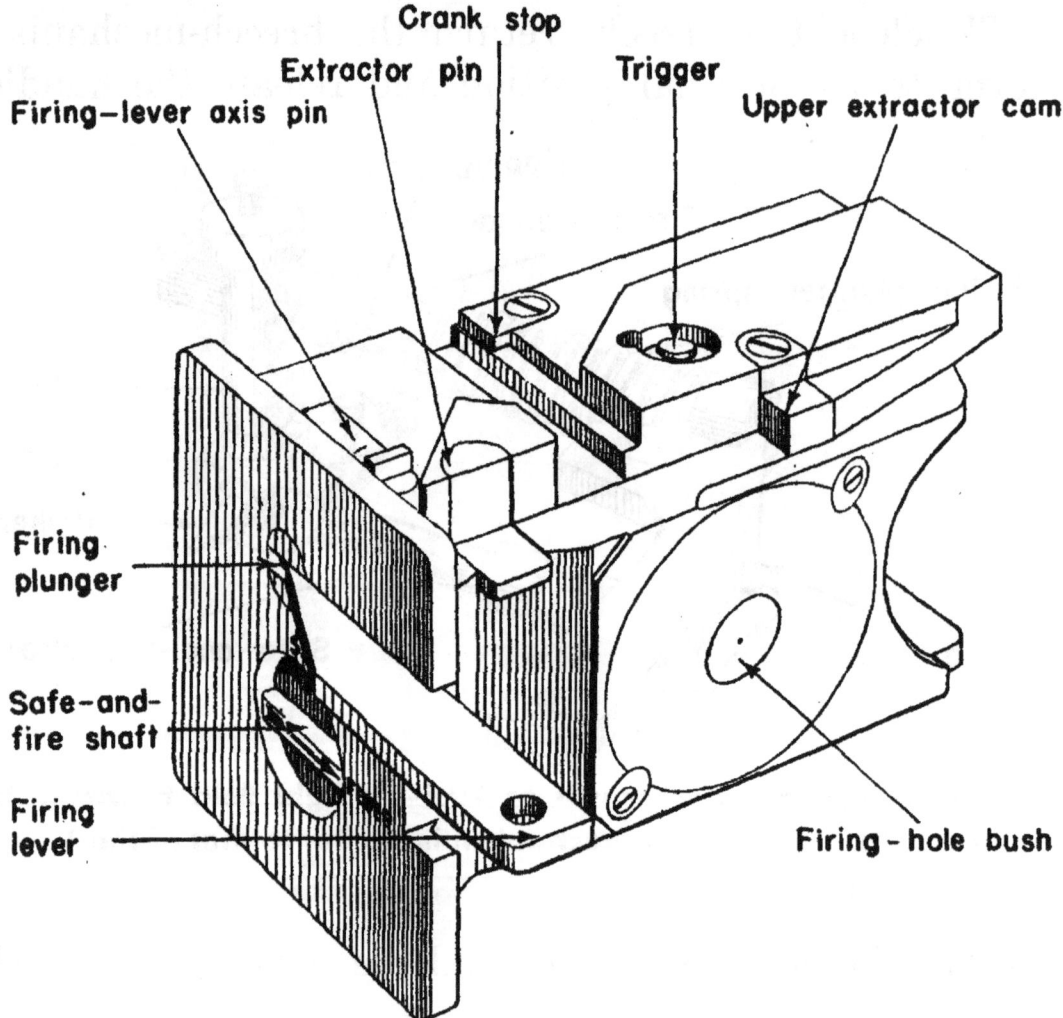

Figure 84.—Breechblock of 10.5-cm light field howitzer 18 (*l.F.H. 18*). (This breechblock is similar to that of the 15-cm infantry howitzer.)

head of the firing plunger, forcing it into the block against its spring. The recess in the plunger in which the upper projection of the trigger is engaged

ANTITANK GUNS AND INFANTRY HOWITZERS 155

turns the latter in a clockwise direction. The toe of the trigger engages the toe of the tripping-piece, which is pivoted on the firing pin, so that both the firing pin and tripping piece are forced back against the firing-pin spring. As the rotation of the trigger continues,

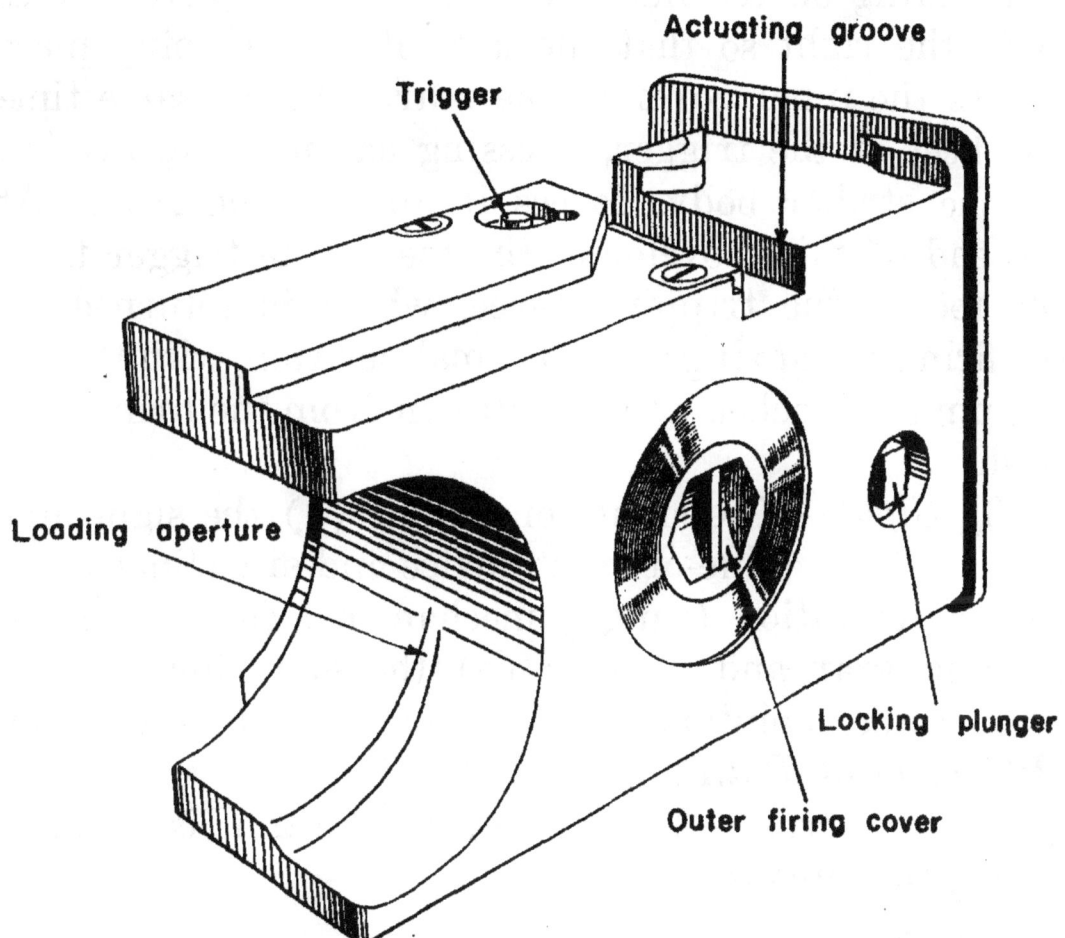

Figure 85.—Breechblock (rear view) of 10.5-cm light field howitzer (I.F.H. 18).

its toe clears the toe of the tripping piece, and the spring of the firing pin asserts itself, driving the striker forward on to the primer of the cartridge. The firing lanyard is now released, and the firing plunger, under pressure of its spring, moves to the right. The upper projection of the trigger, being engaged in the recess of the plunger, turns the trigger in a counterclockwise direction. The toe of the trigger, riding on the inside of the tripping piece, forces it to the right so that the heel of the tripping piece forces the inner cover to the rear. At the same time the heel of the trigger, pressing against a projection on the striker body, forces it, too, to the rear. At the end of this movement, the toe of the trigger trips the toe of the tripping piece, which is returned by the firing-pin spring to the normal position, with the firing pin half cocked and withdrawn from the firing-hole bush.

(3) *Sight.*—The sight consists of (a) the sight and socket; (b) the line-of-sight device and site clinometer; (c) the elevation (range) mechanism; (d) the cross-leveling gear and bubble; (e) the elevation pointer and cradle pointer; (f) the panoramic dial sight (*Rbl.F. 16* or *Rbl.F. 32*).

(4) *Gun crew.*—The service of the gun is divided among the gun crew as follows:

- (a) The chief of section is responsible for seeing that all duties are properly performed, all commands executed, and all safety precautions observed.
- (b) The gunner operates the sights.
- (c) No. 1 operates the breech.
- (d) No. 2 rams the round home.
- (e) No. 3 operates the elevating mechanism.
- (f) Nos. 4, 5, 6, and 7 handle the ammunition.

d. Ammunition

(1) *General.*—The following two types of high explosive shells are used in this infantry howitzer: (a) *15-cm Igr. 38* and (b) *15-cm Igr. 33*. There is also a smoke shell.

The only point of difference between these two types is that the *Igr. 33* has a screwed-in baseplate, whereas the baseplate of the *Igr. 38* is in one piece with the shell body. The high-explosive capacity is large (21.8 percent). The *Igr. 33* is obsolescent, and no more ammunition of this type will be issued when present stocks are exhausted.

(2) *15-cm Igr. 38 and 15-cm Igr. 33 (HE shell).*— (a) *Projectile.*—

Weight (fuzed)	38 kg (84 pounds).
Length (fuzed)	589 mm (23.19 inches).
Diameter at base	145 mm (5.71 inches).
Diameter at driving band	152 mm (5.98 inches).
Driving band, single, width	11 mm (.43 inch).
HE filling	Pressed TNT with smoke box and standard *Zdlg. 36* exploder system; weight of filling, 18¼ pounds.
Packing	1 shell in wicker basket.
Weight of packed basket	42 kg (92 pounds).

(b) *Fuze.*—The fuze *s.Igr.Z. 23* is a highly sensitive, nose-percussion fuze with an optional delay of .4 second. It operates on impact or graze.

(c) *Cartridge.*—The rimmed brass cartridge case, with a *c 12 n/A* percussion primer, has the following dimensions:

External diameter at mouth	155 mm (6.10 inches).
External diameter above rim	158 mm (6.22 inches).
External diameter at rim	169 mm (6.65 inches).
Thickness of rim	4 mm (.16 inches).
Length	133 mm (5.24 inches).
Packing	2 cartridges complete in wooden box, stenciled *Kart. s.I.G. 33*
Weight of box (packed)	9 kg (19.5 pounds).
Markings: on base	4 P131 G Wa A50 6303 s F H 13 (design no.) (equipment)

The markings *s F H 13* suggests that the cartridges for the 15-cm *s.Inf.G. 33* and the 15-cm *s.F.H. 13* are interchangeable.

The cartridge case is closed at the top by a cardboard closing cap.

The propellant consists of six removable parts so that the shell may be fired with any one of six charges. Charge 1 consists of Part 1; charge 2 of Parts 1 and 2; charge 3 of Parts 1, 2, and 3, etc.

Each part is contained in a silk bag on which the details of the weight and type of propellant are stencilled, as follows:

Part 1:
Large flat circular bag, with axial hole	130 gm *Ngl.Bl.P.*[1]–12.5—(40.40.0,2).[2]
Small hole	40 gm *Digl.Bl.P.*[3]–10.5—(3.3.0,8).
Part 2: Crescent-shaped bag	101 gm *Digl.Bl.P.* –10.5—(3.3.0,8).
Part 3: Crescent-shaped bag	106 gm *Digl.Bl.P.* –10.5—(3.3.0,8).
Part 4: Circular bag	101 gm *Digl.Bl.P.* –10.5—(3.3.0,8).
Part 5: Circular bag	26 gm *Digl.Bl.P.* –10.5—(3.3.0,8).
Part 6: Circular bag	41 gm *Digl.Bl.P.*—105—(3.3.0,8).

---

[1] *Ngl.Bl.P.* is the German abbreviation for *Nitroglyzerin Blättchen Pulver* (nitroglycerin flaked powder).

[2] This is the dimension of the flakes in millimeters: that is 40mm x 40mm x .2mm.

[3] *Digl.Bl.P.* is the German abbreviation for *Diglykolnitrat Blättchen Pulver* (diglycolnitrate flaked powder).

(3) *15-cm Igr. 38. Nebel (smoke shell).*—This smoke shell may be identified by the white letters "Nb" on a field-gray projectile which weighs 38.50 kg (85 pounds). The bursting charge consists of picric acid, and the exploder system comprises a detonator set in penthrite wax enclosed in an aluminium container. The shell produces a smoke cloud 50 meters (55 yards) thick.

e. Maintenance

(1) *General.*—Because of the complexity of the mechanism and because of the lack of definite authoritative information on this weapon, the description under the heading of maintenance cannot be made complete.

(2) *To disassemble breech mechanism.*—The breech mechanism may be removed in the following order: (a) set the safety catch to *Feuer* ("fire"); (b) by means of breech-mechanism lever, open the breech mechanism until the extractor bolt is clear; (c) hold the firing lever in the "fire" position and remove the extractor bolt; allow the firing lever to return to its normal position and remove the extractor; (d) crank the breechblock clear of the cam and withdraw; (e) remove the breech-mechanism lever by aligning the key with the keyway and lifting.

f. Carriage

(1) *General.*—The carriage is of the box type. It is fitted with a fixed spade and is also provided with an attachable sand spade. Toward the front are the trunnion bearings which receive the trunnions of the cradle, and there is a spring compensator on each side piece. The elevating handwheel is mounted on the right of the car-

riage, and the traversing handwheel on the left. A shield is fitted at the front, and a box for spares at the rear.

When traveling, the cradle is secured by a clamp to the carriage, to the center of which the sand spade is also secured.

(2) *Cradle.*—The cradle is trough-shaped and is provided with guide ways, in which guides on the gun move as it recoils and runs out. On either side at the front is a pad to receive the unabsorbed force of run-out, and between them is the expansion chamber which receives the buffer fluid forced from the buffer by expansion as it becomes heated. Towards the rear are the two cradle arms to which the trunnions are fixed. Each trunnion is provided with a cranked compensator lever which compresses the compensator spring. The elevating arc is secured underneath, and the recoil indicator at the right rear. The clamp is at the front of the carriage, and is operated by a lever secured to the clamp shaft.

(3) *Elevating gear.*—The elevating gear is operated from the right of the carriage. It consists of a worm gearing, rack, pinion, and shafting.

(4) *Traversing gear.*—The traversing gear is operated from the left by a system of gear wheels and shafting.

(5) *Spring compensators.*—The spring compensators are fitted longitudinally, one on each side of the carriage. They neutralize muzzle preponderance at all angles of elevation.

Section V. AMMUNITION

20. INTRODUCTION

The primary purpose of this section is to describe the ammunition suitable for use in German infantry weapons. Since unidentified ammunition cannot be used without danger to the user, considerable information is included on the system by which the Germans label and pack ammunition. Labels and methods of packing ammunition can be changed easily; therefore, the markings on the cartridge cases and bullets are also described in detail.

21. CALIBERS

The calibers of small arms (weapons with a caliber below 20 millimeters) are measured by the Germans in millimeters, whereas weapons with calibers of 20 millimeters and higher are measured in centimeters: for example, the *9-mm Pistole 08,* the *7.5-cm Kanone.* This should not cause any confusion, as the conversion from centimeters to millimeters is simply a multiplication by 10.

Some confusion, however, may be caused by the German practice of referring to calibers approximately. The Germans refer to their rifle and machine-gun ammunition as caliber 7.9 mm, whereas in reality it is caliber 7.92 mm (.312 inch). Their 8-cm mortar ammunition is actually 8.1 cm. In many instances the exact caliber is used: for example, *3.7-cm Pak.*

22. LABELS

a. General

All German ammunition containers bear labels. A knowledge of the practice used in labeling ammunition will enable identifications to be made readily.

b. Color of Labels

The usual practice is to have white labels with black printing. The following special colors are used for further identification:

(1) *Yellow* labels for tracer ammunition;
(2) *Pale blue* labels for pistol ammunition;
(3) *Brick-red* labels for blank ammunition.

c. Special Marks on Labels

Overprintings and other special marks are sometimes used by the Germans. The following marks have been reported:

(1) "i.L." in large black or red letters is used to indicate that the ammunition is loaded in clips;

(2) "Ex." on the labels is used to indicate dummy ammunition;

(3) "S. m. K." printed in red is used to identify armor-piercing ammunition;

(4) "für M. G.", printed usually in red, indicates cartridges are for use in machine guns;

(5) "für Gew." or "nur für Gewehr", printed usually in red, indicates cartridges are for use in rifles only;

(6) "Patr. 318" indicates cartridges for use only in antitank rifles (the cartridge case being larger than that of the standard 7.92-mm rifle and machine-gun ammunition);

(7) "Pist. Patr. 08" indicates 9-mm pistol and submachine-gun ammunition;

(8) A green diagonal band is used to indicate ball cartridges with the "l.S.", or light-weight bullet.

(9) A blue band of considerable width, running vertically, indicates steel cartridge cases (rather than brass).

d. Special Labels

When a special label is used, it is often for the purpose of marking unreliable ammunition. In some instances, special labels indicate specially loaded ammunition. The following (figs. 86 to 90, incl.) are examples of some special labels:

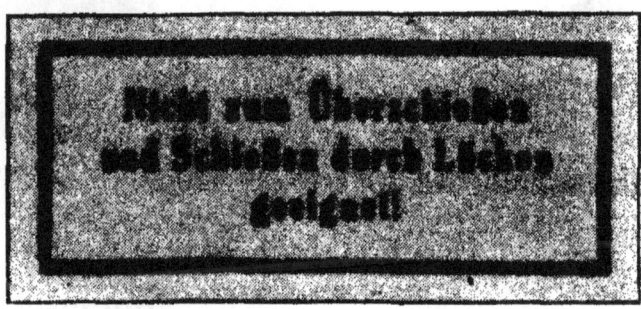

Figure 86.—"Not suited for overhead fire or firing through gaps in lines!"

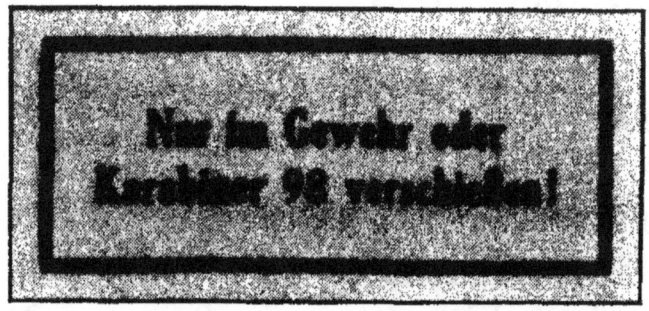

Figure 87.—"To be fired only in rifles or 98Kl"

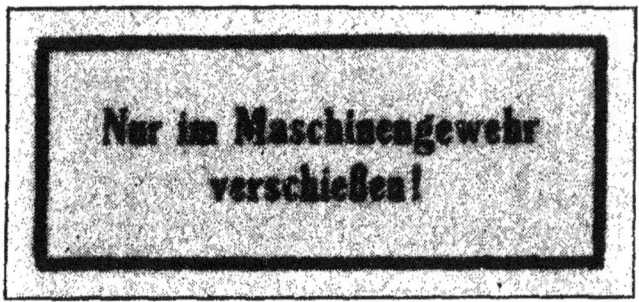

Figure 88.—"To be fired only in machine guns!"

Figure 89.—"Only for sighting in."

Figure 90.—"Only for practice purposes."

e. Method of Reading Labels

(1) *General.*—On labels for small-arms ammunition, the Germans omit in nearly all instances any reference to the caliber. The ammunition cases are labeled to indicate the name of the weapon for which the enclosed ammunition is intended. The standard caliber for pistols and submachine guns is 9 mm. Where the caliber differs from 9 mm, it is shown on the label: for

example, *Pist. Patr. 7.63 mm* ("7.63-mm pistol cartridges"). Where the caliber of 9 mm is shown on the label, it will indicate that the ammunition is made for use with non-standard 9-mm weapons.

Labels may be expected to contain the following information: (1) number and type of cartridges; (2) lot number and the year of loading of the cartridges; (3) type of powder, and also the type of weapon for which it is intended; (4) place and year of manufacture; (5) specifications of the cartridge case and bullet; (6) specifications of the primer; (7) composition of the tracer (if any). In order to place all this information on a label, abbreviations are used. To facilitate the translation of the labels, a list of abbreviations [1] and a glossary [2] are given in sections VI and VII (pp. 185–190, below). The Germans use two alphabets, roman and German gothis,[3] and consequently labels may be printed in either, or both of them.

(2) *Examples.*—Set forth below (figs. 90 to 101, incl.) are some typical labels for small-arms ammunition.

The label illustrated in figure 91 reads:

Line
(1)   1500 Patronen s. S.
(2)   P. 24. L. 35
(3)   Nz. Gew. Bl. P. (2.2.0,45):
(4)   Rdf. 17. L. 35

---

[1] A more extensive list of German abbreviations is given in "German Military Abbreviations," MIS *Special Series*, No. 12 (April 12, 1943).

[2] See also TM 30–255, "Military Dictionary, English-German, German-English."

[3] See figs. 92 and 94.

(5) Patrd: S.* P. 7. L. 35—Gesch.: P. 55. L. 35
(6) Zdh. 88: S. K. D. 98. L. 35

The following information is contained on this label:

Line
(1) Number and type of cartridges
(2) Lot number and year of loading of cartridges
(3) Type of powder, including type of gun for which intended
(4) Arsenal, serial number, and year of manufacture
(5) Specifications of cartridge case; specifications of bullet
(6) Specifications of primer.

A translation of this label reads as follows:

Line
(1) 1,500 rounds, heavy, pointed ball ammunition
(2) Lot 24; delivery 1935
(3) Nitrocellulose rifle flaked powder (?)
(4) Rdf.(?) arsenal; 17th delivery 1935
(5) Brass-cartridge case, lot 7, delivery 1935—Bullet lot 55, year 1935
(6) Primer capsule 88, (???) 98, delivery 1935

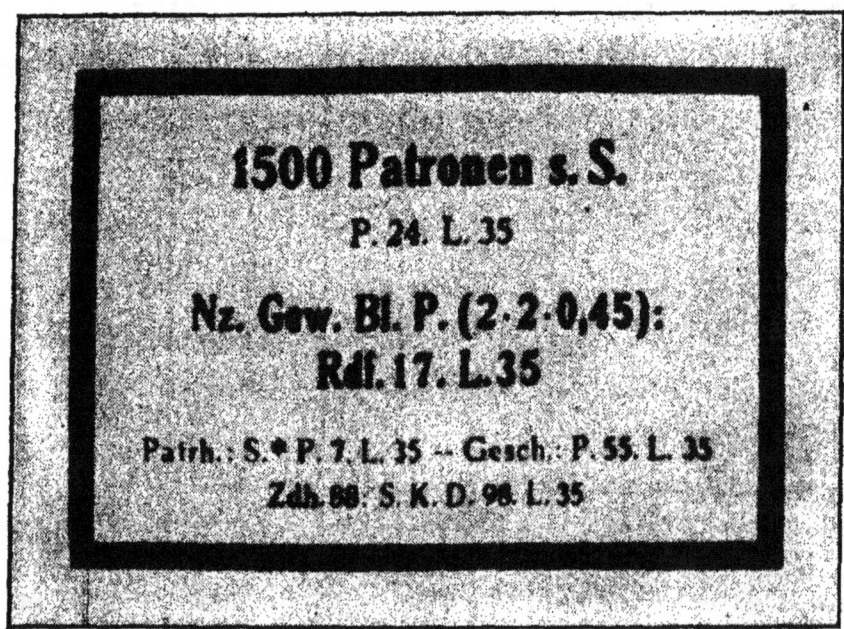

Figure 91.—Label for case of 1,500 rounds of heavy, pointed ball ammunition (*Patronen s. S., Patronen schweres Spitzgeschoss*). (The label is white with black printing.)

Figure 92.—Label for super armor-piercing bullet, with tungsten carbide core (*Patr. S. m. K. (H), Patronen Spitzgeschoss mit Stahlkern gehärtet*). (This label is white with a red triangle, black border and printing. The letters "S. m. K. (H)" are in color after Patr. but they are not reproduced in this photograph.

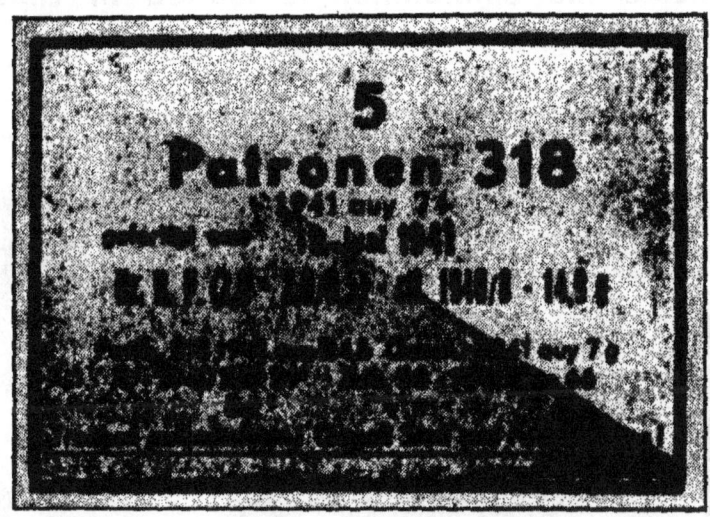

Figure 93.—Label for 5 rounds of armor-piercing bullet (*Patronen 318*). (This label consists of two triangles, one red and the other yellow; the border and the printing are black; the edging is white.)

Figure 94.—Label for armor-piercing incendiary bullet (*Patr. P. m. K., Patronen Phosphor mit Stahlkern*). (This label is green with black printing.)

Figure 95.—Label for heavy, pointed ball ammunition (*Patr. s. S., Patronen schweres Spitzgeschoss*). (This label is white with black printing. The letters "i. L." are overprinted in red ink; they indicate the ammunition is loaded in clips—*i. L., im Ladestriefen.*)

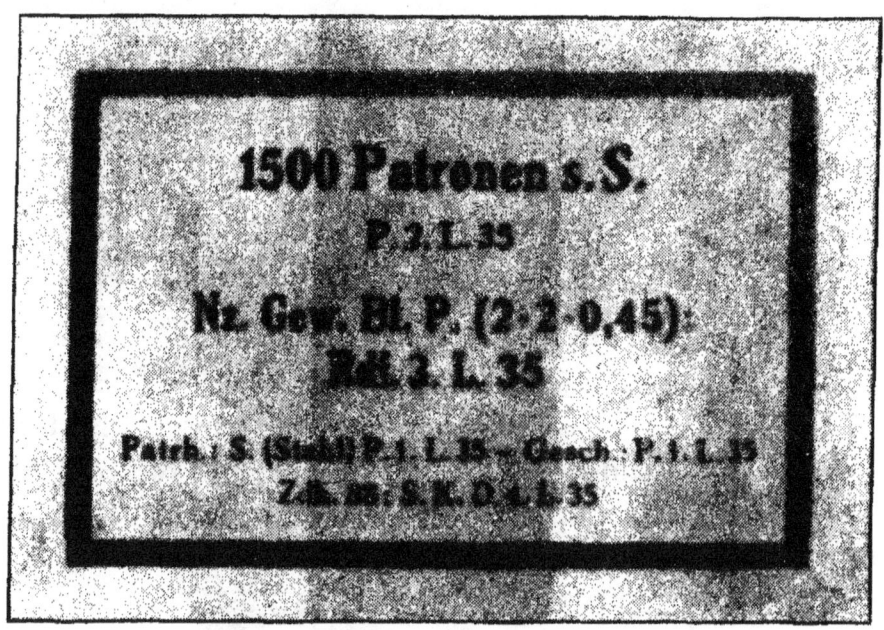

Figure 96.—Label for 1,500 rounds of heavy, pointed ball ammunition (*Patr. s. S., Patronen schweres Spitzgeschoss*). (The label is white with black printing. A vertical blue band runs through the center, indicating the cartridge cases are steel instead of brass; notice also the word *Stahl* ("steel").)

Figure 97.—Labels for steel-core, armor-piercing ammunition (*Patronen S. m. K., Patronen Spitzgeschoss mit Stahlkern*). (The labels are white with black printing; "S. m. K." is printed in red. The different sizes of the same label are used on different sizes of packing boxes.)

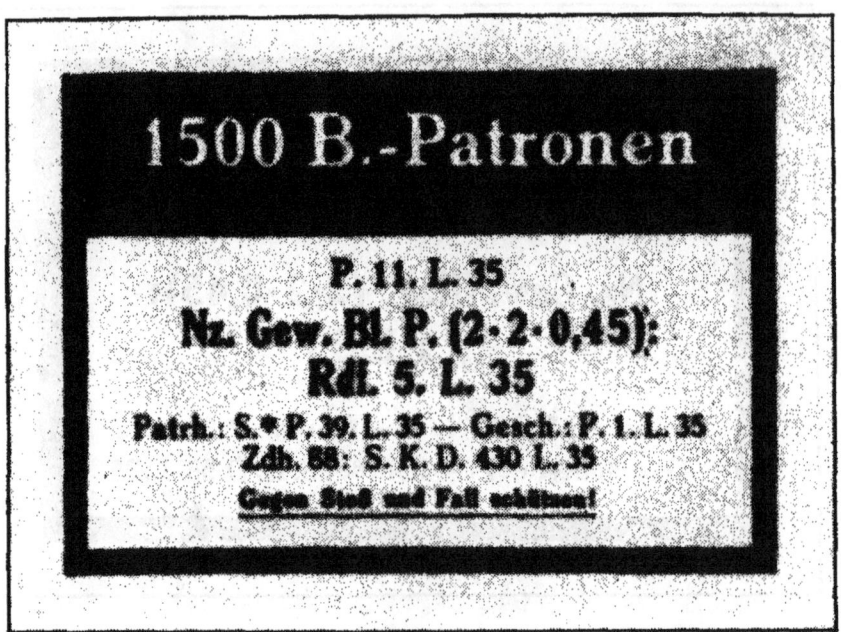

Figure 98.—Label for 1,500 rounds of observation (explosive) bullets (*B.-Patronen, Beobachtungsgeschoss Patronen*). (This label is white with black printing. The underlined printing is a caution: *Protect against shock and dropping!*)

Figure 99.—Label for light, pointed ball ammunition (*Patronen l. S., Patronen leichtes Spitzgeschoss*). (This label is white with black printing; a green diagonal band runs from the lower left to upper right corners.)

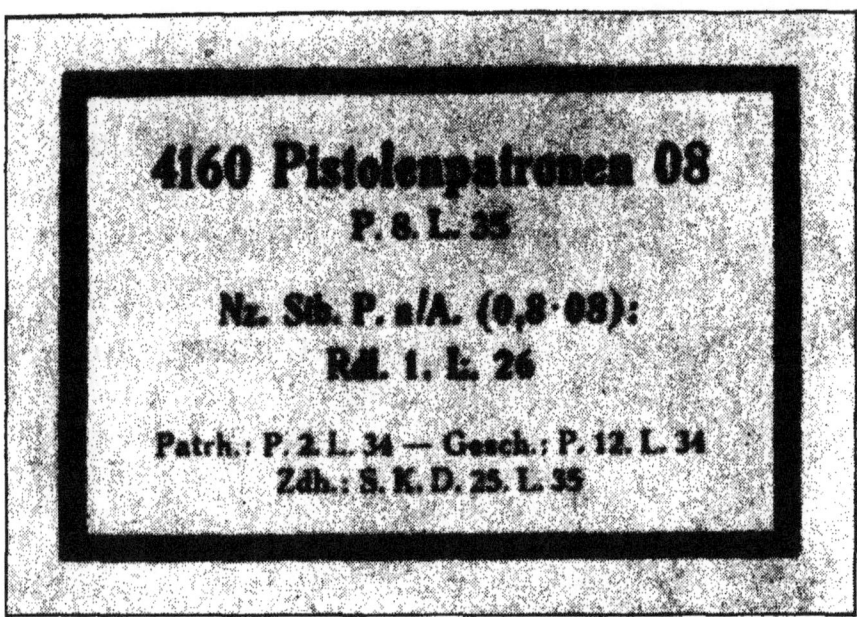

Figure 100.—Label for model 08 pistol cartridges (*Pistolenpatronen 08*). Model 08 pistol cartridges are the regular ammunition for the Luger, the Walther, and the M. P. 38 and 40; this label is pale blue with black printing.)

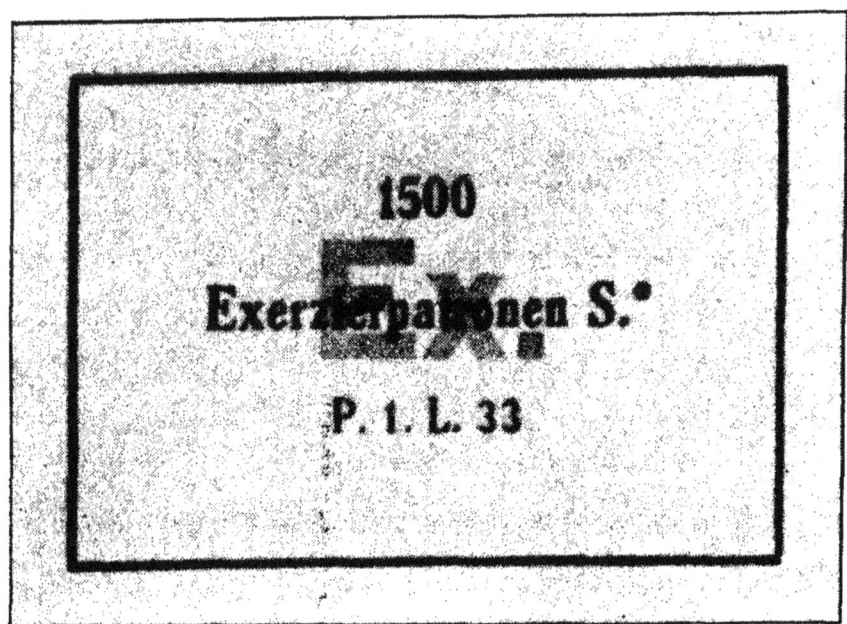

Figure 101.—Label for dummy, drill cartridges, model S (*Exerzierpatronen* S.). (This label is white with black printing and a red overprinting of "Ex.")

23. BASE MARKINGS

The following information is stamped on the base (fig. 102) of German small-arms ammunition: (1) the manufacturer's mark (for example, *P* for *Polte*); (2) the type of case (for example, *S** for brass cartridge case [4]); (3) the delivery number (for example, *2* means delivery 2; (4) the year of manufacture (for example, *38* means 1938).

Figure 102.—Markings on base of German small-arms cartridge.

Colors are used on various parts of the ammunition itself to provide another means of identifying each cartridge. The coloring may be applied in the primer seat, on the tip, or as a colored band around the case.

24. BELTED AMMUNITION

German machine-gun ammunition is packed in cases, and is not supplied in ready-belted form. The German nondisintegrating metallic-link belts are non-expendable, being used over and over. The cartridges are belted by the unit to which they are issued. Sometimes belted ammunition is placed in canvas bags, which are used to carry small-arms ammunition for machine guns mounted on tanks.

25. POSSIBLE DANGERS

All ammunition which is exposed to the sun and heat is likely to produce dangerous pressures, even in

---

[4] *St* is for "steel."

weapons that are in good condition. In addition, ammunition may be dangerous for any of the following reasons:

(a) Removal (either deliberate or accidental) of safety devices from fuzes;

(b) Use as booby traps laid deliberately by the enemy;

(c) As a result of subjection to shelling or fire.[5]

Consequently, care should be exercised in the use of any enemy matériel to be sure that both the ammunition and the weapon are in good working order.

26. STANDARD PISTOL AND SUBMACHINE-GUN AMMUNITION

a. *Pist. Patr. 08, Pist. Patr. 08 für M. P., or Pist. Patr. 9 mm.*

The above-named pistol ammunition types are all standard ball ammunition for German pistols and submachine guns. Each type consists of a rimless cartridge case and a round-nosed bullet. The bullet has a lead core, and a steel jacket with a copper or gilding metal coating to cut down wear on the rifling. This ammunition may be identified by the label reading: *Pist. Patr. 08*, *Pist. Patr. 08 für M. P.*, or *Pistol Patr. 9 mm (P)* (of Polish manufacture). The primer seat is colored black.

b. *Pist. Patr. 08 S. m. E.*

The cartridge case of this standard 9-mm semi-armor-piercing ammunition is the same as the ball ammunition, but the bullet has an iron or mild-steel core and a steel jacket. This ammunition may be identified by the black coloring of the bullet.

---

[5] The mechanical safety devices may have been so disarranged as to arm the ammunition.

27. RIFLE AND MACHINE-GUN AMMUNITION (7.92-MM)

a. General

Caliber 7.92-mm ammunition is standard for German rifles and machine guns (see figs. 103 to 114, incl.). Various types of this ammunition are used for special purposes. The modifications are made in the size and character of the bullet, the cartridge case being the same for all of the various types. The case is a rimless bottleneck case, much like the U. S. caliber .30 case but somewhat shorter.

b. Patr. s. S.

Patr. s. S. (*Patronen schweres Spitzgeschoss*) (fig. 103) is the heavy, pointed ball ammunition. This is the standard rifle and machine-gun ball round, having a heavy, pointed bolt-tail bullet consisting of a lead core and a steel jacket coated with gilding metal.

This ammunition is identified by its green primer seat.

c. Patr. S. m. K.

Patr. S. m. K. (*Patronen Spitzgeschoss mit Stahlkern*) (fig. 104) is the cartridge with a steel-core, pointed bullet. This type of ammunition has a steel core and a feed sleeve with a steel jacket that is coated with gilding metal.

This ammunition is identified by its red primer seat.

d. Patr. S. m. K. L'Spur

Patr. S. m. K. L'Spur (*Patronen Spitzgeschoss mit Stahlkern und Leuchtspur*) (fig. 105) is the cartridge with a pointed armor-piercing bullet and tracer.

This ammunition is identified by the red coloring on its primer seat and a black-tipped bullet.

e. Patr. S. m. K. (H)

Patr. S. m. K. (H) (*Patronen Spitzgeschoss mit Stahlkern gehärtet*) (fig. 106) is a cartridge with a pointed, armor-piercing (tungsten carbide core) bullet.

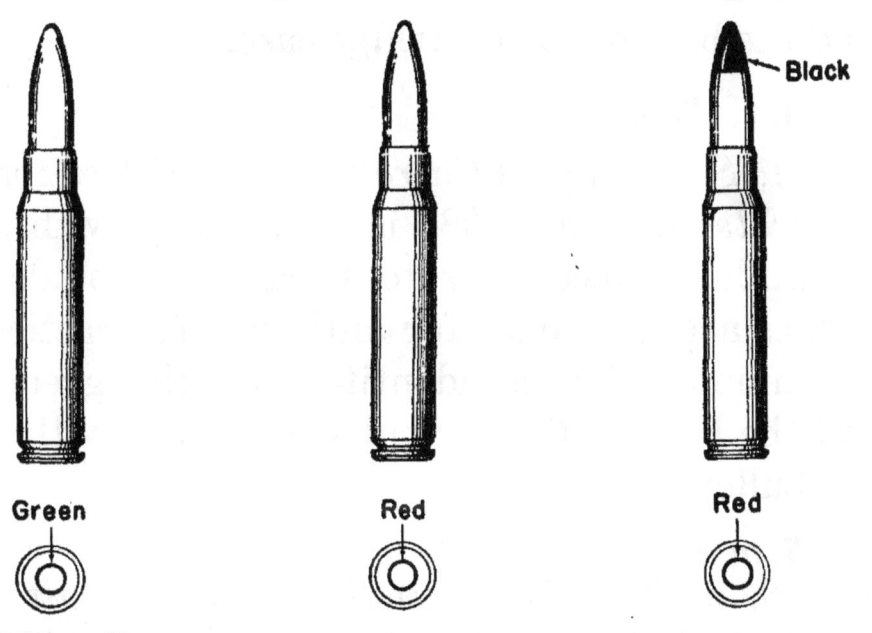

Figure 103.—Heavy, pointed ball (*Patronen schweres Spitzgeschoss*).

Figure 104.—Armor-piercing (*Patronen Spitzgeschoss mit Stahlkern*).

Figure 105.—Armor-piercing tracer (*Patronen Spitzgeschoss mit Stahlkern und Leuchtspur*).

This ammunition may be identified by the red primer and the red base of the clip, and a black bullet. Earlier issues had a plain uncolored bullet but did have the red primer.

f. Patr. l. S.

Patr. l. S. (*Patronen leichtes Spitzgeschoss*) (fig. 107) is similar to the *Patr. s. S.* heavy, pointed ball ammunition, except that instead of a lead core the core is of aluminum. This decreases the range, and German documents state that this type of ammunition is used for antiaircraft practice only.

This ammunition is identified by a green band around the base of the cartridge case.

g. Patr. l. S. L'Spur

Patr. l. S. L'Spur (*Patrone leichtes Spitzgeschoss mit Leuchtspur*) (fig. 108) is a cartridge with a light, tracer bullet. According to German manuals, these cartridges are used only for antiaircraft practice.

This ammunition is identified by the green band around the base of the cartridge case and by the black-tipped bullet.

h. Patr. S. m. E.

Patr. S. m. E. (*Patronen Spitzgeschoss mit Eisenkern*) (fig. 109) is a semi-armor-piercing cartridge with an iron or mild-steel core and pointed bullet.

This ammunition is identified by the blue color on its primer seat.

i. Patr. P. m. K.

Patr. P. m. K. (*Patronen Phospor mit Stahlkern*) (fig. 110) is an incendiary armor-piercing cartridge with a standard case. It is said to be used only against aircraft. It has a steel core, and a phosphorus charge in the base cavity.

This ammunition is identified by the black or red color of its primer seat; it may have a red band across the base.

j. B. Patr.

B. Patr. (Beobachtungsgeschoss Patronen) (fig. 111) is an observation bullet containing a smoke producer

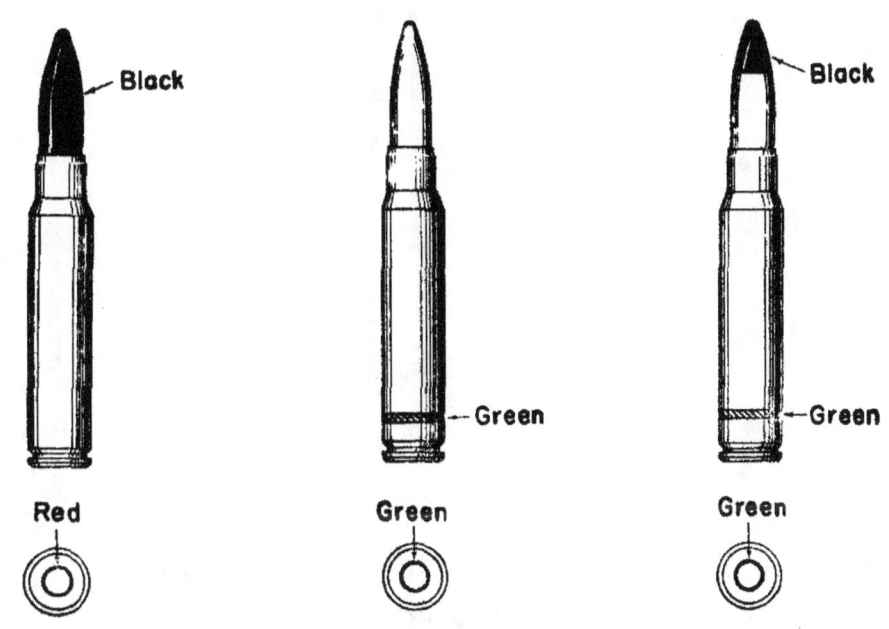

Figure 106.— Super-armor-piercing with tungsten carbide core (Patronen Spitzgeschoss mit Stahlkern gehärtet).

Figure 107.— Light ball, special practice (Patronen leichtes Spitzgeschoss).

Figure 108.—Practice tracer (Patronen leichtes Spitzgeschoss mit Leuchtspur).

and explosive, and is said to be used only in peacetime firing for checking ranges.

This ammunition is identified in earlier issues by its chromium-tipped bullet, and in later issues by a bullet painted black (except for the tip).

28. STANDARD ANTITANK RIFLE AMMUNITION

a. Introduction

The ammunition used in the *Pz.B. 38* and *Pz.B. 39* (antitank rifles) is of the armor-piercing type. The round itself can be identified by the large cartridge

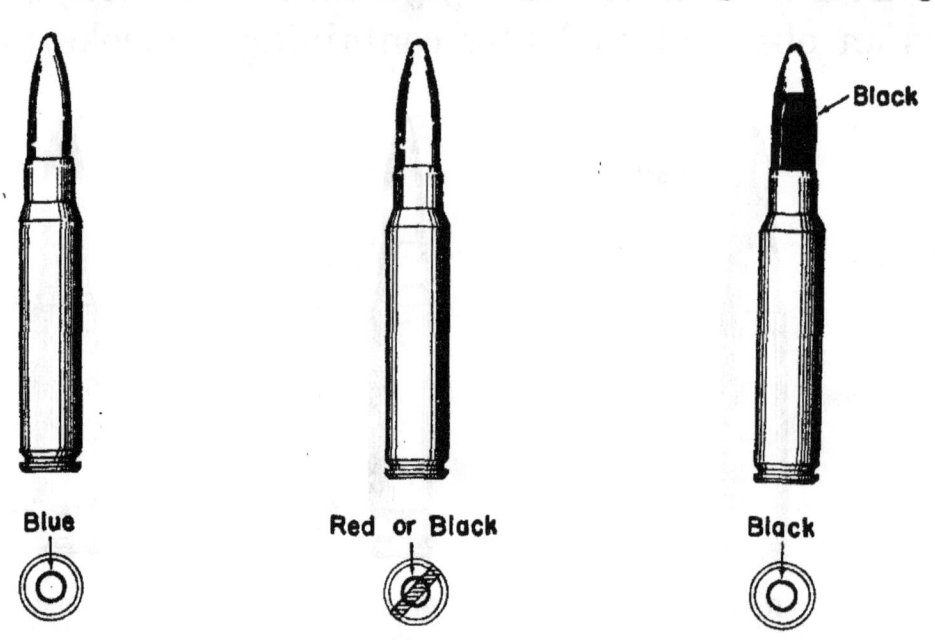

Figure 109.—Semi-armor-piercing (Patronen Spitzgeschoss mit Eisenkern).

Figure 110.—Armor-piercing incendiary (Patronen Phospor mit Stahlkern). (The bullet is black or red in the primer seat, or has a red band across the base.)

Figure 111.—Observation (explosive) bullet (Beobachtungsgeschoss Patronen). (The bullet is black except for the tip; early issues have chromimum-plated tip only.)

case, necked down to take the 7.92-mm (.312-inch) bullet.

The German labels distinguish this ammunition from the regular 7.92-mm rifle and machine-gun ammunition by the words "Patr. 318" in front of the distinguishing "S.m.K." Labels having the distinguishing "Rs." have a small amount of tear gas in the bullet.

b. *Patr. 318* or *Patr. 318 S.m.K.*

This is the regular armor-piercing ammunition for the *Pz.B. 38* and *Pz.B. 39* antitank rifles. It consists of a large cartridge case (like the U. S. caliber .50 car-

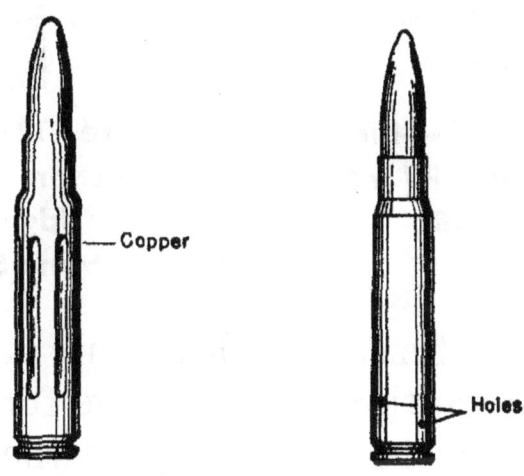

Figure 112.—Dummy cartridges (Exerzierpatronen).

tridge case) with a small projectile of 7.92-mm (.312 inch). The projectile has a gilded metal jacket and a tungsten carbide core. Sometimes it will have a tracer and sometimes a small charge of tear gas in the base of the projectile.

29. MORTAR AMMUNITION

a. *5-cm Wgr. 36, Wgr. Z. 38* [6]

This is the standard shell used in the 50-mm model 36 mortar. It is a high-explosive shell and has a

---

[6] *5-cm Werfergranate 36, Werfergranatzünder 38* (50-mm model 36 mortar shell, with model 38 mortar fuze).

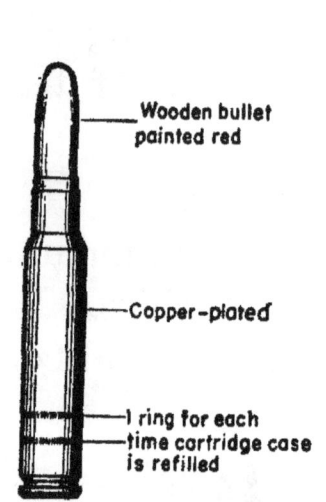

Figure 113.—Blank cartridge *Platz-Patrone 88)*.

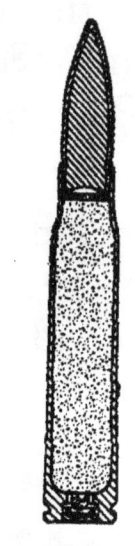

Figure 114. — Cross section of ball cartridge (scharfe Patrone S.).

percussion-nose fuze. It has only one propellant charge, and an ignition charge in the form of a shotgun shellcase that fits into a cavity at the center of the tail-fin assembly. This shell may be identified by its size and maroon color (fig. 115).

b. 8-cm Wgr. 34, Wgr. Z. 38 [7]

This is the standard high-explosive shell for the German 81-mm mortar (*s.Gr.W. 34*). It has a percussion fuze. Each shell has three increments, or charges, which are clipped into a slot in the ammunition container which is provided for carrying the mortar shell. This shell may be identified by its size and maroon color.

---

[7] *8-cm Werfergranate 34, Werfergranatzünder 38* (80-mm (actually 81-mm) HE model 34 mortar shell with model 38 mortar shell fuze).

c. 8-cm Wgr. 34 Nb., Wgr. Z. 38 [8]

This is the standard smoke shell for the German 81-mm mortar (*s.Gr.W. 34*). It has a percussion fuze. Each shell has three increments, or charges, which are clipped into a slot in the ammunition container that is

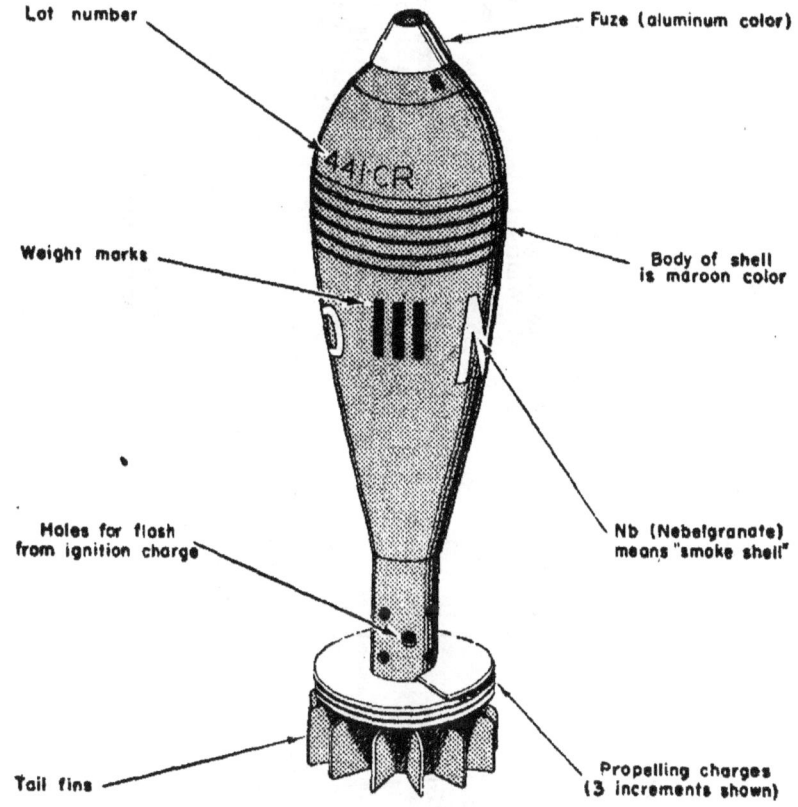

Figure 115.—8-cm mortar shell.

provided for carrying the mortar shells. This shell may be identified by its size, its maroon color, and the letters "Nb".

---

[8] *8-cm Werfergranate 34 Nebel, Werfergranatzünder 38* (89-mm (actually 81-mm) model 34 smoke shell with model 38 mortar shell fuze).

30. CHART OF PISTOL, RIFLE, MACHINE-GUN, AND MORTAR AMMUNITION

SMALL-ARMS AMMUNITION

Caliber	German abbreviation	Type	Identification		Suitable for use in—	How packed	Weight of container
			Color of primer seat	Color of bullet			
9 mm (.354 in)	Pist. Patr. 08	Pistol, ball	Black	Copper or nickel	Pistole 08 (Luger); Pistole 38 (Walther); M.P. 38; Bergmann and Solothurn submachine guns.	Tin-lined wooden case holding 4,160 rounds in multiples of 16 rounds—5 cartons of 832 rounds each.	127.87 lbs.
9 mm (.354 in)	Pist. Patr. 08 S. m. E.	Pistol, semi-armor-piercing	Black	Black	Pistole 08 (Luger); Pistole 38 (Walther); M.P. 40; Bergmann and Solothurn submachine guns.	Tin-lined wooden case holding 4,160 rounds in multiples of 16 rounds—5 cartons of 832 rounds each.	127.87 lbs.
7.92 mm (.312 in)	Patr. s. S. (i. L.) clipped, (o. L.) not in clips	Heavy, pointed ball	Green	Plain	Mauser Gew. 98; Kar. 98K; Kar. 98B; Kar. 98; M. G. 34; M. G. 42; and 7.92-mm aircraft machine guns.	Wooden case holding 1,500 rounds packed in 5 cartons, each holding 300 rounds packed in 20 cardboard packages holding 15 rounds each.	Patr. s. S. (i. L.) clipped, 117.95 lbs. Patr. s. S. (o. L.) not in clips, 113.54 lbs.
7.92 mm (.312 in)	Patr. S. m. K.	Armor-piercing	Red	Plain	Mauser Gew. 98; Kar. 98K; Kar. 98B; Kar. 98; M. G. 34; M. G. 42; and 7.92-mm aircraft machine guns.	Wooden case holding 1,500 rounds packed in 5 cartons, each holding 300 rounds packed in 20 cardboard packages holding 15 rounds each.	109.13 lbs.
7.92 mm (.312 in)	Patr. S. m. K. L'Spur.	Armor-piercing tracer	Red	Black tip	Mauser Gew. 98; Kar. 98K; Kar. 98B; Kar. 98; M. G. 34; M. G. 42; and 7.92-mm aircraft machine guns.	Wooden case holding 1,500 rounds packed in 5 cartons, each holding 300 rounds packed in 20 cardboard packages holding 15 rounds each.	106.04 lbs.
7.92 mm (.312 in)	Patr. S. m. K. (H)	Super-armor-piercing with tungsten carbide core	Red	Black	Mauser Gew. 98; Kar. 98K; Kar. 98B; Kar. 98; M. G. 34; M. G. 42; and 7.92-mm aircraft machine guns.	Wooden case holding 1,500 rounds packed in 5 cartons, each holding 300 rounds packed in 20 cardboard packages holding 15 rounds each.	118.61 lbs.

AMMUNITION

Caliber	Designation	Type	Color marking	Used in	Packing	Weight
7.92 mm (.312 in)	*Patr. l.S.*	Light ball, special practice	Green (Green band around cartridge case)	Plain	Mauser *Gew.* 98; *Kar.* 98*K*; *Kar.* 98*B*; *Ka. 98*; *M.G. 34*; *M.G. 42*; and 7.92-mm aircraft machine guns.	Wooden case holding 1,500 rounds packed in 5 cartons, each holding 300 rounds packed in 20 cardboard packages holding 15 rounds each.	
7.92 mm (.312 in)	*Patr. l.S. L'Spur*	Practice tracer	Green band around base of cartridge case	Black tip	Mauser *Gew.* 98; *Kar.* 98*K*; *Kar.* 98*B*; *Kar. 98*; *M.G. 34*; *M.G. 42*; and 7.92-mm aircraft machine guns.	Wooden case holding 1,500 rounds packed in 5 cartons, each holding 300 rounds packed in 20 cardboard packages holding 15 rounds each.	
7.92 mm (.312 in)	*Patr. S.m.E.*	Semi-armor-piercing	Blue	Plain	Mauser *Gew.* 98; *Kar.* 98 *K*; *Kar.* 98 *B*; *Kar. 98*; *M.G. 34*; *M.G. 42*; and 7.92-mm aircraft machine guns.	Wooden case holding 1,500 rounds packed in 5 cartons, each holding 300 rounds packed in 20 cardboard packages holding 15 rounds each.	
7.92 mm (.312 in)	*Patr. S.m.K.*	Armor-piercing	Black or red or red band across base	Plain	Mauser *Gew.* 98 *K*; *Kar.* 98 *B*; *Kar. 98*; *M.G. 34*; *M.G. 42*; and 7.92-mm aircraft machine guns.	Wooden case holding 1,500 rounds packed in 5 cartons, each holding 300 rounds packed in 20 cardboard packages holding 15 rounds each.	
7.92 mm (.312 in)	*B. Patr.*	Incendiary explosive	Black	Plain with chromium tip or black except for tip sometimes with green band	Mauser *Gew.* 98; *Kar.* 98 *K*; *Kar.* 98 *B*; *M.G. 34*; *M.G. 42*; and 7.92-mm aircraft machine guns.	Wooden case holding 1,500 rounds packed in 5 cartons, each holding 300 rounds packed in 20 cardboard packages holding 15 rounds each.	
7.92 mm (.312 in)	*Patr. 318* or *Patr. S. m. K.(H R s.) L'Spur*	Armor-piercing tracer with tear gas	Red	Black tip	*Pz.B. 38* and *Pz.B. 39* antitank rifles only.	5 in cardboard carton; 250 rounds in each case.	72.75 lbs
7.92 mm (.312 in)	*Patr. 318 (P)*	Armor-piercing	Red	None	Polish Maserzek, model 35, antitank rifle only (bolt-operated shot magazine weapon)	5 in cardboard carton; 250 rounds in case.	72.75 lbs
9 mm	*Ex. Patr. 08*	Dummy pistol	Silver finish all over		*Pistole 08* (Luger); *Pistole 38* (Walther); *M.P. 38* and *M.P. 40*; Bergmann and Solothurn submachine guns.	4,160 in case.	
7.92 mm (.312 in)	*Ex. Patr. s. S.*	Rifle and MG dummy	Copper finish all over; round-nose bullet		Mauser *Gew.* 98; *Kar.* 98 *K*; *Kar.* 98 *B*; *Kar. 98*; *M.G. 34*; *M.G. 42*; and 7.92-mm aircraft machine guns.	1,450 in case.	

Chart of Pistol, Rifle, Machine-Gun, and Mortar Ammunition—Continued

MORTAR AMMUNITION AND HAND GRENADES

Caliber	German abbreviation	Type	Identification - Color of primer seat	Identification - Color of bullet	Suitable for use in—	How packed	Weight of container
50 mm	5-cm Wgr. 36 Nb.	Light mortar, model 36, smoke shell.	Maroon except for fuze and "Nb" in white.		5-cm light mortar, model 36.	10 or 40 rounds to a case.	10 rounds—26.90 lbs; 40 rounds—154.32 lbs
50 mm	5-cm Wgr. 36	Light mortar, model 36 shell (HE).	Maroon except for fuze.		5-cm light mortar, model 36.	10 or 40 rounds to a case.	10 rounds—26.90 lbs; 40 rounds—154.32 lbs
81 mm	8-cm Wgr. 34	Heavy mortar, model 34, shell (HE).	Maroon except for fuze.		8-cm heavy mortar, model 34.	Packed 3 or 12 rounds per case, with 3 increments per shell packed.	3 rounds—31.97 lbs; 12 rounds—175.05 lbs
81 mm	8-cm Wgr. 34 Nb.	Heavy mortar, model 34, smoke shell.	Maroon except for fuze and "Nb" in white.		8-cm heavy mortar, model 34.	Packed 3 or 12 rounds per case, with 3 increments per shell packed.	3 rounds—31.97 lbs; 12 rounds—175.05 lbs
81 mm	8-cm Wgr. 38	Heavy mortar, model 38, smoke shell with delay.	Maroon except for fuze and "Nb" in white.		8-cm heavy mortar, model 34.	Packed 3 or 12 rounds per case, with 3 increments per shell packed.	3 rounds—31.97 lbs; 12 rounds—175.05 lbs
	Stielhdgr. 24	HE stick grenade, model 24.	Gray green color, unpainted wood handle.		(Thrown by hand)	15 rounds in steel or wooden case, with 15 detonators packed.	33.07 lbs.
	Nebelhdgr. 34	Smoke stick grenade, model 34.	Gray green head, broken white line, and "Nb."		(Thrown by hand)	15 rounds in steel or wooden case, with 15 detonators packed.	33.07 lbs.
	Eihdgr. 39	Egg grenade, model 39.	Gray green body.		(Thrown by hand)	30 or 90 rounds packed in airtight case, with 30 detonators packed.	30 rounds—19.84 lbs; 90 rounds—105.38 lbs

Section VI. GLOSSARY OF GERMAN TERMS[1]

aus	out
Beobachtungsgeschoss Patrone	observation (explosive) bullet
Dauerfeuer (D)	continuous fire, sustained fire
Ein	in
Einzelschuss	single-shot
Ersatzstücke (E)	spare parts, replacements
Exerzierpatrone	drill cartridge (dummy or blank cartridge)
Feuer (F)	fire
geballte Ladung	concentrated charge, pole charge
gehärtet (H)	hardened *(tungsten carbide core)*
geladen	loaded
gesichert	made safe ("safed")
Eierhandgranate	egg-type hand grenade
Kanone	cannon
Kern	core
Ladestreifen	clips, rifle magazine clips
Ladung	charge, propelling charge, load
leichter Granatwerfer (l.Gr.W.)	light mortar
Leuchtspur (L 'Spur)	tracer
Maschinengewehr (M.G.)	machine gun
Nebel (N)	smoke
Nebelhandgranate	smoke hand grenade
Parabellum	trade name of 9-mm German pistol ammunition
Patrone (Patr.)	cartridge, semi-fixed shell; round of ammunition
Patrone leichtes Spitzgeschoss (Patr. l. S.)	heavy, pointed ball ammunition with core of aluminum

[1] This is a list of the German words used in the text. For an extensive German military dictionary see TM 30-255, "Military Dictionary, English-German, German-English" (Aug. 5, 1941).

Patrone mit Spitzgeschoss mit Stahlkern (Patr. S. m. K.)	cartridge with steel-core, pointed bullet
Patrone schweres Spitzgeschoss (Patr. s. S.)	heavy, pointed ball ammunition
Patrone schweres Spitzgeschoss mit Leuchtspur (Patr. s. S. L'Spur)	cartridge with heavy tracer bullet
Patrone Spitzgeschoss mit Eisenkern (Patr. S. m. E.)	cartridge with iron or mild steel-core, pointed bullet
Patrone Spitzgeschoss mit Stahlkern (gehärtet) (Patr. S. m. K. (H))	cartridge with pointed, armor-piercing (*tungsten carbide core*) bullet
Patrone Phosphor mit Stahlkern (Patr. P. m. K.)	incendiary armor-piercing cartridge case
Patrone Spitzgeschoss mit Stahlkern (Patr. S. m. K.)	round cartridge with steel-core, pointed bullet
Patrone Spitzgeschoss mit Stahlkern und Leuchtspur (Patr. S. m. K. L'Spur)	cartridge with pointed, armor-piercing bullet and tracer
Pistole	pistol
Pistolenpatrone	pistol cartridge
Rundblickfernrohr	panoramic sight
schwer	heavy
schweres Infanteriegeschütz (s. G.)	heavy infantry gun
sicher (S)	safe
Spitzgeschoss	pointed bullet
Spitzgeschoss mit Stahlkern (S. m. K.)	pointed bullet with steel core
stahl (St)	steel
Stielhandgranate (Stielhandgranate 24)	stick hand grenade (hand grenade, model 24)
Stielhandgranate PH 39	stick hand grenade, model PH 39
Tankbüchse	antitank rifle (model 35) (*Polish*)
Zünder (Z)	fuze

Section VII. GERMAN ABBREVIATIONS[1]

Al.	Aluminum	*indicates inclusion of a granular aluminum flash composition in filling of shell*
Az. *or* A.Z.	Aufschlagzünder	percussion fuze
B	Büsche	rifle
Bd. Z	Bodenzünder	base percussion fuze; base detonator fuze
B. Patr.	Patrone mit Beobachtungs Geschoss	an observation bullet containing a smoke producer and explosive
D	Dauerfeuer	sustained fire
Digl.	Diglykolnitrat	diglycolnitrate
Digl. Bl. P.	Diglykolnitrat Blattchen Pulver.	diglycolnitrate flaked powder
Dopp. Z. (S/60)	Doppelzünder (60 Sek. unden Brennlänge)	combination fuze (60 seconds burning time)
D.Z.	Druckzünder	pressure fuze, pressure igniter
E	Ersatzstücke	spare parts, replacements
Ex.	Exerzier	dummy (*used to indicate dummy or practice ammunition*)
F	Feuer	fire
Flak	Flugabwehrkanone	antiaircraft gun
Geb.	Gebirgs-	mountain
Gesch	Geschoss	projectile, bullet
Gew.	Gewehr	rifle
H. *or* 'H	gehärtet	hardened (*tungsten carbide core*)
I. G.	Infanteriegeschütz	infantry gun
Igr.	Infanteriegranate	infantry grenade
I.Gr.Z. (s.I.Gr. Z.)	Infanteriegranatz zünder (schwerer Infanteriegranatz zünder)	infantry grenade fuze (heavy infantry grenade fuze)
i.L.	in Ladestreifen	in clips (rifle)
k	kurz	short

[1] This is a list of German abbreviations used in the text. For an extensive dictionary of German military abbreviations, see MIS, *Special Series*, No. 12, "German Military Abbreviations" (April 5, 1943).

Kar.	Karbiner	carbine
Kar. 98B	Karbiner 98B	carbine 98B
Kar. 98K	Karbiner 98 kurz	short carbine 98
Kart.	Kartätsche	case shot; canister shot *(semi-fixed ammunition)*
Kart.	Kartusche	cartridge
L.	Lieferung	delivery
L	Ladung	charge, propelling charge, load
l.F.H.	leichte Feldhaubitze	light field howitzer
l.Geb.I.G.	leichtes Gebirgsinfanteriegeschütz	light mountain infantry howitzer
l.Gr.W	leichter Granatwerfer	light mortar
l.I.G.	leichtes Infanteriegeschütz	light infantry gun (howitzer)
l.S.	leichtes Spitzgeschoss	light weight, pointed bullet
m	Meter	meter
M	Mark, Modell	model
M.G.	Maschinengewehr	machine gun
Mod.	Modell	pattern, model
M.P.	Maschinenpistole	machine pistol, submachine gun
m.V.	mit Verzögerung	with delay action *(fuze)*
N	Nebel	smoke, fog *(used to designate gas as well as smoke)*
n.A.	neuer Art	new type
Nb.	Nebel	smoke, fog
Ngl.	Nitroglyzerin	nitroglycerine
Ngl.Bl.P.	Nitroglyzerin-Blättchenpulver	nitroglycerine, flaked powder
Nz.	Nitrozellulose	nitrocellulose
Nz.Gew.Bl.P.	Nitrozellulose Gewehr Blättchenpulver	nitrocellulose rifle powder *(flaked)*
o.L.	ohne Ladestreifen	without clips; not in clips
o.V.	ohne Verzögerung	without delay, instantaneous
P.	Pulver	powder
Pak	Panzerabwehrkanone	antitank gun
Patr.	Patrone	cartridge; semi-fixed shell; round of ammunition
Patrh.S.	Patronenhülse-Stahl	brass cartridge case
Patr.l.S.	Patrone leichtes Spitzgeschoss	light, pointed ball ammunition with core of aluminum
Patr.P.m.K.	Patrone Phospor mit Stahlkern	incendiary armor-piercing cartridge with steel core

Patr.S.m.E.	Patrone Spitzgeschoss mit Eisenkern	cartridge with iron or mild steel-core, pointed bullet
Patr.S.m.K.	Patrone Spitzgeschoss mit Stahlkern	cartridge with steel-core, pointed bullet
Patr.S.m.K.H.	Patrone Spitzgeschoss mit Stahlkern gehärtet	cartridge with pointed armor-piercing *(tungsten carbide core)* bullet
Patr.S.m.K. L'Spur	Patrone Spitzgeschoss mit Stahlkern und Leuchtspur	cartridge with pointed armor-piercing bullet and tracer
Patr.s.S.	Patrone schweres Spitzgeschoss	heavy, pointed ball ammunition
Patr.s.S. L'Spur	Patrone schweres Spitzgeschoss mit Leuchtspur	cartridge with heavy tracer bullet
Patr.318 S.m.K.	Patrone 318 Spitzgeschoss mit Stahlkern	cartridge 318, bullet with steel core
Patr. 318 S.m.K. (H)	Patrone 318 Spitzgeschoss mit Stahlkern gehärtet	cartridge 318, bullet with hardened steel core
Patr. 318 (P)	Patronen 318 Polnisch	Polish cartridge No. 318
Pist.	Pistole	pistol
Pist. Patr.	Pistolpatrone	pistol cartridge
Pz.	Panzer	armor, armor-plate
Pz.B.	Panzerbüchse	antitank rifle
Pzgr.	Panzergranate	armor-piercing shell
Rbl.F.	Rundblickfernrohr	panoramic sight
Rdf.	Rheindorf	*an arsenal*
Rh	Rheinmetal	*arms manufacturing company*
Rs.	Reizstoff	irritant gas
s.	schwerer	heavy, medium *(artillery)*
S	sicher	safe
S*		*manufacturer's mark for brass cartridge case (72% copper and 28% zinc)*
S 274, 222, etc.		*manufacturer's mark for a type of alloy*
s.F.H.	schwere Feldhaubitze	heavy (medium) field howitzer
s.Gr.W.	schwerer Granatenwerfer	heavy mortar
s.I.G.	schweres Infanteriegeschütz	heavy infantry gun (howitzer)
S.Inf.G.	schweres Infanteriegeschütz	heavy infantry gun (howitzer)
S.K.	Schnellfeuerkanone	rapid-fire cannon

S.K.D.	Selve-Kornbegel-Dornheim, A. G.	*small-arms ammunition factory*
S.m.K.	Spitzgeschoss mit Stahlkern	pointed bullet with steel core
S.m.K.(H)	Spitzgeschoss mit Stahlkern gehärtet	super armor-piercing bullet with hardened steel core
S.m.K.L'Spur	Spitzgeschoss mit Stahlkern und Leuchtspur	pointed bullet with steel core and tracer effect
Spgr.	Sprenggranate	high-explosive shell
Spr.	Spreng-	explosive
St.	Stahl	*mark for steel cartridge*
Ub.	Übungsmunition	practice ammunition
Wgr.	Werfergranate	mortar shell
Wgr.Z.	Werfergranatzünder	mortar shell fuze
Z.	Zünder	fuze
Zdlg.	Zündladung	primer charge
Zdh:88	Zündhütchen 88	primer capsule 88